ROUTLEDGE LIBRARY EDITIONS:
WORLD EMPIRES

Volume 12

THE BUILDERS OF THE MOGUL EMPIRE

I0887481

THE BUILDERS OF THE MOGUL EMPIRE

MICHAEL PRAWDIN

Routledge
Taylor & Francis Group
LONDON AND NEW YORK

First published in 1963 by George Allen & Unwin Ltd

This edition first published in 2018
by Routledge
2 Park Square, Milton Park, Abingdon, Oxon OX14 4RN

and by Routledge
711 Third Avenue, New York, NY 10017

Routledge is an imprint of the Taylor & Francis Group, an informa business

© 1963 George Allen & Unwin Ltd

All rights reserved. No part of this book may be reprinted or reproduced or utilised in any form or by any electronic, mechanical, or other means, now known or hereafter invented, including photocopying and recording, or in any information storage or retrieval system, without permission in writing from the publishers.

Trademark notice: Product or corporate names may be trademarks or registered trademarks, and are used only for identification and explanation without intent to infringe.

British Library Cataloguing in Publication Data
A catalogue record for this book is available from the British Library

ISBN: 978-1-138-47911-1 (Set)
ISBN: 978-1-351-00226-4 (Set) (ebk)
ISBN: 978-1-138-48562-4 (Volume 12) (hbk)
ISBN: 978-1-138-48563-1 (Volume 12) (pbk)
ISBN: 978-1-351-04856-9 (Volume 12) (ebk)

Publisher's Note
The publisher has gone to great lengths to ensure the quality of this reprint but points out that some imperfections in the original copies may be apparent.

Disclaimer
The publisher has made every effort to trace copyright holders and would welcome correspondence from those they have been unable to trace.

THE EMPEROR BABUR READING

MICHAEL PRAWDIN

THE BUILDERS OF THE MOGUL EMPIRE

London

GEORGE ALLEN & UNWIN LTD

RUSKIN HOUSE MUSEUM STREET

FIRST PUBLISHED IN 1963

This book is copyright under the Berne convention. Apart from any fair dealing for the purpose of private study, research, criticism or review, as permitted under the Copyright Act 1956, no portion may be reproduced without written permission. Enquiry should be made to the publishers.

© *George Allen & Unwin Ltd*, 1963

PRINTED IN GREAT BRITAIN
in 11 on 12 pt. Ehrhardt type
BY C. TINLING AND COMPANY LTD
LIVERPOOL, LONDON AND PRESCOT

CONTENTS

PART ONE: BABUR

PART TWO: HUMAYUN

PART THREE: AKBAR

ILLUSTRATIONS

MAPS

PART ONE
BABUR

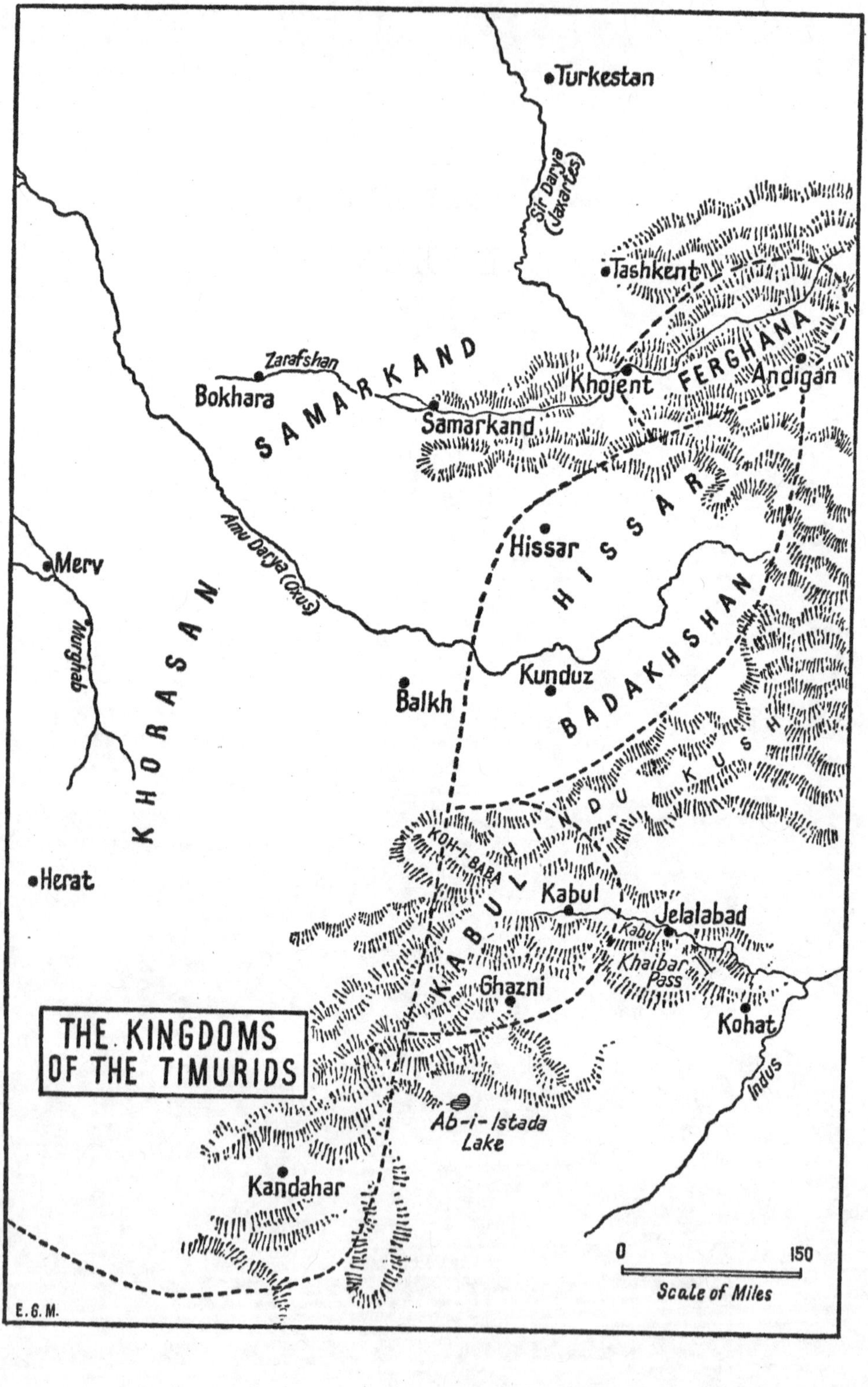

THE KINGDOMS OF THE TIMURIDS
Turkestan
Sir Darya (Jaxartes)
Tashkent
SAMARKAND
Zarafshan
Bokhara
Samarkand
Khojent
FERGHANA
Andigan
HISSAR
Hissar
Amu Darya (Oxus)
Merv
Murghab
KHORASAN
BADAKHSHAN
Kunduz
Balkh
HINDU KUSH
KOH-I-BABA
KABUL
Kabul
Jelalabad
Kabul
Khaibar Pass
Ghazni
Kohat
Indus
Herat
Ab-i-Istada Lake
Kandahar
0
150
Scale of Miles
E. G. M.

1

SAMARKAND GAINED AND LOST

Over two and a half centuries had passed since Jenghiz Khan, out of the vastness of East Asia, had irrupted into the lands of the Sir Darya and Amu Darya and smashed the Moslem Empire then stretching from the Pamir to beyond the Caspian Sea. Forty years later the Mongols, under Jenghiz Khan's grandson Hulagu, had subjugated all the realms to the west of the Oxus, nearly as far as the Mediterranean, and were only stopped by the Egyptian Mamelukes from conquering the whole of Syria. Then, in the space of a few generations, the Empire of the Il-Khans, which Hulagu had founded, changed its character, as had happened so often in the history of western Asia, where the settled world of Persian civilization had absorbed wave after wave of invaders from the steppes. Hulagu's descendants, and more and more of the Mongolian nobles, went over to Islam; the nomad rulers surrounded themselves with scholars and poets, building palaces and towns to their glory, and spending their time in festivities or wars against one another. Real power was wielded by the viceroys and amirs in the various provinces. As soon as one of them felt strong enough, he discovered some descendant of Jenghiz Khan, proclaimed him Khan, and in his name started wars against his neighbours in the hope of annexing their provinces.

It was about a century after the creation of Hulagu's Empire that in the region of the Amu Darya (the Oxus) and the Sir Darya (the Jaxartes of old) a new power arose. This region, Jenghiz Khan's original target, did not really belong to Hulagu's Empire. The land beyond the Amu Darya had been allocated to the realm of Jagatai, Jenghiz Khan's second son, whose central Asian empire was intended to form a bridge between China and Western Asia. But the eastern half of Jagatai's realm, Turkistan, poor in cities and rich in steppes, remained a typical nomad land, while its western part,

Transoxiana, between the Amu Darya and Sir Darya, was populous, industrious, and culturally and economically much more akin to the empire of the Il-Khans which bordered it to the south-west.

In this frontier land between Iran and Turan a chieftain of the Barlas Turki-tribe, Timur, had himself proclaimed Grand Amir of Transoxiana in the year 1369, and with a Jenghizid as nominal Khan started on the superhuman task which he had set himself: that of re-establishing Jenghiz Khan's empire. When he died thirty-six years later, he left what is known in Europe as Tamerlane's Empire, reaching from the Aral Sea to the Arabian Sea and from the Mediterranean nearly to the Altai Mountains. But he had not, like Jenghiz Khan, created a warrior nation, since he made his conquests with an army of mercenaries held together in the main by his personality and the expectation of spoils. And in spite of the frightful destruction which accompanied his campaigns, it was the Iranian-Islamic civilization which not only survived but re-emerged from the slaughter strengthened and enhanced.

Timur's descendants felt themselves heirs more to a culture which they wanted to enjoy and foster than to the ambition of world conquest. Fighting one another for the throne, for a province, for a fief they often sought help from the nomadic warriors of Turkistan or of the northern steppes against their immediate neighbours, only to discard their helpers at the moment of success in order to pursue a life of culture and pleasure as the previous rulers had done. Proud of their learning and their manners, they considered themselves not Mongols but Turks, superior to the rough Mongolian riders of the steppes. And the nomads, whether they came from outside the province or were wandering with their cattle in its hills or wastes, felt themselves in no way bound to the man by whom they had been engaged for a campaign. When the fortunes of battle turned against him, they simply plundered his camp before fleeing themselves.

This struggle for the succession started immediately after Timur's death. Nevertheless, when after four years of strife his youngest son Shah Rokh established his supremacy, he managed to bring back a great part of the empire under his rule and to leave the throne, after a prosperous reign of nearly forty years, to his son Ulugh Beg, a great scholar, poet, theologian, and eminent mathematician, whose astronomical tables became world-famous. Yet, after a short reign Ulugh Beg was dethroned, and then murdered, by one of his sons.

A fratricidal war plunged the country again into chaos, until a great-grandson of Timur from another line, Abu Said, established himself on the throne of Samarkand with the help of the Uzbegs, the nomad Mongols from the northern steppes.

An able ruler and a keen warrior, Abu Said kept order in his realm, but before engaging on a campaign against Irak, where he was defeated and killed, he divided it amongst his sons. The lands of Samarkand and Bokhara he apportioned to his eldest son Sultan Ahmed, the Amu Darya basin with Hissar and Badakhshan to his son Sultan Mahmud; another son, Omar Sheikh, inherited the kingdom of Ferghana, lying eastwards on both sides of the upper Sir Darya; and still another son, Ulugh Beg, held the far-off mountainous kingdom of Kabul. The rich kingdom of Khorasan to the south and west of these realms, stretching from Afghanistan to the Amu Darya, was conquered by another great-grandson of Timur, Sultan Husain Baikara, who, an admirer of art and literature, made his capital Herat one of the greatest cultural centres of the Asian Mohammedan world.

The little kingdom of Ferghana, Omar Sheikh's domain, was, as Babur later wrote in his memoirs, 'situated on the extreme boundary of the habitable world'. It was surrounded on three sides by mountains and open only to the west, towards Samarkand. Beyond it, on the other side of the mountain passes, was the land of the Jagatai Mongols, but their Khan, Yunus, a descendant of Jenghiz Khan, had spent his youth as an exile at the courts of descendants of Shah Rokh and loved town life. Three of his daughters had married sons of Abu Said, and with one of them, his son-in-law Omar Sheikh, the King of Ferghana, he struck up a particular friendship and often spent the winter months in his kingdom. When Omar Sheikh's wife, early in 1483, gave birth to a boy and he was named Zahir-ud-din Mohammed—Defender of the Faith—it is said that the Mongols, finding the name difficult to pronounce, called him Babur—Panther; and it was under this soon generally adopted name that the boy, the descendant of both Timur and Jenghiz Khan, made his entrance into history.

Ferghana was, as he described it, a beautiful country 'abundantly supplied with running water and extremely pleasant in spring'. Its orchards and gardens were celebrated, full of tulips and roses. It abounded in corn and fruits, particularly peaches, apricots, melons, and pomegranates. The people liked to take the stones out of the apricots and insert almonds in their place, (which is very pleasant). It had a rich soil and sheltered meadows of clover. It had good hunting grounds with plenty of game. 'Its pheasants were so fat that four persons could dine on one and not finish it'. In the hills there were delightful summer retreats to which the people retired to avoid the heat. There were 'mines of turquoise, and the people in the valley wove cloth of purple colour'. But the country was small and its revenue just sufficient to maintain 4,000 troops. Omar Sheikh, ambitious and adventurous, often set out for inroads into the neighbouring domain of Samarkand, and sometimes it needed the mediation of Yunus Khan and the menace of his Mongols to prevent Sultan Ahmed, the lord of Samarkand, from overrunning the kingdom of his unruly brother. However, when after the death of Yunus Khan the adventurous Omar Sheikh did not stop his pillaging invasions, Sultan Ahmed and his brother-in-law, Mahmud Khan of Tashkent, the elder son of Yunus Khan, decided to divide Ferghana between themselves and marched in the spring of 1494 from west and north into the country. Omar Sheikh was at the time in the mountain fort of Akhsi, where his palace buildings were erected at the edge of a precipice, and while he was, perhaps on the look-out for the invaders, feeding his pigeons, the platform with the dovecote gave way under him and he was hurled to his death from the top of the rock.

When the news of the accident reached the capital, Andijan, his eleven-year-old son Babur was immediately proclaimed king, and the begs and amirs, knowing how precarious the position was and what pillage and murder usually accompanied the fall of a city, prepared for defence. In the meantime an embassy went in Babur's name to his uncle Sultan Ahmed, stating that he regarded himself as son and servant of the Sultan and would be happy to govern the country as the Sultan's regent. But the Sultan's ministers rejected the proposal and the army continued to advance. However, while it was crossing a muddy and slimy river the only bridge collapsed, many horses and camels fell into the swamp and perished. Then an epidemic of distemper broke out among the animals, and Sultan Ahmed called off the campaign. On the way back he himself was seized with fever and died. Babur's maternal uncle, Mahmud Khan, who was besieging the fortress of Akhsi, fell ill, too, and returned to his country. Babur notes in his memoirs: 'The Almighty God, by His perfect power, has in His own good time and season accom-

1. Young Babur dangerously ill in Samarkand. A physician sprinkling his face with water.

2. Babur and his uncle's armies saluting the Mongolian horse-tail standards by throwing Kumiss on them.

plished my designs in the best and most proper manner without the aid of mortal strength'; and it was probably in the desire to prove himself worthy of this divine mercy that the boy 'began to abstain from forbidden and dubious meats' and even refrained from alcohol —a most astonishing feat in his surroundings.

After Ahmed's death, his brother, Sultan Mahmud, mounted the throne of Samarkand, but being tyrannical and debauched he soon earned the hatred of the people of the capital. During the twenty-five years of Ahmed's reign they had lived in ease and tranquillity, now they feared to leave their houses 'from a dread lest their children be carried off for slaves'. However, after a few months Sultan Mahmud also fell ill and died within six days.

Now the begs of Samarkand called in Baisanghar, the eighteen-year-old son of Sultan Mahmud, but other Mirzas—as all princes of Timur's stock were called—also raised their claim to the throne of Samarkand and, accompanied by their begs and retainers, began incessant warfare. In reality they were only puppets in the hands of their begs, who eager for spoil and power readily changed one Mirza for another or even blinded or assassinated an uncomfortable one if he did not manage to escape in time to a domain or town in the power of another war-lord.

Babur's begs of Ferghana had used the general commotion, first to regain some towns and forts which had been lost after Omar Sheikh's death; then they set out, with the now thirteen-year-old Babur, towards Samarkand. However, the armies of the various pretenders had finally exhausted the resources of the country, 'great scarcity of provisions prevailed everywhere and as the winter season was fast approaching' the campaign was postponed to the next year.

When in 1497 Babur's army advanced again in the direction of Samarkand, it proved to be somewhat better disciplined and behaved than the others, and various towns and forts surrendered and were spared. A number of nomad bands joined him, and when these Mongols plundered a few peaceful villages, the leading beg 'ordered two or three of them to be cut to pieces as an example'. The result was that when Babur encamped before Samarkand 'so many townspeople and traders arrived that the camp was like a city and one could buy there whatever was procurable in the town'. One day the soldiers could not resist the temptation and raided the stalls, but on the order 'that everything should be restored without reserve before the end of the first watch next day, there was not a thread or a broken needle that was not restored to its owner', writes Babur.

Nevertheless, the siege lasted seven months, deep into the winter, before Baisanghar, 'with two or three hundred hungry and naked wretches', fled from the city and Babur was welcomed by the begs and chief townsmen of Samarkand. The capital of his great ancestor Timur made an overwhelming impression on the fourteen-year-old boy and it exercised a fascination on him which was to last throughout his whole life, making him ready more than once to sacrifice all he had won for a chance to regain possession of this city. Its palaces, its mosques, its gardens, its baths, its halls, its colleges, everything was incomparably magnificent. 'In the whole inhabitable world there are few cities so pleasantly situated as Samarkand . . . I directed its wall to be paced round the ramparts, and found that it was five miles in circumference.'

In his description of Samarkand he does not forget the observatory, by means of which 'Ulugh Beg composed the Astronomical Tables which are followed at the present time, scarcely any other being used. Before they were published, the Il-Khani Astronomical Tables were in general use, constructed in the time of Hulagu, in his observatory . . .

'Samarkand is a wonderfully fine city. One of its distinguishing peculiarities is that each trade has its own bazaar; so that different trades are not mixed together in the same place. The established customs and regulations are good. The bakers' shops are excellent, and the cooks are skilful. The best paper in the world comes from Samarkand . . . Another product of Samarkand is crimson velvet, which is exported to all quarters . . .'

But the town had been taken after severe resistance. It had been pillaged according to custom, and as it soon proved so completely, that instead of being taxed the inhabitants had to be given 'seed-corn and supplies to enable them to carry on till the harvest'. The soldiers had acquired considerable booty when the city fell, but now they could only expect hardship. There were no riches left to plunder, Babur had nothing to give them, and so they began to desert him. First the Mongol tribes went away, then the troops from Ferghana, with even the most important begs, returned home, and then the news arrived that these begs, considering Babur now to be the lord of Samarkand, had proclaimed his younger brother Jahangir as King of Ferghana. It was quite customary that each son of a ruler should receive a separate appanage, but as Babur's whole strength derived from Ferghana his governors refused to surrender the capital Andijan, and the rebels laid siege to the city.

Urgent letters from Babur's mother called on him to hasten with his remaining troops to the relief of his old capital, but just at this moment the boy fell so seriously ill that he could neither speak nor take nourishment, and even the men who had loyally remained with him despaired of his life. However, he recovered and a hundred days after his entry into Samarkand he left the city with his little army to hurry to Ferghana. But when after a week he reached Khojent, less than half way to his capital Andijan, news came that, in the belief that he was dying, the garrison of Andijan had made terms with the enemy and surrendered the fortress, while immediately on his departure from Samarkand his cousin Ali Mirza had occupied the city. Babur had lost both his kingdoms, his own Ferghana and his beloved Samarkand. Now the begs, captains and soldiers who had wives and families in Andijan, about seven to eight hundred men, left him altogether. Not more than two to three hundred followers of all ranks stuck to him, 'voluntarily choosing a life of exile and hardship'. To make matters worse, Khojent was such a small place that it could not maintain even two hundred men, and Babur confesses that he became 'a prey to melancholy and vexation, and wept a great deal'.

Then his grandmother and mother arrived from Andijan. As the widow and the daughter of Yunus Khan, they had many connections. One of his mother's brothers, Mahmud Khan of Tashkent, gave Babur a detachment of Mongols; a number of Babur's officers and begs were sent out into the hills to gain the help of the mountain tribes; and slowly, as the news spread that Babur was gathering forces to fight for his heritage, the country, discontented with the arbitrary rule of the new masters, became restive. One after the other, forts and towns drove out the imposed governors and opened the gates to Babur's envoys. Various engagements ended in his favour, and finally Andijan declared itself for him: 'Thus by the grace of the Most High I recovered my paternal kingdom, of which I had been deprived for nearly two years'.

But fortunes changed quickly. A great part of his forces consisted of mercenary Mongol tribes who had first joined his adversaries and lately, seeing his success, changed over to his side, each time using the opportuniy to plunder the losers. Now Babur's retainers came to him complaining that the Mongols 'are riding the horses which were ours, wearing our garments, and killing and eating our own sheep before our eyes. What patience can possibly endure all this?' Babur found that their complaints were just and allowed them to 'resume possession of whatever part of their property they recognized'.

The Mongols were not the men to give back any of their spoils. There were about three to four thousand of them, and they immediately rose and departed to his enemies. Babur learned: 'In war and statecraft a thing may seem reasonable at first sight, but it should be weighed and considered in a hundred lights before it is finally decided. This ill-judged order of mine was in fact the ultimate cause of my second expulsion from Andijan.'

The begs of his brother Jahangir, reinforced by the Mongols, resumed the offensive, a series of skirmishes and battles followed without either side achieving a decisive victory, and finally, in the spring of 1500, an agreement was patched up by the begs that Ferghana should be divided and that both parties were jointly to proceed against Samarkand. Once the city was conquered and Babur became King of Samarkand, he would give the whole of Ferghana to his brother Jahangir.

Samarkand, which Babur's cousin Ali Mirza had occupied immediately after Babur's departure, was still in his hands, although he was only a figurehead for the leading nobles there, the Terkhans, in the same way as Babur and Jahangir were in the hands of their own war-lords. But the Terkhans had just fallen out with the prince and appear to have called in Babur, promising to deliver the city to him, for he suddenly set out with only a few hundred men he happened to have with him. He was still on his way when he received the information that he had been forestalled: Sheibani, Khan of the Uzbegs, had taken Samarkand.

Sheibani Khan was a much more formidable adversary than any of the Timurid Mirzas who were contending for power. The Uzbegs were Turko-Mongolian tribes from the steppes to the north of the Sir Darya. Long ago they had been crushed and dispersed by the Jagatai Mongols under Yunus Khan. Sheibani, the little grandson of the Uzbeg Khan, who was slain, had taken refuge in Samarkand and risen in the service of Sultan Ahmed, who was then the ruler of Samarkand. Fifteen years later Sultan Ahmed made war against Mahmud Khan of Tashkent, and Sheibani suddenly changed sides and saved Mahmud Khan from defeat. As reward he received from Mahmud Khan the city of Turkestan, situated at the edge of his ancestral steppes. There he began to rally about him the tribal warriors, and as his inroads into the crumbling remains of the Timurids' empire to the south of the river were successful, more and more of the adventurous riders of the steppes joined him and his forces grew. Again ten years later, when Babur's army besieged Samarkand, Baisanghar Mirza had called for help from the Uzbeg Khan. Sheibani came, observed both defenders and attackers, and withdrew without taking part in the contest. When now the quarrels between the new ruler, Ali Mirza, and the Terkhans started, he captured Bokhara, the second most important town in the kingdom of Samarkand, and it was here that he received the call for help from Ali Mirza's mother, herself an Uzbeg. Some sources maintain that she even promised him the throne of Samarkand as her dowry if he would marry her and settle an appanage upon Ali. In any case, he moved in, put Ali to death and seized the town. Then, leaving a small garrison, he put up his own camp in the plains beyond the city and distributed the main bulk of his army in the neighbourhood.

Babur, once again in a desperate position, since immediately after his departure Jahangir's begs had occupied Andijan and his other provinces, decided to make, with his few hundred men, a foolhardy dash for Samarkand. In a November night they rode to the walls, scaled them, and overwhelmed the sleeping garrison. When the townsmen woke up and saw him and his soldiers, they fell upon the remaining Uzbegs and clubbed and stoned them. As soon as Sheibani got the news of what had happened, he galloped with the men at hand to the city, but he was too late. The gates were guarded, the walls manned. As soon as Babur's success in Samarkand became known, many districts declared themselves for him, in forts and towns the people rose and expelled the Uzbeg garrisons, and the peasants in the villages started to resist their marauding soldiers. In the end, Sheibani collected his troops and drew away to Bokhara.

The seventeen year-old Babur was for the second time lord of Samarkand. He writes in his memoirs: 'For nearly a hundred and forty years, Samarkand had been the capital of my family. A foreign robber, who knew not whence he came, had seized the kingdom, which dropped from our hands. Almighty God now restored it to me, and gave me back my plundered and pillaged country'. He now sat enthroned in Timur's Garden Palace, was feted and congratulated by men of rank and consequence in the offices of the city, and listened with enjoyment to the laudatory verses of the local poets. He sent for his mother, grandmother and wife, who was a daughter of Sultan Ahmed, the previous King of Samarkand, and to whom he had been betrothed as a child; and later on while still in Samarkand she gave birth to a girl who, however, 'in a month or forty days went to share the mercy of God'.

In general, the first joy soon gave way to serious apprehensions. The territory which had been so rich and fertile had recently suffered too much from the continuous changes of government and from the ravages of both hostile and friendly armies. Its wealth was destroyed, its resources reduced, and the forces that it could put into the field were inadequate for its defence, for in Bokhara Sheibani was recruiting swarms of riders from the steppes. Babur repeatedly despatched ambassadors and messengers, 'one after the other, to all the Khans and Sultans, Amirs and Chiefs to request their aid and assistance. These messengers I kept going back and forward without intermission'. But none of the war-lords of Transoxiana thought it necessary to get involved on Babur's behalf. At best, some sent small detachments, and he had to depend on returning refugees, deserters, adventurers, levies which he raised in the towns and villages of the territory. Nevertheless, during the winter his force grew, and when in May Sheibani advanced, Babur was also able to take the field and marched along the river which flows from Samarkand to Bokhara until he came to Sar-i-pul (The Bridgehead) where he met Sheibani's army. Here Babur encamped and fortified his camp with a palisade and trenches. For a few days there was some undecisive skirmishing, one night Sheibani tried to take the fortified camp by surprise, but found Babur's troops on the alert and withdrew to his own camp. At last Babur decided to give battle and was met, for the first time in his life, with the age-old tactics of the riders of the steppes. His right wing was covered by the river; thus, while both centres met in head-on attack, Sheibani's best troops hurled themselves at the extreme end of his left wing and, turning his flank, attacked at a breakneck gallop from the rear, letting their deadly arrows fly. Babur's troops were surrounded and routed, and he himself with his nearest followers plunged, heavily armed as they were, into the river and succeeded in swimming across with their horses. Then they rode for their lives to Samarkand.

The mighty walls of Samarkand provided sufficient protection even when manned only by the remnants of his troops, but as no supplies came into the beleaguered town, soon famine and distress prevailed. People ate donkey-meat and dogs, horses were fed on tree leaves and sawdust soaked in water. Help was not to be expected from any quarter, and soldiers and even men high in Babur's confidence 'began to let themselves down over the walls and make their escape'. After nearly five months of siege Sheibani agreed to a capitulation on terms: Babur, with his mother and two other ladies, and with the few men who still wanted to remain with him, should leave the city by night, while his sister was to remain behind and and become Sheibani's wife. Babur, who in his memoirs has no good word to say of Sheibani, is ashamed of this agreement to the marriage and writes: 'My eldest sister Khanzada Begam was intercepted and fell into the hands of Sheibani Khan, as we left the city on this occasion'.

For the populace of Samarkand the change did not signify much; they would humble themselves before another lord, perhaps have to work a bit harder, but they would get enough to eat. For the eighteen-year-old Babur this capitulation meant the loss of the throne of Samarkand for the second time, a complete downfall from his grandeur, but his resilience had grown in the intervening years. On the flight, probably in fear that Sheibani might change his mind and pursue the fugitives, he undertook, just for amusement, a race with two of his followers, and when after two days and nights of riding they reached a village where they found 'nice fat flesh, bread of fine flour well baked, sweet melons, and excellent grapes in great abundance', he composed these lines:

From famine and distress we have escaped to repose;
We have gained fresh life and a fresh world.
The fear of death was removed from the heart;
The torments of hunger were taken away.

And he continues: 'In all my life I never enjoyed myself so much nor felt at any time so keenly the pleasures of peace and plenty. Enjoyment after suffering, abundance after want, come with increased relish and afford more exquisite delight.'

He is proud of his ability to write verses and to express himself in a refined manner, whether in Turki or in Persian. He knows the sayings of the wise men, and the verses of the great poets. The pleasures of a cultured life are for him just as important as the art of war, and when he describes his contemporaries he always appraises them as fighters, as bowmen, and as writers of verses. The appropriate etiquette must be maintained under all conditions, for it is a sign of cultured behaviour and the loss of face is worse than death.

And so Babur added to his fame as a soldier and conqueror that of the writer of a book of memoirs which gives a unique picture not only of his own personality, of his adventures and achievements but equally of the habits and customs of his time and country. A keen observer and lover of nature, who knew every animal and every bird and flower, an indefatigable rider and hunter, of avid curiosity, he is always in search of new experience and knowledge and knows how to communicate his impressions and feelings to the reader. We do not know when he started to write his famous memoirs, and although they are undoubtedly written from memory, they have several gaps, some for long periods, and the later parts are more sketchy, as if they had not been worked out as the earlier ones had been. Nevertheless the work is an invaluable document showing the vicissitudes, the character and the everyday moods of an outstanding personality, and bringing to life a particular society at the beginning of the sixteenth century with its mixture of culture, decadence and savagery.

2

THE FUGITIVE

AFTER a few days rest the fugitives, Babur with his mother and his companions, proceeded to another village deeper in the mountains, a village of shepherds, where they took up lodgings in the peasants' houses. Babur describes how he lived in the house of the head-man, about seventy or eighty years old, whose mother was still alive, and she told them stories of Timur's invasion of India a century earlier, as she had heard them as a little girl from her relatives. These tales may have taken root in his imagination, but now he was only a wretched refugee, so poor that when his grandmother, who had remained behind in Samarkand and had been set free by Sheibani, arrived 'with the family and heavy baggage, and a few lean and hungry followers', he was even obliged to give the men leave to return to Andijan because he could not maintain them.

Ferghana was in the hands of his brother Jahangir and his begs, and although they barred his return, the customary etiquette had to be observed, and with the men Babur sent some presents to Jahangir and his courtiers. Now winter was coming on, and he spent his days walking on foot about the hills. In his poverty he usually went barefoot, and was astonished to find that soon his feet became so hardened that he did not mind rock or stone in the least. One day, wanting to bathe for religious purification, he found a rivulet which was frozen at the banks but not in the middle because of the swift current, and he plunged into the water and dived sixteen times, though the biting chillness penetrated him.

When the spring came, he organized a hunting party, he tried a raid, but this type of life offered no prospects for the future; at last, in June 1502, he went to Tashkent, to his maternal uncle Mahmud Khan. It would be shameful to come as a suppliant; it was already a loss of face that he had to appear at his uncle's court with only a couple of attendants. He regarded himself as fortunate 'that this did not happen among strangers but with my own kinsmen'; and he was relieved to find the customs at this Mongol court so different from the etiquette reigning at the courts of the Timurids. He notes with astonishment that he could 'wait on Shah Begam—the mother of the Khan—bareheaded and barefooted with as much freedom as a person would do at home in his own house'. Nevertheless, officially, he came to present to the Khan a quatrain which he had just composed:

> No one remembers him who is in adversity;
> A banished man cannot indulge his heart in happiness;
> My heart is far from joy in this exile;
> However brave, an exile has no pleasures.

He was accepted as a poor relative and 'endured such vexation and misery that life itself became burdensome for me. I debated with myself whether it would not be far better to flee from the sight of man, as far as my feet could carry me, rather than exhibit myself as a spectacle in such distress and abasement'. A trusted friend submitted to the Khan and Shah Begam a plan that Babur should go to Turkistan, to his other maternal uncle, Ahmed Khan, to put to him the necessity of joining all forces and acting together against the ambitions of Sheibani. Actually, Babur's idea was to use this journey into the Mongolian vastness as the first stage of an even longer journey into China, about which many legends were circulating, and to try his luck there. But when Mahmud Khan and Shah Begam heard of his desire to go to Ahmed Khan, they had the feeling that Babur wanted to leave because of the poor reception they had given him. That would be a blemish on their reputation as hosts, and they insisted on some delay in his departure. And very soon after that there came a messenger that Ahmed Khan himself was on the way to visit his brother, whom he had not seen for over twenty years.

Ahmed Khan was a Mongol of the steppes without the refinement and the cultural aspirations of the Timurids. He and his men wore strange garments: frocks of China satin ornamented with flowered needlework, caps embroidered with gold threads, Chinese cuirasses with a whetstone and purse hanging from the belt, and on the pursepocket there hung various trinkets, such as perfume-cases. Their quivers and saddles were of shagreen leather, and their horses were decked and caparisoned in a strange fashion. Babur, who was presented with such a dress and horse, delights in telling that even his friends did not recognize him. Then he describes the procedure of the meetings, of the military show where everything was executed with the precise ceremonial which was still based on Jenghiz-Khan's Mongolian customs and differed vastly from that at the courts of the Timurids.

However, the visit does not seem to have been as incidental as Babur tries to present it, since its purpose was to unite forces in order to take Ferghana from the begs who were holding it in the name of Jahangir. Babur was given a strong detachment to create a diversion and in rapid marches started the reconquest of his land. Some of the towns declared themselves for him, the wandering tribes flocked to his standard, but in an encounter with the main adversary before Andijan he was defeated and wounded by an arrow in the leg. When he rejoined Ahmed Khan's camp he was received as a hero, but there he learned his uncles' decision that the main part of Ferghana, with the capital Andijan, was to become the property of Ahmed Khan in order to interest him in the affairs of the West and have him at hand, while Babur was to have only Akhsi. But then both Khans would ride with him against Samarkand and install him there.

That was a bitter disappointment, but he could do nothing against the decision. He remarks only about the habits of the future lord of Ferghana: 'As he had been brought up in a rude and remote country, the tent in which he lived was far from being distinguished by neatness and had much the air of a marauder's. Melons, grapes and stable utensils were lying huddled about in the tent in which he was sitting'. However, for the Mongolian surgeon whom Ahmed Khan had sent to him is he full of praise: 'He was wonderfully skilful in surgery. To some wounds he applied a kind of plaster, to other wounded persons he gave a medicine to swallow. To my thigh wound he applied the skins of some fruits which he had prepared and dried, without inserting a seton. He told me many strange and wonderful stories of cures, such as the surgeons of our parts are totally unable to effect.'

Indeed Babur's wound healed so well that he could soon resume his campaign in the provinces which were now allotted to him, but he fell into a trap, was scarcely able to save himself by headlong flight, and only after various hair-raising adventures extricated himself from the danger of being caught and put to death, and finally joined his uncles just when the news arrived that Sheibani Khan with his Uzbegs was marching against them.

Sheibani advanced with lightning speed, surprised and crushed the Mongol army and took both Khans prisoner. But he remembered that he had only been able to start his phenomenal career as conqueror thanks to the patronage of Mahmud Khan, who fifteen years earlier had allotted to him the town of Turkestan. Therefore he set both Khans free to return home to their steppes in the east.

Ahmed Khan, the true Mongol, was so broken by the defeat that he died within a few months. It is said of him that when his doctor suspected that he had been poisoned by Sheibani and wanted to give some antidote, he answered: 'Yes, Sheibani has poisoned me. That man who rose from the lowest dunghill to the highest rank took me prisoner and then dared to set me free! If you know an antidote against that kind of poison, give it to me.' Mahmud Khan survived, but accustomed to the pleasures of the settled town-life, he could not stand the rough nomadic existence of the steppes. Many years later, distrusted by the Jagatai Mongols, he tried to return to Tashkent but was slain together with his sons.

Babur, who had managed to escape after the battle in which the Mongol armies were crushed, fled into the mountain ranges in the south of Ferghana and there found a precarious refuge for himself, his mother and his family with a few men-at-arms who still adhered to him in his misfortune.

For nearly a year he wandered there as a fugitive and outlaw among the mountain shepherds, experiencing privation and distress, sometimes hunted from village to village or from forest to mountain. The news that Sheibani had defeated and killed the begs who had once been Babur's enemies was poor consolation, as now the whole of Ferghana irretrievably became Sheibani's possession. Sheibani was already making ravaging incursions into the lands of the Amu Darya basin, the only escape route still open to Babur. And so, in June 1504, Babur took the decision to cross with his small band of some two hundred men, women, and children the ice-bound passes of the mountain ranges south of Ferghana. Most of the party was on foot, miserably equipped, with brogues of raw-hide as shoes, in tattered cloaks, with clubs in their hands. 'We were so poor that we had only two tents. My own I gave to my mother; and at every halt they put up for me a felt tent on crossed poles in which I took up my quarters', writes Babur.

When they reached the province of Hissar on the other side of the mountains, they found it in a chaotic state. Sheibani had invaded the country. In order to be spared, the towns, one after the other, declared themselves for the Uzbeg Khan. The ruler of the province, Khosrou Shah, had quarrelled with the wandering tribes of his country and even alienated his brother Baki, who governed the eastern districts. At the appearance of Babur, already known as a Timurid of indomitable spirit and famous for his adventurous enterprizes, Khosrou Shah's alienated brother Baki joined him with his followers, to become one of his chief advisers. This was a stroke of luck. Some of Khosrou's vassals followed his example; the Mongol tribes hurried to Babur in expectation of new and profitable exploits, and suddenly Babur saw himself again at the head of a growing force. Finally, Khosrou Shah himself, sudenly a powerless fugitive, officially rendered his submission on condition that he could depart to Khorasan with all his property.

Babur's intention had been to go to Khorasan, the mightiest of all Timurid kingdoms, in the hope of inducing its sovereign, Sultan Husain Baikara, to take up arms against Sheibani Khan. But the old man, who in his thirty-seven years' reign had brought his kingdom to unprecedented splendour and made his capital Herat the most magnificent city in the East and his court the resort of philosophers, poets, historians, and artists, had no inclination to go to war. His answer to Babur's messages was that his line of fortresses was sufficient to check Sheibani, and Babur, not daring to face the approaching Uzbegs although his forces had grown to about 4,000 men, changed his plans. He decided to ride in a totally different direction, to the south, towards Kabul.

The kingdom of Kabul was separated from the other kingdoms of the Timurids by the mountain ranges of the Hindukush. It had been the realm of the youngest of Babur's paternal uncles, Ulugh Khan, and after his death in 1501 it had been inherited by Ulugh's young son Abdur-Razzak, who in the following year had been deposed by one of his vassals, Muhammed Mokim. Trying to regain his throne, Abdur-Razzak had appealed to his cousins for help, and with this appeal as pretext Babur now led his troops against the usurper. It was not an easy undertaking to cross the Hindukush with his undisciplined bands along precipices and over mountain passes up to 12,000 feet, and at the same time to prevent the prowling groups from marauding, which would have roused the enmity of the whole native population of the country he was entering. Only after one of the culprits had been flogged to death on Babur's orders did the worst abuses stop. A detachment of the usurper's troops was surprised and instantly routed, and learning that his invasion was completely unexpected Babur hurried on to the capital city of Kabul and invested the town and the castle. The place was situated on a steep hill, barren of all vegetation and surrounded by a wide moat, beyond which an immense earthwork rose; but the ostentatious display of the forces now surrounding it, as well as the lack of provisions for a siege, dejected the people in the town. Mokim's soldiers began to desert, the mob started to plunder, and on the promise of unmolested departure for himself and his adherents with all their property and families, Mokim surrendered the capital after a few days' siege. Less than four months after his departure from Ferghana as a homeless fugitive, as a poor and ragged adventurer, the twenty-two year-old Babur now saw himself in possession of a kingdom mightier and bigger than Ferghana and, with one of those swift reversals of fortune in which the history of his time abounds, he had gained it almost 'without battle or contest'.

3

THE KINGDOM OF KABUL

BABUR declared himself King of Kabul, donating only a small appanage to his cousin Abdur-Razzak, and maintained that in taking over the kingdom he had restored the legitimate line of succession. He assigned fiefs to his followers, showing himself particularly generous to the men who had been faithful to him through all his misfortunes and giving them, in addition to lands, clothing, cattle and gold, as they possessed nothing. His brother Jahangir, who had managed to escape from his begs and had accompanied Babur on his trek, was made governor of Ghazni, the second town of the kingdom, far to the south-west; and his still younger brother Nazir Mirza was put in command of a province in the east, down the river Kabul. For the wandering tribes he levied a contribution of thirty thousand loads of grain from the country and exacted them, only later recognizing that 'the amount was excessive for the revenue and resources of Kabul and the country suffered extremely'.

He was delighted with his new land: 'It is surrounded on all sides by hills and difficult of access to foreigners and enemies. Its warm and cold districts are close to each other. You may go in one single day to a place where snow never falls, and in two hours you may reach a place where snow lies always.' Nevertheless, as the caravan route from India to Persia leads through Kabul, he found that 'the country is situated in the midst of the inhabited world. The caravans from Hindustan amounted every year to eight to ten thousand horses and brought twenty thousand pieces of cloth, and also slaves, sugar, candy, drugs and spices'. And all caravans had to pay transit duties.

The population of the country was very diverse, Babur writes: 'The various districts of Kabul lie amidst mountains which push out like so many mounds, with valleys and level plains expanding between them; and the greater part of the villages and the people live on these intermediate spaces'. The inhabitants of the plains were Persian-speaking Tajiks, either of Persian origin or having belonged to the Persian Empire since ancient times. In the hill country there lived countless tribes of every possible origin speaking different languages like Turki, Mongolian, Arabic, Hindu, Afghani and half a dozen dialects. They were wanderers and shepherds, but some were also plunderers who infested the plains and highroads and demanded contributions from travellers passing through their territory. When Babur imposed 'a large contribution of horses and sheep' on one such group of tribes, the Hazaras, they rebelled, and he had to take the field and smash them in a sudden raid. 'This country was to be governed by the sword and not the pen', was his conclusion.

Yet he had to recognize that the country was too poor to provide enough to feed and clothe and satisfy his numerous retainers. He needed more grain, more cattle, more stuff for clothing for his men who had helped him to his sudden success but could just as suddenly melt away, if he was not able to meet their wants. He had to do something, and it was only three months after his conquest of Kabul that, in January 1505, 'it was determined in council to make an irruption into Hindustan'. The stories of India's riches were everywhere alive in Babur's surroundings. He was now on the threshold of India, which his great ancestor Timur had invaded and from which he had brought home legendary booty that would more than satisfy his men and keep them in his service. And so Babur mustered his army and set out along the river Kabul. It was to be no more than a foraging expedition, one of those pillaging raids his ancestors had made into neighbouring lands since time immemorial.

After six days, on reaching Jelalabad, Babur was struck by the total change of climate and nature. Up to now he had known only countries of temperate climate, with cold winters and brief summers, high-lying grassland and mountain torrents. Now, 'I all at once saw a new world; the vegetables, the plants, the trees, the wild animals, all were different. The birds were of different plumage, 'and even the manners and customs of the tribes were of a different kind, although they were also Afghans. He proceeded through the Khaibar Pass, the gateway to India for all invaders from the north. The first town they fell upon and plundered was Kohat, where they found 'immense quantities of grain and a great many bullocks and buffaloes'. Their advance plundering parties reached the upper Indus but nowhere discovered the riches that Baki, Babur's chief adviser, had led them to expect, 'and Baki was greatly ashamed'.

Now a council was held. The heat and moisture made the men sweat under their heavy jackets and armour, and blistered their

3. The feast in Kabul held to celebrate the birth of Humayun.

4. Babur at a rhinoceros hunt.

skin. It was therefore decided not to cross the Indus but to proceed westward along the hills. They ravaged the land of the Afghans, they stormed every hill on which the Afghans entrenched themselves, they pillaged everything on their way, killing the men and erecting pyramids of their heads as a warning to others. Soon Afghan chieftains began to come at their approach 'with grass between their teeth, this being as much as to say: I am your ox'—and then they were sometimes spared.

This foray was regarded by Babur as a useful exercise for teaching his unruly soldiers discipline. To guard against surprises, the army was drawn up in battle-array every night, with foot-soldiers on watch and the most trusty chiefs taking turns in making the round of the camp with torches; those who were not found at their posts 'had their noses slit, and were led through the camp in that state'.

After ravaging Banu, they heard of other wealthy towns along good roads and continued their march to the south, down the bank of the Indus, but in the end the horses of the army became so exhausted that every day two to three hundred had to be left behind. The main booty consisted of bullocks and cows in such masses 'that the meanest retainer picked up three or four hundred of them'. But then the real rainy season started, water flooded the tents knee-deep, and the exhausted army turned west, back towards the mountains and came into a completely barren country where no fodder for the horses was to be found so that more and more luggage had to be left behind, even Babur's own tent. But then the mountains opened to the view of a great lake, Abi-Istada, and Babur felt overpowered:

'The water seemed to touch the sky; the further hills and mountains appeared inverted, like in a mirage, while the nearer hills and mountains seemed suspended between earth and heaven . . . From time to time, between the water and the sky some reddish appearance was to be seen, like the rosy dawn, to vanish and to reappear again until we came nearer and discovered that this appearance was caused by immense flocks of wild flamingoes, not ten or twenty thousand, but simply innumerable, beyond counting; and in their flight, as they moved their wings, their red feathers sometimes appeared and sometimes were hidden.'

From here they were on known ground and took the way to Ghazni, where Jahangir, as governor, played the host 'and did the honours of the place for a day or two'. Then, after four months absence, Babur returned to Kabul and had to pay for the strain of this arduous expedition with a sudden attack of fever. Scarcely had he overcome his illness when he had a grievous loss: his mother, Kutluk Nigar, who had shared his fortunes and misfortunes, helping him always, died; and a few days after her death Shah Begam, her step-mother, the mother of Babur's Mongolian uncle Mahmud Khan of Tashkent, arrived, with quite a large family following. Her arrival was a sign of the regard which Babur's standing already enjoyed in the neighbouring countries, and it also illustrates the important position occupied by women at these courts.

After Mahmud Khan's defeat by Sheibani, Shah Begam had followed him to Mongolistan, but, used to being obeyed, she very soon quarrelled with the obstinate Mongolian chieftains and left for Samarkand under the pretext of trying to get Sheibani to assign some province to Mahmud. When she arrived in Samarkand, Sheibani was occupied with the task of getting rid of all Mongols of distinction to whom the hordes were attached and whom they were used to follow, in order to prevent the emergence of rivals. He either got them to flee by circulating rumours that he intended to assassinate them, or actually imprisoned and killed some of the less prominent. Nevertheless, Shah Begam made herself comfortable in Samarkand. She was related to Sheibani, who after his victory had married her grand-daughter, as well as to his son, who was married to one of her daughters, and she began to play a game of intrigues. At last Sheibani, about to start a campaign, ordered her to be sent to Herat; but she did not feel happy at this court of splendour and intellectual refinement, and with a step-daughter who was an elder sister of Babur's mother she decided to set out for Kabul. They arrived too late, for Kutluk Nigar had just died, but their coming to Babur's residence only three years after Babur had appeared as a homeless adventurer at her court at Tashkent, was a confirmation of his achievement, and he repaid her hospitality in a magnificent way. He sent a ceremonial procession to meet the guests, received them with the utmost distinction and made them as comfortable as he could, bestowing on Shah Begam a choice district of Kabul.

He now had the feeling that if he was not to remain a mere figurehead in his own kingdom, as almost all of the Timurid princes were in the hands of their begs and advisers, the time had come to assert his personal authority. Already for some time there had been tension between him and his chief minister Baki. Baki had joined Babur in Hissar, when he was a fugitive, in the expectation of finding in him simply an adventurous youth whose name and descent would legalize all future conquests and acquisitions, while he himself would wield the real power and reap the benefits. And that was exactly what he had done since the conquest of Kabul, as chief minister, as commander of the guards, and as governor of Kabul. It was to him that the transit duties had been assigned as well as the property tax from large mountain tribes, but nothing would satisfy him. At any hint of opposition to his orders he declared he would resign, and as he had too many personal followers and a great prestige in the army Babur drew back every time. But now, when on the occasion of some dispute he declared that he would retire from his office, Babur accepted his resignation. Baki had second thoughts and reminded the king of his promise not to call him to account until he had committed nine offences—a privilege which Jenghiz Khan had conferred on his highest dignitaries. Babur immediately sent him a list of eleven offences against his sovereignty of which he had been guilty and maintained the dismissal. Baki departed with his family, his followers and possessions, went to Hindustan but fell foul of one of the Afghan chiefs and was killed. 'He was caught in the toils of his own evil-doing' noted Babur in his memoirs.

He appointed other ministers, but never again did he allow anyone to become powerful enough to threaten his personal authority. Henceforth he himself held the reins of government firmly in his own hands, and dealt personally with all important problems.

Babur's youngest brother, Nazir Mirza, had left the province assigned to him and gone north to Badakhshan, following an invitation by some unruly mountain tribes who had rebelled against Sheibani and fought the Uzbegs sent by the Khan. It was a foolhardy step, undertaken without Babur's knowledge while he was in Hindustan; but at the moment the rebels were successful, and as they were bound to encumber Sheibani, Babur could not really be too displeased. He himself was busy leading his troops in lightning forays against the mountain tribes in his own land, subduing them or punishing them for their marauding raids, and even winter and deep snow did not deter him. During one of these expeditions he suffered such a severe attack of lumbago that for forty days he was unable to move and had to be conveyed on a litter. Another time he was afflicted with boils on a cheek and had them lanced, but nothing could subdue his spirit.

Now he was the sovereign ruler and that seems to have made him more difficult. His brother Jahangir, somehow offended, fled from Kabul, taking two Mongolian tribes with him, to try to establish himself in the north-west, in the hilly frontier district. There was a danger that, together with the tribes living there, Jahangir would proclaim his independence.

But just at that time there came to Babur a call from Herat. The old Sultan Husain Baikara, King of Khorasan and mightiest of all descendants of Timur, who until now had turned a deaf ear to any request for help against Sheibani, saw his own kingdom menaced. The Uzbeg Khan was reducing its strong outposts one after the other and it was only a question of time before the wild hordes from the north would ride against the heart of his kingdom. Sheibani had to be checked and the old man himself took the field, summoning all his sons and amirs with their armies and sending messengers to the still remaining princes of Timur's house, summoning them to join him.

Babur immediately responded to the appeal: 'It was right that I should go—against such a foe as Sheibani Khan. If others had to go on foot, I would go even on my head; if others took up clubs, I would take up a stone!' Moreover, the way to Khorasan led through the district where Jahangir had fled, and Babur's appearance there with a strong army and the routing of some plundering Uzbeg parties in the neighbourhood sent all the chieftains from the hills to pay him homage; finally, the dejected Jahangir, too, came to beg his pardon and submissively joined his troops.

Babur continued his march, but before he had gone far an ambassador from Khorasan brought him the news that the old Sultan Husain Baikara had died; the ambassador also carried an invitation from the Sultan's sons to come and join them at the camp on the bank of the river Murghab, where the armies were assembled. Babur moved on and at the end of October 1506, after a march lasting four months and covering a distance of 800 miles, he joined up with the Sultan's sons. The reception was magnificently arranged, in the highest form of traditional etiquette.

The younger of the princes rode out a mile to greet him. Both dismounted, advanced and embraced. Then both mounted again and proceeded to the Hall of Audience. There the eldest Mirza sat on an elevated platform. On entering the state-tent, Babur bowed and advanced without stopping; the Mirza rose and stepped forward to meet him. They embraced precisely on the pre-arranged spot, at the extremity of the elevated platform. Everything poceeded according to rule. As Babur's movements were too hasty, his master of ceremonies tugged at his girdle, and he advanced at a more deliberate pace. When at the second meeting the host seemed to behave not as respectfully as he should, remonstrations were made to his master of ceremonies, and the Mirza immediately modified his conduct and showed Babur 'every mark of regard and esteem'. At the festivities and drinking parties that followed the hosts were informed that Babur drank no wine, and they did not press him. Later on, in Herat itself, at a particularly merry party, they tried to make him drink, and he confesses in his memoirs that he had a secret longing for wine and thought: 'as I had come to a refined city like Herat, in which every means of heightening pleasure and gaiety was possessed in perfection; in which all the incentives and circumstances of enjoyment were combined with an invitation to indulgence—if I did not seize the present moment, I never could expect such another. I therefore resolved to drink wine'. But at this moment it occurred to him that he had declined a cup at the banquet of the elder brother, and to take one from the younger would be an affront. He mentioned this difficulty at once, and all agreed. Thus his courtiers, out of respect for him, had to hide their goblets with their hands and to swallow their drinks quickly while he looked away.

He enjoyed his stay in Herat, which lasted for twenty days. Like a curious tourist he rode out every day to visit some new place, 'the marvellous gardens, the marble palaces, the mausoleums, the mosques, the bazaars, the colleges, the tombs of famous men, the baths and hospitals, the paper mills'. He admired all the luxury and beauty that Persian civilization could produce and concluded: 'In the whole habitable world there is not another such city'. Herat was the magnificent converging point of all the great highways from East and West, its mosques and public buildings were the admiration of the Mohammedan world, and the old Sultan had surrounded himself with the most learned men, with the best poets, painters, dancers and singers. His sons 'had all the virtues that ornament the relations of men with men', but, as Babur had already recognized at the camp on the banks of the Murghab, 'they were total strangers to the art of war'. Forty miles from their camp a party of four to five hundred men were plundering their land and they did not even send a detachment to cut up the marauders. Babur offered to do so for them, 'but afraid for their reputation they would not suffer me to move'. There was no question of an immediate campaign against Sheibani, the winter was coming and it was decided that the army should break up, each Mirza going with his troops to his own winter quarters, ready to begin operations in the spring. They also invited Babur to stay on in Khorasan, but after lengthy vacillation, with the foreboding that his long absence from Kabul might be dangerous, he decided to return and take the shortest route home across the mountains.

He had waited too long. It was the end of December and he had not gone far on the mountain road when snow began to fall. It snowed incessantly and soon all traces of the route were obliterated. The further the troops advanced, the deeper lay the snow. When it reached above the stirrups, so that sometimes the horses' hoofs no longer touched the ground, they went back to a place where there was firewood, camped around the fires, and sent a detachment down along the road they had come to look for some mountain people who might be wintering somewhere. After three or four days the men returned without having found anybody who could act as a guide. So they advanced again and continued for a week, 'trampling down the snow and being able only to make two or three miles a day. We all dismounted. At each step we sank up to the waist or still deeper, but we still continued trampling it down. After a few paces the man at the head of the file was exhausted; then he stood still and another man advanced to take his place. Next, the advancing party succeeded in dragging on a horse without a rider. The first horse sank up to the stirrups and girths, and after advancing ten or fifteen paces was worn out and replaced by another. In this manner, ten or twenty of us trod down the snow and brought our horses on. The rest of the troops, even our best men, rode along the road thus beaten down for them, hanging their heads. It was not the time for harassing them or displaying authority; if a man has vigour or fortitude he will of his own accord join in such work . . .'

After several days they reached a cave at the foot of Zard Sang (the pass over the Kohi Baba range). 'That day the storm was terrible. The snow fell so heavily that we all expected to die together. While the first of the troops reached the cave it was still daylight. When it became dark further troops ceased to arrive. Every man had to halt and dismount where he was. The cave seemed to be small and I took the shovel and, clearing the snow away at the entrance of the cave, made a resting place for myself. I dug down breast deep and yet did not reach the ground. In this hole I sat down sheltering from the gale.

They urged me to go into the cave, but I did not. I felt that for me to be within in comfort while my men were in trouble and distress was not to do my duty as I should. Whatever their hardships and difficulties were, I had to share them. So I remained sitting in the hole that I had dug out for myself till bed-time prayers, when the snow fell so fast that, as I had all the time been sitting crouched on my feet, I found four inches of snow on my head, lips and ears. That night I caught cold in the ear. About bed-time prayers a party which had explored the cave found it sufficiently large to hold us all. Then I shook off the snow, went into the cave and sent to call in all those who were at hand. A comfortable place was found for fifty or sixty people . . .'

Next morning the storm was over and the snow had stopped; they continued trampling the snow down and crossed the pass, although the cold was frightful and many lost their hands and feet through the frost. After another day's ride down the glen, they reached a village and were hospitably received by the astonished peasants, as 'it was not in the memory of the oldest man that this pass had ever been descended when there was so much snow on the ground; nay, it was never known that anybody even conceived the idea of passing it at such a season'. After a day's rest Babur and his troops were sufficiently restored to beat and plunder a nomad tribe who did not take kindly to having their sheep taken away. But then Babur pressed on at full speed to Kabul, for he received the news that a rumour had been deliberately spread that he was a captive in Khorasan, whereupon some tribes had declared his cousin Mirza Khan, a grandson of Shah Begam, king. The rebels, Mongols who were adherents of Shah Begam, besieged the citadel. Babur's approach took them by surprise and they were routed, but as the instigators were his next of kin who enjoyed much reverence among the seditious tribes, Babur reassured them, and particularly Shah Begam, of his continuing affection, and only ensured that Mirza Khan and other leaders departed to Khorasan.

Spring came. Jahangir, who had returned from Herat on a litter, very ill, died. Nazir, expelled by the Badakhshan tribes, came back and was installed in Ghazni. Babur was undertaking one of his punitive expeditions against Afghan tribes who had refused to pay tribute, and as a warning to others erected pyramids of the heads of those who had put up resistance. The raid was so successful that the one-fifth of the spoil which was set aside for Babur amounted to sixteen thousand sheep. As a celebration a hunt was arranged in the old Mongolian tradition, going back to Jenghiz Khan, according to which the troops formed a large ring and drove the deer and the wild animals to the centre, where first the king, then the nobles and then the lower ranks chased them down. Then, returning to Kabul, Babur heard the momentous news: Sheibani Khan had taken Herat after the sons of Husain Baikara had fled, and was hunting them down.

Sheibani was lord of Khorasan! This meant that the whole of what had been the heritage of the Timurids had become the possession of this Uzbeg Khan, with the sole exception of Babur's Kabul, and the only and last barrier between him and Kabul was the district and fortress of Kandahar, previously a dependancy of Khorasan, where Mokim, the man whom Babur had driven out of Kabul, ruled with his brother. Afraid of Sheibani, the brothers seem to have asked for Babur's help, and so he set out for Kandahar demanding naturally that they should recognize his overlordship. On his march he met masses of refugees from Khorasan, remnants of the beaten army, also some ladies of the royal house, among them Maham, whom he had met in Herat and to whom he was affianced.

Before he reached Kandahar, however, its rulers had offered their submission to Sheibani and so averted his attack. They no longer needed Babur, and at his approach, instead of welcoming him as an ally, they led their troops against him. They were far superior in numbers, but, as Babur writes, he had for the first time a really well drilled and disciplined army and he accepted the challenge. Their attacks were repulsed, his troops charged in turn, and in the end the enemy was put to flight. The citadel of Kandahar opened its gates and the booty was immense. Babur writes that because of a reconnaissance ride he arrived rather late at the camp: 'It was no longer the same camp, and I did not recognize it. There were horses, strings of long-haired camels, and mules laden with silk-cloth and fine linen. Everywhere there stood chests containing thousands of pounds of property and effects, carefully arranged and packed as in a treasury. There were trunks upon trunks and bales upon bales of cloth and other effects heaped one upon the other; cloak-bags on cloak-bags, and pots upon pots filled with money. In every man's tent there was a superfluity of spoil.'

However, Babur's cautious adviser, Kasim Beg, warned him not to tarry in the land of Kandahar and, bestowing it on his brother Nazir, he returned to Kabul. Only a week later he heard that, called by

Mokim, Sheibani had hastened by forced marches from Herat in the hope of surprising Babur himself and laid siege to Kandahar.

Now the last barrier was gone. A war council was held at once, and such was the alarm at the Uzbeg threat that it was decided not to wait for the fall of Kandahar but to withdraw from Kabul altogether. Since Babur was the last still independent Timurid on the throne, Sheibani was certain to turn with all his might upon him, and Babur knew that in spite of all his successes he would not be able to face the onslaught. It was better to clear out of the country undefeated and the only question was: where to flee? He had the choice of two ways: to the north, into the hills of Badakhshan, or to the south into Hindustan. But in Badakhshan he would be surrounded on all sides by Sheibani's forces. Moreover, Shah Begam, who was the daughter of the hereditory king of Badakhshan, claimed that her grandson Mirza Khan, who had returned with the fugitives from Khorasan, could easily gain it for himself. Thus Babur let her go there with her clan, and himself set out for Hindustan. As governor in Kabul he appointed his cousin Abdur-Razzak, who as the son of the last king of Kabul had hereditory rights to the throne which he had even occupied for a year before he was overthrown by Mokim. If Sheibani invaded the kingdom the native tribes might fight for him.

On the way to Hindustan, Babur encountered unexpected obstacles. His march to the south led through Afghan country and the Afghans, whom he had so often raided, now occupied the passes and obstructed his progress so that he had to fight all the time, 'for even the best disposed of them were bent on mischief'. It was this delay that saved Kabul for Babur. While he was fighting the Afghan tribes, Sheibani's attention was called to events nearer home. Babur received from his brother Nazir Mirza, whom he had left in charge of Kandahar, the news that Sheibani, on hearing that a castle near Herat where he had left his family and treasures was being attacked by some rebels, had offered him a free retreat if he surrendered the citadel of Kandahar. In his helpless position Nazir Mirza was only too glad to accept the offer and to be able to go with his troops to Ghazni, while the Uzbeg Khan hurried off to Khorasan. In the meantime winter had come, there was no danger of an immediate attack by Sheibani, and Babur felt that he could safely return to Kabul.

Now, as the only sovereign of Timur's descent in undisputed possession of a kingdom, he assumed the title of Padishah—Emperor—which before him had been used by Husain Baikara, the

King of Khorasan. The purpose of this title was to raise his prestige as the head of the illustrous dynasty and it elevated his little mountain kingdom to special eminence. He had married Maham after her flight from Khorasan, and a few months earlier she had borne him his first son, Humayun. The happy father, having seen what marvels his ancestors and relatives had done in Samarkand and Herat, now threw himself into the task of accomplishing similar splendours in the land and city of Kabul to make it worthy of the new dynasty.

His expectation that all his troops and people would proudly share in his new glory were suddenly shattered. He had owed his successes in Kabul and afterwards chiefly to the troops who had deserted to him in Hissar while he was still no more than an enterprising adventurer, and whether they were Mongolian tribes under native chieftains or bands following some leader or other, they all regarded the land where they were staying, together with its inhabitants, to a certain extent as their prey. They smarted under the discipline which Babur maintained; they thought his punishments for marauding and other offences outrageous, and a conspiracy was formed to seize him and to restore Abdur-Razzak to the throne. One night, as Babur was returning from a palace in a garden outside Kabul, an ambush was laid, and when, having escaped seizure by a hair's breadth, he reached the camp of his guards many of his officers and soldiers left him and rushed into the town to protect their families and possessions, as plundering and other outrages were to be expected. In the morning he could not muster more than about five-hundred horsemen while the insurgents counted at least two to three thousand. But he rode against the rebels at once and perhaps never before did he risk his life so recklessly as in this desperate battle, exposing himself in every encounter. It is said that in single combat he slayed or put to flight, one after the other, five champion fighters of the enemy, and finally, in hand to hand fighting, he broke and routed the foe. The Mongols fled from Kabul, and Babur re-established his sovereignty, henceforth undisputed.

Sheibani was still in the north; the threat of invasion had for the moment receded and Babur could dedicate himself wholly to peaceful exploits. He laid out more gardens on the banks of the rivers, he directed fountains to be built, he had the cherry-tree sap brought and planted, which later produced excellent fruit, and he also boasted: 'It was I who planted the sugar-cane'. In his gardens were orange trees and pomegranates, there bloomed 'arghwan' flowers clustered around small artificial lakes, 'the yellow mingling with red, so that no place on earth was to compare with it'. There he received his friends and held his feasts. As a man of culture and refined living he composed verses, and as the art of writing itself was highly regarded in the East he even designed a new style of caligraphy, which was called 'the Baburi hand'. It was a life of pleasure in continuous succession, in which the feasting alternated with delightful hunting parties. And as a great warrior he also liked the punitive expeditions against insubordinate hill tribes in between the pleasures.

This delightful life had continued for well over two years, when, at the end of December 1510, a courier from Badakhshan arrived from his cousin Mirza Khan, who had managed to establish himself there, although his grandmother Shah Begam had fallen into the hands of one of his opponents and had lost her life. The courier had sped in all haste, in icy winter conditions, over the snow-clad passes of the Hindukush to bring Babur the incredible message: Sheibani Khan had been defeated and killed. He had encountered a superior power beyond the confines of Transoxiana, and that power was Persia.

4

FROM SAMARKAND TO DELHI

IN the decade in which Sheibani Khan and his Uzbegs had been effecting the piecemeal conquest of the eastern part of what had been Timur's empire, the western part, the original Persia, went through a similar political convulsion. A devout religious brotherhood of Shiites which, for over a century and a half, had grown to considerable strength, had been crushed after their religious and military leader was slain in a battle; his children, with the exception of one, Ismail, were massacred by a relative, a Turkoman lord. When the boy, whose life had been saved by divine intervention, reappeared with his adherents some years later, in 1500, all the faithful of the brotherhood rallied around him. His opponents were defeated one after the other and he was enthroned in Tabriz. The next seven years saw his triumph over a dozen princes who ruled over various parts of Persian territory, culminating in the conquest of Baghdad. At twenty-one Ismail was the Shah of an empire which reached in the east to the frontiers of Khorasan.

With Sheibani's conquest of Khorasan the two conquerors became neighbours, and Sheibani's Uzbegs, riding in pursuit of the sons and adherents of the Sultan Husain Baikara, or simply marauding, did not refrain from carrying their raids into the neighbouring kingdom and ravaging its adjoining province. Shah Ismail sent an envoy to Sheibani, asking for redress and the assurance that such inroads would not happen again. In reply, Sheibani returned a pilgrim's staff and a dervish's bowl—an insolent recommendation that the Shah should return to the profession of his forbears. Ismail, proud of his descent from holy dervishes of ascetic piety, who gloried in voluntary poverty, immediately sent to Sheibani in return a spindle and a distaff, indicating that it would be safer for the Khan to spend his time spinning rather than insulting his neighbours. Then, without losing a moment, the Shah betook himself to Khorasan with the flower of the Persian cavalry. Sweeping the scattered Uzbeg detachments before him, he rushed through the northern part of the country to Meshed, to the shrine of the holy Imam Reza, a place of pilgrimage for the Shiites, thus giving additional offence to the Moslems of the eastern countries, who were orthodox Sunnites; and from Meshed he hastened to Merv, where Sheibani was waiting for reinforcements.

Near Merv the Persian Shah defeated the Uzbeg army which tried to stop him and pitched his camp in sight of the city. But recognizing that the siege would be long and that he would soon have to face the whole force of the Uzbegs from Turkistan and Transoxiana, he faked a retreat after writing a taunting letter to Sheibani. Sheibani, quick to take offence, did not wait for reinforcements, but proclaiming that this was a holy war against the accursed Shiites, he at once set out in pursuit of the retreating enemy. Easily routing Ismail's intentionally weak rearguard, he pushed on across a river, when he was suddenly faced by the Shah's army in battle array; the Shah immediately attacked him with 17,000 men of the best Persian cavalry. The Uzbegs were beaten and, trying to retreat, found that the Shah had thrown a body of his troops to the other side of the river, and had destroyed the bridge. The retreat was cut off. Although Sheibani and his Uzbegs tried to take refuge in an enclosure at the river, the gate of the enclosure was soon stormed; and as the enemy poured in, the Khan and his entourage tried to leap over the high stockade, but the horses failed to clear it, and the riders, falling one upon the other, were slain. Sheibani was among the dead. The story goes that his body was dismembered and that the pieces were sent to the still restless Persian princes as a reminder. The skin of his head, stuffed with straw, was conveyed to Bayazid II, the Sultan in Constantinople, while Ismail himself kept the skull, mounted in gold, to serve as a drinking cup on great occasions.

Following up his victory, Shah Ismail rode to Herat, entered the town and ordered the Khutba—the prayer for the sovereign—to be read in the Shiite fashion. The Shiites recognized only the fourth Caliph, Ali, the cousin and son-in-law of Mohammed, as the Prophet's rightful heir .To read prayers in the Shiite creed was tantamount to proclaiming the first three Caliphs accursed usurpers, and the preacher in Herat declared that he would not save his life at the cost of the true faith. He was killed on the spot. Then Shah Ismail asked the Sheikh-ul-Islam, the highest Moslem authority in Herat, to pray in the Shiite way. He refused and was shot down with an arrow; his body was burned in the market-place. A new type of hatred, a religious one, arose between the local population and the conquerors.

In the meantime Babur, after the receipt of Mirza Khan's letter announcing Sheibani's death, had left his kingdom of Kabul and 'started out for Kunduz with the utmost speed, although it was mid-winter and the high passes were closed'. When he arrived in Kunduz, he found that the main forces on which he could rely in Badakhshan were Mongol tribes who, having plundered the fleeing Uzbegs, had found their way into the mountains. Most of them were returning to their eastern steppes; but some of the clans, who had previously lived in the province of Hissar, were prepared to join him. However, he heard that the Uzbegs had recovered a little from their defeat. The various reinforcements who were on the way to Sheibani had quickly elected a new Khan, the provinces which were in their hands were re-distributed among his own and Sheibani's relatives, and their fighting forces still had their old strength and the chieftains their old ability.

Babur sat in Badakhshan, in Kunduz, burning for the reconquest of his old domains but powerless to undertake anything against the superior Uzbeg forces, when his sister Khanzada arrived, who ten years earlier had been left in Samarkand to become Sheibani's wife. She had been taken prisoner in Merv; Shah Ismail had restored her possessions, given her her freedom and sent her with all her baggage, her servants and an escort of honour to Babur. Babur understood the meaning of this gesture and immediately despatched his cousin Mirza Khan with presents and congratulations to the Shah. That was a corresponding gesture on his part, implying that he would welcome Persian friendship and assistance.

The Shah, already preoccupied with disturbances in the west, on his Turkish frontier, came to an agreement with the Uzbegs that the lands south of the Amu Darya were to be his. He confirmed Mirza Khan as ruler of Badakhshan and agreed that Babur could have whatever he was able to wrest from the Uzbegs. The guards which had accompanied Babur's sister, and even certain Persian reinforcements which Mirza Khan had brought back when he returned, were to help him, naturally on condition that he became a Shiite. It was clear that in these circumstances the utmost Babur could expect to achieve would be a position as viceroy under the Shah's authority. Then there was the vexed religious question. Whether Babur hoped that, once installed in Transoxiana, he would be able to satisfy the

Shah with lip service to the Shiite faith, or whether the lure of Samarkand and the chance to take revenge on the hated Uzbegs were stronger than anything else, including religion, he accepted the terms and crossed the Amu Darya. A pitched battle against the Uzbegs was won, and the fall of Hissar was the prize. Other wandering tribes flocked to his banner at once, new reinforcements from the Shah arrived, and, outflanking another Uzbeg army, Babur rushed to Bokhara. He occupied the city and the Uzbegs evacuated the whole region and retired to the north.

In October 1511, for the third time in his life, Babur, now in his twenty-ninth year, made a triumphant entry into Samarkand. He was received with immense joy; the streets were hung with brocades and velvets and thronged with the delighted population. Everybody welcomed the expulsion of the hated Uzbegs and the restoration of the traditional sovereign of Timur's descent.

But the gladness did not last long. The people saw in his train the accursed Kizil-Bashi—the Redheads—as the Shiite soldiers were called because of their red conical caps with twelve points (signifying the twelve Imams) and a long strip of red cloth hanging down behind. Even though Babur soon sent his Persian auxiliaries away, he had to keep some of the officers, and the new coins which he struck bore the name of the Shah in the place of honour above his own. In addition he received from Shah Ismail a reminder that the Khutba was to be read strictly in accordance with the Shiite rules and he had to obey. The population of Transoxiana, always untainted orthodox Sunnites, were enraged; unable to offer resistance they used their wits to ridicule Babur and his followers and to make sarcastic remarks about them. His popularity vanished overnight.

When spring came, the Uzbegs, encouraged by Shah Ismail's return to the west, poured into Transoxiana from the steppes and marched to Bokhara. Babur tried to stop them but was defeated and fled to Samarkand, followed by the enemy, who began to encircle the city. With empty granaries and with the population averse to his present form of rule, he could not consider resistance and in May 1512 was for the third time forced to leave the capital of his dreams.

He sent to the Shah an appeal for aid and Ismail despatched a new army. But this army was not to serve under Babur. On the contrary, he, together with his troops, was put under the command of the Persian general. The Uzbegs retreated. The Persian general, after storming their stronghold, Karshi, put not only the garrison but, in spite of Babur's protests, the whole population of 15,000 men, women and children to death. In any case, they were accursed Sunnites. The struggle took on the character of a religious war of extermination.

Now the Uzbegs, meanwhile collecting all their forces from the districts and towns, retreated further and further without making a stand until they were at the edge of the desert lying north of Transoxiana, and here at last they halted in a well protected camp. When the Persian cavalry charged in close array a hail of deadly arrows wrought havoc among the massed riders. Once the enemy was shaken a terrible countercharge followed, and the Persian army fled in disorder after its commander had been killed. Babur, who had been placed by the Persian general in command of the reserve, did not try to intervene but withdrew and hastened with his troops to Hissar. Did he hold his command back in order to preserve his forces, or had the slaughter of Karshi taught him a lesson? This period is not covered by the memoirs, and we have no first hand account of his motives and aspirations during that time.

Now the bulk of his forces once more consisted of Mongols who had fled from the Uzbegs or had been pushed by the Uzbeg commanders outside their territories because they were thought unreliable. These unsettled tribesmen, who belonged nowhere and owed allegiance to no one, regarded it as their legitimate right to rob and plunder wherever they were and whatever they could. They were not in the mood to let this defeated and disposessed man, Babur, prescribe what they ought or ought not to do or restrict their opportunities to pillage. One night, in the camp at Hissar, they fell upon his quarters, killing and wounding all who opposed them. Babur, awakened by the hubub, leaped out of bed and just managed to escape into the citadel while the Mongols plundered whatever they found.

Recognizing that he was unable to oppose them, he fled, again in the dark of night, and went over the hills and the Amu Darya to Kunduz, where his cousin Mirza Khan was. Nominally, Babur regarded himself still as the overlord of Badakhshan, of which Kunduz was the capital, but that Mirza Khan had been confirmed as ruler there by Shah Ismail was more important than any question of overlordship.

In Kunduz Babur remained with his cousin for over a year on the watch, waiting and hoping for an opportunity to march and regain the lost dominions. But the opportunity did not arrive. When the

Uzbegs dared to cross the Amu Darya and raid the northern provinces of Khorasan Shah Ismail returned from the west, and they retreated in haste. The Shah executed the officers who had fled before the Uzbegs and punished the inhabitants who in their hatred of the Shiites had welcomed them. Babur, however, could no longer apply to the Persians for help, for his retreat in the face of the Uzbegs was regarded by the Shah as treason. The Mongols who, after Babur's flight to Kunduz, became masters of the province and the town of Hissar, had robbed the inhabitants of all cattle, grain and other possessions and caused a terrible famine in the devastated land. Then, when the winter came, the masters saw themselves in need of food and in want of forage for their horses, and it was the turn of the Uzbegs to fall upon them and to cut them to pieces. If this punishment of the predatory Mongol tribes gave Babur some satisfaction, it deprived him at the same time of every hope of winning back any of the Timurid possessions to the north of the Amu Darya. Everything was lost, and in 1514, after nearly four years of abscence, he returned to Kabul. This little kingdom was all that he could call his own.

Babur was fortunate enough to find his kingdom secure and at peace. He had left it under the rule of his brother Nazir Mirza, who handed over the government at once and retired to Ghazni, which he had previously held as his brother's vassal. He died there the following year from overindulgence in wine, according to some chroniclers. Under his soft and smooth government there had been no revolts and no disturbances in Kabul, and after his bitter experiences of the last years Babur could resume the same life which he had led before his departure to Badakhshan—with one additional enjoyment, that of drinking wine.

During his sojourn in Transoxiana he had given up the abstinence which he had strictly observed all his life and began to drink wine. Describing the merits of Bokhara he remarks: 'There is no wine superior in spirit and strength to that of Bokhara. When I drank wine in Samarkand in my drinking bouts, I used the wine of Bokhara'. Now in Kabul he wrote to its praise:

> 'Drink wine in the land of Kabul, and send round the cup without hesitation;
> For it is at once a mountain and a sea, a town and a desert!'

And he added opium and hemp to the pleasure of wine.

But all was not ease and pleasure-seeking. His position depended as much as ever on his ability to satisfy the needs and desires of his followers, and the resources of the country of Kabul itself were not sufficient to give them what they wanted. The continuing expeditions against the hill tribes, while consolidating his hold on the country, brought in little. His men remembered the enormous booty they had found when they invaded Hindustan, but Babur remembered the exertions and the hardships, too, and he had learned caution. Before attempting a campaign across the mountain ranges, he wanted to make his passage secure. The road to Hindustan led through the mountainous territory in the hands of the Yusufzai Afghans and Babur marched first against them and ended the campaign with marrying the daughter of the chief of the clan, in this way gaining their allegiance.

From his stay in Transoxiana he had brought a new knowledge: the use of gunpowder. In 1514 the Ottoman Turks had inflicted a heavy defeat on Shah Ismail with the aid of their artillery, and Babur must have used the following years in Kabul to engage a 'Rumi'—Ottoman—gunner and matchlock-men, because in his memoirs he mentions them and also a gun, which he calls 'the foreign piece'.

At the end of 1518, all preparations complete, he finally set out with his army to invade the Punjab, once conquered in a lightning campaign by Timur. In an attack upon the little mountain fortress of Bajaur the foreign gun was discharged twice, and the matchlocks also were fired. Babur describes the effect of the fire-arms: 'As the people of Bajaur had never seen any matchlocks, at first they were not in the least apprehensive of them, so that when they heard the report of the matchlocks, they stood opposite them, mocking and making unseemly and improper gestures' But when the unseen bullets, piercing shields, leather jackets, or even coats-of-mail, brought down about a dozen Bajaur fighters 'the men of the fort were so alarmed that, for fear of the matchlocks, not one of them would venture to show his head'.

The fortress was taken and pillaged, the men were killed, it is said up to 3,000, and a pillar erected of their heads. Their wives and children were taken prisoner and made slaves: 'In any case they were infidels'. For the first time Babur mentions religion as justifying cruelty.

Then a drinking party was held, a hunt arranged, and a quantity of grain was seized in a valley near-by. Next month, in February, the upper Indus was crossed above Attok, the infantry and the heavy baggage were floated across the river on rafts, and Babur pushed on through the hilly country of the North Punjab.

He was now in the land under the sway of the ruler of Lahore, Daulat Khan, who himself held it as a fief from the Sultan of Delhi, an Afghan of the dominating Lodi clan. In his first expedition to Hindustan, fourteen years ealier, Babur had been content with carrying away all the plunder he could find. Now he raised a new claim: 'From the time that Timur had invaded Hindustan and on leaving it appointed some amirs as rulers, all these countries were the rightful possession of the family of Timur and of his descendants'. Being the last sovereign of Timur's house he started to regard them as his rightful domain 'and was resolved to acquire possession of them'. This view had for the inhabitants the advantage that he issued strict orders to his troops not to molest or trouble the flocks or herds of the natives, forbidding all plundering and pillage. The result was that as they pressed forward, 'in several places men were coming, bringing some gifts as tribute and a caparisoned horse or a camel, and offering their submission.' On reaching Bhera at the river Jhelum, Babur had the satisfaction of seeing that the town, too, submitted, and it was spared although it had to pay a heavy contribution. When he heard that in spite of his order some of his troops had maltreated a number of its inhabitants, he sent out a party who seized the evil-doers, slit their noses and led them about the camp in that condition. The news spread, and he received the submission of various other towns and forts or forced the recalcitrants by sudden assault into submission and into accepting his officers and begs as governors.

Enjoying the ease with which he was able to secure a grip on the country, Babur used every excursion and every suitable occasion for drinking bouts or for hemp and hashish parties. When they were near a river, the revelry took place on a boat or on a raft. They drank until they were utterly drunk, and when they had to ride back to the camp, they were 'falling sometimes on one side of the horse, and sometimes on the other'. In between, he with his companions had the pleasure of hunting a rhinoceros or a tiger. But now the rainy season had come. 'There was such a fall of rain, that the whole plain was covered with water. Between Bhera and the hills where we were encamped, there was a little stream. By the time of noonday prayers, it was equal in breadth to a considerable lake.'

It was high time to think of returning to Kabul, and he was still on his way home when he was joined by the governors and officers whom he had left behind to rule the country and who were immediately expelled as soon as his troops were gone. Before he started on his return journey he sent an ambassador to Sultan Ibrahim of Delhi with letters informing him that he, Babur, had already taken the Upper Punjab and was claiming the whole province once conquered by Timur. The ambassador had to travel first to Lahore, to Daulat Khan, with similar letters and instructions, and the result was, as Babur writes in his memoirs: 'Daulat Khan detained my ambassador some time in Lahore, neither seeing him himself, nor suffering him to proceed to Sultan Ibrahim; so that my envoy, five months after, returned to Kabul without having received any answer.'

But Daulat Khan had very good reasons for not letting the ambassador go to Delhi. The kingdom of Delhi was in fact a conglomerate of nearly independent principalities, provinces and fiefs, each one ruled by a hereditory Afghan chief who had absolute power in his domain. Every one had the support of the Afghan clan to which he belonged and so there was continuous rivalry between the men as well as the clans. The chiefs feared that the monarchy might gain too much power and become despotic, and that the men of the Lodi dynasty who ruled in Delhi would grow too strong. When Sultan Ibrahim had ascended the throne in 1518, only a short time before, a group of Afghan leaders insisted that his brother should have a separate domain carved out; but that again was opposed by other chieftains, who rallied round Ibrahim, and Ibrahim managed to beat down the rebels and put his brother to death. Then, instead of trying afterwards to conciliate his amirs, he began to strengthen his rule by imprisoning or putting to death all those whom he considered dangerous, and a new rebellion flared up, particularly in the more distant provinces. Civil war broke out and Daulat Khan found it imprudent to let Babur's ambassador reach Delhi, whatever message he carried.

Next winter, Babur again invaded the Punjab to punish the rebels of the districts he had forced into submission, but he had to break off this campaign as his own kingdom of Kabul was suddenly in peril. The ruler of Kandahar, Shah Beg, the brother of Mokim, who had died, had taken advantage of Babur's absence to invade his land. Babur rushed home, expelled the invaders and laid siege to Kandahar. However, there was famine and pestilence in the land; the disease spread to Babur's camp and forced him to raise the siege and to withdraw. By now it was clear to him that he could not risk any prolonged campaigns in far-off Hindustan with an independent Kandahar at his back, so next year he invaded it again.

Shah Beg, aware of Kandahar's precarious position between the now Persian Khorasan and Babur's Kabul, was just about to carve out for himself a safer domain in the south, in the hills leading to the valley of the lower Indus. He made a peace proposal: Babur should give him a year to remove his adherents and tribes with their cattle and effects, and probably pay some compensation, and then the city and the provinces of Kandahar would be delivered to him. Babur agreed, and the following summer he was able to take possession of the whole land of Kandahar without further fighting.

In Badakhshan, to the north of Kabul, his cousin Mirza Khan had died two years earlier, and Babur had immediately appointed his then thirteen year-old son Humayun governor of Badakhshan, sending him to his post accompanied by trustworthy begs, who were to rule the province in his name. Thus both approaches to Kabul, from the north and the west, were now safeguarded, and Babur could devote himself to his plans for Hindustan.

In the meantime, events in the kingdom of Delhi showed all signs of an impending crisis. Sultan Ibrahim, having again crushed the rebels, took his revenge. A proud and arrogant youth, he wanted to make a true autocracy of his sultanate. The amirs, who were used to be honoured with a feast when they came to Delhi, were now asked to stand, with their hands crossed before them, at the throne as slaves of royalty. He commanded Daulat Khan to appear in Delhi, and Daulat Khan, informed that his life was at stake, declared the Punjab independent. Sultan Ibrahim raised an army against him, whereupon Daulat Khan sent one of his sons to Kabul, offering to acknowledge Babur as his sovereign in return for his help. At the same time, an uncle of Sultan Ibrahim, Alim Khan, also solicited Babur's assistance in his aspirations to the throne of Delhi.

It may be that this request directed Babur's ambitions to the far greater target, the whole kingdom of Delhi instead of only the Punjab, its northern province. Had Timur's invasion not culminated in terrible destruction at Delhi?

When finally, in the autumn of 1523, Babur set out for Lahore, Daulat Khan had already been driven from his capital by the approaching Delhi army. Babur defeated this army; in pursuing the fugitives his troops entered Lahore and plundered it, and then advanced to Dipalpur, storming and sacking the town. Here he was joined by Daulat Khan, who was expecting to be re-instated as governor in Lahore. But Babur, who considered it his own dominion, gave him only a minor fief. Deeply disappointed, Daulat Khan pretended to depart to his *jagir*—his fief—but immediately withdrew with his followers into the foothills of the Himalayas, waiting, beyond Babur's reach, for an opportunity to assert himself again. In any case, when Babur heard of his flight he returned to Lahore, apportioned the command of the various districts and forts to his officers—and was once more obliged to rush back to Kabul on the news that Shah Ismail had died and the Uzbegs had started a campaign.

As soon as he left, Daulat Khan reappeared in the Punjab, and after some fighting, in which he defeated Alim Khan, the two came to an understanding that they would march together against Delhi, hoping to conquer it without Babur's help. They advanced and laid siege to Delhi, but in the end were both put to flight by Sultan Ibrahim.

Babur in the meantime collected all the troops he could. It was the largest army he had ever led. 'Great and small, good and bad, servants and no servants, the force numbered twelve thousand persons'. Leaving Kabul in the nominal charge of his second son Kamran, now about sixteen years old, he set out in November 1525. On the way, in his beloved Garden of Fidelity, his son Humayun was to join him with the troops from Badakhshan, but he was late in arriving, and while sending him severe reprimands Babur enjoyed the rest: 'The garden was in great glory. No one can view it without acknowledging its beauty. During the few days we stayed there we drank a great quantity of wine at every sitting and regularly took our morning cup. When I had no drinking parties—one of the sources mentions that the drinking days were Saturday, Sunday, Tuesday and Wednesday—I had bhang-opium-parties'. After Humayun arrived, and the troops from Ghazni too, the combined armies continued their march, and Babur writes: 'I embarked on a raft and proceeded down the river, drinking all the way'. A couple of days later he caught fever and coughed blood. But he knew the reason: it was a punishment for turning contemptible and despicable thoughts into verse for amusement. So he wrote there:

> What can I do with you, oh my tongue!
> On your account I am inwardly covered with blood.
> How long will you delight to compose vituperative verses,
> One of which is impure and another lying?

He resolved to do penitence and religiously abstain 'from such idle thoughts and such unworthy amusements'; and he concluded that 'every servant of the Almighty who feels and benefits from such punishment has cause to regard it as mercy overflowing'. At the next halt his tents were pitched on a hill and 'the blaze from the fires of the troops in the camp below was wonderfully brilliant and beautiful', and so he drank wine. In the morning before sunrise he took 'bhang' and they continued their march.

Then some rhinoceroses were discovered, a hunt followed and two of them were killed. Babur was curious to know how an elephant and a rhinoceros would behave if brought face to face. The elephant keepers set out with their elephants, but the rhinoceros ran off at once. In this manner, proceeding comfortably, the army progressed and was joined by various amirs and also by the troops left behind in Lahore. Reports came that Daulat Khan and his sons had assembled a big army, but at the news of Babur's approach the army had dispersed. On the promise of pardon Daulat Khan surrendered the fortress he held. He had to wait on Babur as a suppliant and was humiliated, but after a harangue about his ingratitude was allowed to retire with his family to the hills and villages where his Afghan clan lived. However, knowing his own troops, Babur took the precaution of being near the fortress gate through which the Khan with his family was to leave and had himself to 'shoot various arrows to prevent the departing from being pillaged. Several officers were sent to secure and safeguard the treasures in the fortress, and then Babur went there to inspect the library collected by Daulat Khan's son, giving some of the books to Humayun and sending others to Kamran in Kabul.

Some further hill forts were taken, some more Afghan amirs with their troops joined Babur, and then he marched towards Delhi against Sultan Ibrahim, constantly sending out reconnaissance detachments on all sides. On the report that an enemy army was approaching from the side, Babur despatched a specially selected force against them under Humayun. It was Humayun's first engagement and he distinguished himself by scattering the enemy and bringing in about a hundred prisoners and seven or eight elephants. Humayun received a dress of honour and was given other presents; the prisoners Babur 'ordered to be shot by matchlock-men as an example'.

Then an advance body of Ibrahim's army was attacked and

beaten and again 'several of the prisoners were put to death, to strike terror into the enemy'.

Now both armies were approaching each other slowly and carefully. Sultan Ibrahim advanced three or four miles at a time and halted two or three days at each station. Babur let his troops march in battle order, each formation in its precisely prescribed place. And every time the camp was formed, it was secured against surprise attack. The guns were placed in front, the gun-carriages being linked together with twisted bull-hides 'as with chains, according to the custom of the Rumi—Ottoman Turks', to break any possible cavalry charge. Between each pair of carriages there were movable breast-works or bags filled with earth, behind which the matchlock-men could load and fire their weapons. In a war council it was decided to advance to the plain of Panipat and to arrange the camp there in such a way that the right flank was covered by the city, while on the left ditches were dug and barricades of tree branches put up. One of the begs said to Babur: 'You have fortified our camp in such a way that the enemy will never think of coming here'. Babur retorted that he was judging Ibrahim by the Khans and Sultans of the Uzbegs. 'Our present enemies have not the ability to discriminate when it is proper to advance and when to retreat'.

For a week he waited in vain for the vastly superior enemy forces to attack. Many of his troops 'were in great terror and alarm' and he agrees that 'they had some reason, for they had come two or three months' journey from their own country and had to engage in arms a strange nation, whose language we did not understand and who did not understand ours'. However, in Babur's judgment Ibrahim was 'a young man of no experience. He would not part with his treasure even to satisfy his troops. If he had chosen to spend enough money, he might have engaged 100,000 more men. But he was negligent: he marched without order, retired or halted without plan, and engaged in battle without foresight'.

Nevertheless in the mood prevailing in Babur's army it was dangerous to wait longer, so one night he sent out four to five thousand men to attack the enemy's position. They failed and were driven back, and elated by the ease with which the invaders were repulsed, Ibrahim advanced next day in battle array. Babur arranged his troops in battle order and placed on the extreme left and the extreme right flanking parties of Mongols, flying columns whose task it was to execute an enveloping movement around the enemy and engage him from the sides and the rear with clouds of arrows, after the pattern of the Uzbeg tactics. While the Delhi army pressed straight on it became engaged all round, was met with arrows from all sides, while in front the gun and matchlock fire wrought havoc among the attackers. Their charges were met by counter-charges, and by noon the great army of the King of Delhi was broken and in flight, pursued and slaughtered, while Sultan Ibrahim was found dead among thousands of his soldiers.

This battle at Panipat, fought on April 20, 1526, decided the fate of Hindustan. On the very day of the battle, Babur sent detachments to Delhi and Agra to occupy the towns and to seize the treasure. Three days later he himself arrived at Delhi, and on April 27th the Khutba was read in his name in the main mosque and money was distributed among the poor. A few days later he reached Agra.

In the meantime Humayun, who had been sent forward with the advance detachment, had blockaded the fort. In the fort was the family of the Raja of Gwalior who had fallen with Ibrahim at Panipat. The family tried to escape and was caught, but Humayun protected them and did not allow them to be plundered. Out of gratitude they presented him with jewels, among them an enormous diamond. When Babur arrived, Humayun offered it to his father as a present. Babur had the stone valued by a jeweller, and 'the judge of diamonds estimated its value at half of the daily expenses of the whole world'. Then Babur gave this stone back to Humayun, and, according to various investigators who have tried to trace the history of this great diamond, it appears to have been the Great Mogul or Koh-i-noor, the diamond which was presented to Queen Victoria in the year 1850.

5

IN THE FOREIGN LAND

THE kingdom of Delhi was conquered. Immense treasure was found accumulated in Agra and Delhi, and Babur's first concern was to examine it and to reward the men who had helped him to gain the throne. He distributed the bounty with open hands, not only to his amirs and officers but to everybody in the army. 'I bestowed gratuities suited to their rank and circumstances.—Every merchant, every man of letters, in a word every person who had come along with me, received presents and gratuities, which marked their good fortune and superior luck.' Even men whom he had left at home were to receive presents, and to every person in the country of Kabul, 'man or woman, slave or free, of age or not' a rupee was to be sent as a gift. This generosity earned him the name of 'Kalandar' —meaning a mendicant who had devoted himself to voluntary poverty—but his lavishness had its purpose. It spread his fame and the importance of his conquest far and wide, and he knew that he needed more and more recruits.

Even under Sultan Ibrahim and before him, the kingdom of Delhi had been an agglomeration of little states under local rulers who had resented any interference from the distant capital of Delhi. Babur's invasion was regarded as a passing phase, an irruption which would pass away just as suddenly as it had come. When against all expectations Babur started to establish himself in earnest in Agra and Delhi, the Afghan chiefs in the different provinces and fortified towns lost no time in strengthening their fortifications and preparing for resistance. The amirs in the east especially, who had already formed a confederacy against Ibrahim, drew closer together, elected Sultan Muhammad of Bihar as their king and raised troops. The Khans in other more centrally situated districts came to an understanding to place a brother of Sultan Ibrahim on the throne of Delhi. And in the country around Delhi and Agra the inhabitants left their villages and fled in terror from Babur's soldiers, so that soon the victors with all their booty could not find food for themselves or grain for their horses and cattle. Enforced requisitions increased the hatred, and the villagers who fled became robbers and formed bands, infesting the highways and making the roads impassable.

Moreover, when Babur and his army reached Agra it was May. The sun was burning, the wind blew in fierce blasts and filled the air with hot dust. The men from the north were not accustomed to the native habit of not leaving their houses until the sun had set, and, heedlessly exposing themselves, they suffered sunstroke in masses: 'Many dropped down as if struck by the Simum wind and died on the spot'. Under these conditions many of his begs and even the best men 'began to lose heart and objected to remaining in Hindustan. Some even began to make preparations for their return'.

Babur saw the great achievement of his life suddenly in danger. When he had started on this last Indian campaign, he had, in his need of troops, raised many men of low rank to the dignity of begs, 'in the expectation', as he writes, 'that if I went through fire and water and came out again, they would have gone in with me unhesitatingly and with me have come out, that wherever I went they would be present at my side'. Now he had heaped gifts upon them, distributed fiefs which would maintain them and their adherents in a state of wealth they could scarcely have hoped for, and yet had to see that they were determined to oppose 'every measure, plan and opinion which I put forward in the council and assembly'.

His whole quest for an empire was about to be destroyed in the moment of fulfilment, because these men knew no higher satisfaction than to squander in their established manner whatever spoils had come their way, and when they fell back into the wretched condition in which they had always lived, to look out for fresh spoils. If he wanted to save what he had achieved he had to act at once, so he summoned all his nobles to a big council. 'I told them that empire and conquest could not be got without the means of war; that sovereignty and nobility could not exist without subjected peoples and lands. By the labours of many years, by encountering hardship, long travel, by flinging myself and the army into battle, and by deadly slaughter, we, through God's grace, had succeeded in beating these masses of enemies in order that we may take their broad lands. And now what force compels us, what necessity has arisen that we should, without cause, abandon countries taken with such risk of life, and flee from our conquests to retreat to Kabul with every sign of disappointment and discomfiture? . . .' And contemptuously he finished: 'If there is any one amongst you who cannot bring himself to stay, he can depart. He has my permission'.

The men felt ashamed; though unwillingly, they stopped talking of going home and decided to stay with their Padishah. Only Khoja Kilan, Babur's old friend and distinguished counsellor, maintained that his constitution was not suited to the Indian climate. Babur could not quarrel with the old man who all his life had been one of his best and most devoted companions in all his reverses and successes, so he decided to make the best of his departure. Khoja Kilan was the governor of Ghazni and with his large retinue would be the best guardian of the kingdom of Kabul, now without a real government and with only few troops left; in addition, Babur commissioned him to take presents to all relatives, officials and servants there, prescribing precisely how the distribution was to proceed, where the ladies of the royal house had to assemble with their tents in the Garden of the Audience Hall, how they were to make the prostration of thanks for the victory, and in what order the gifts should be conveyed. Besides the gold vessels filled with jewels and other precious things, he sent to each Begam an Indian dancing-girl from the court of Sultan Ibrahim. At the same time an invitation went out to all his kinsmen and friends to come and to share with him the prosperity of Hindustan, promising full favour to all who would enter his service.

The feeling prevailing in Babur's surroundings in Agra and the easy relationship which was habitual between the Padishah and his companions is well illustrated by the following incident. Departing with his enormous baggage, Khoja Kilan could not forgo the pleasure of having inscribed on the wall of his house:

> If safe and sound I pass the Sind
> Shame on me if ever again I long for the land of Hind!

Babur could not let this challenge pass and immediately composed a reply which he sent by messenger to Khoja Kilan:

> Babur, give hundred thanks to God most High,
> Who gave you Sind and Hind and royal kingdoms,
> If ever wearied by the fires of its sky
> You long for cold, remember the frost and ice of Ghazni!

Yet to revive the spirit of his troops, not pleasantries but action were required; and as soon as the heat subsided he despatched various detachments to the scenes of unrest, and their successes raised the army's morale. If the son of an Afghan chief was taken prisoner, Babur received him magnanimously, set him free and sent him home; often thereafter the father would arrive offering allegiance. The tales of Babur's magnanimity spread and other chiefs followed. Soon the leaders of Ibrahim's army, who had been fighting against the rebels in the east, came to him and he bestowed on them and their chief officers much more valuable fiefs than they had held before. These fiefs, however, were situated mostly in the provinces still offering resistance; the officers therefore acquired a vested interest in Babur's success. Then he sent an army with Humayun, some of his best officers, and a number of Afghans who had submitted, to the east, from where the rebels were advancing, and soon the news came that the enemy was retreating and had crossed the Ganges, with Humayun pursuing them.

Babur's resolution to remain in Hindustan and to secure his conquest bore fruit, but in spite of his decision to hold what he had conquered he was in no way enchanted by his new empire. As a man from the north, imbued with the Turko-Persian culture of Transoxiana, and taking the magnificent edifices of Herat and Samarkand and the social splendours of their courts as examples, his judgment is severe:

'Hindustan has few pleasures to recommend it. The people are not handsome. They have no idea of the charms of frankly mixing together, or of sociable intercourse. They have no imaginative mind, no politeness of manner, no amiable feelings, no ingenuity in mechanical matters when planning or executing their handicraft works, nor skill or knowledge in their architecture. There are no good horses, no good dogs, no grapes, musk-melons or good fruit, no ice or cold water, no good food or bread is to be found in their bazaars, no hot baths, no colleges, no candles nor even candlesticks. If you want to read or write by night, you must have a filthy half-naked fellow standing over you, holding a wooden tripod with a wick on which they let trickle a thin thread of oil when necessary.

'Its nature, its climate, everything is different; its mountains, rivers, jungles and deserts, its towns, its cultivated lands, its animals and plants, its peoples and their tongues, its rains and its winds are all different. There are only three seasons: "four months are summer, four are the rains, four are winter". Except their large rivers, which flow in ravines and hollows, and their standing-waters, they have no waters. There is no running water in their gardens or residences. These residences have no charm, air, regularity or symmetry. He agrees that 'while it rains and through the rainy period, the air is remarkably fine, not to be surpassed for healthiness and charm; but the fault is that the air becomes very soft and damp. A bow from our countries, once it has been in the rains in Hindustan, may not be drawn even, it is ruined; and not only the bow, everything is affected: armour, books, clothes and all utensils; even a house does not last long.' And 'sometimes it rains ten, fifteen or twenty times a day; torrents pour down all at once and rivers flow where no water had been'. However, 'not only in the rains but also in the cold and hot seasons the airs are excellent; yet at these times the north-west wind constantly gets up laden with dust and earth. It gets up in great strength every year in the heats, when the rains are near, and it is so strong and carries so much dust and earth that the people cannot see one another.'

But all this was compensated for by the simple fact that 'Hindustan is a large country and has abundance of gold and silver .There are innumerable workmen of every kind, and for every sort of work and everything there is a fixed caste that has done that work or that thing from father to son until now'. This division into castes makes him wonder: 'All artisans, wage earners and official workers are Hindus. In our country the wild folk have tribal names, but here those on farms and in towns are named like different tribes'. And he remarks: 'Most of the inhabitants of Hindustan are pagans; they call a pagan a Hindu. Most Hindus believe in the transmigration of souls'.

What he had to do here was to create for himself the appropriate surroundings for a more pleasant life. He found the countryside around Agra 'ugly and detestable', and ordered a well to be sunk, a large tank constructed, and 'a regularly planned pleasure ground' to be laid out. A grand Hall of Audience was to be built, then private apartments and baths. Later on, when the work, on which 680 stone-cutters were daily employed, was finished he could boast: 'The men of Hindustan, who never before had seen places formed on such a plan or laid out with so much beauty, gave the name of Kabul to the bank of the river Jumna on which our garden palaces were built'. He was particularly proud of his baths: 'We were annoyed with three things in Hindustan: one was its heat, another its strong winds, the third its dust. Baths were the means of removing all three inconveniences. In the bath we could not be affected by the winds. During the hot winds, the cold inside can be rendered so intense that a person often feels as if quite powerless from it. The room of the bath, which contains the tub or cistern, is finished wholly of stone. The waterrun is of white stone; all the rest of it, its floor and roof, is of red stone.' Artificial irrigation made it possible to satisfy all his whims: 'In every corner I planted suitable gardens; in every garden I sowed roses and narcissi regularly, and in beds corresponding to each other', and his courtiers had to follow his example and build their residences in the same fashion.

Yet it was not long after he had started with these cultural amenities and beautifications when, after a meal, he suddenly fell ill and vomited. As he had never before been sick after eating or drinking wine his suspicions arose and an investigation was started. Babur, always eager to try out something new, had kept a few of Sultan Ibrahim's tasters and cooks to prepare native dishes. When the Sultan's mother heard of this she sent one of her maids to the taster with a poisonous powder to put it into Babur's meal. The cook, to whom it was passed, being observed, could not put the powder in the pot itself, from where the dish would in any case first be tried by the tasters, but sprinkled it on the slices of bread on which the meat was placed. Some chroniclers ascribe this poisoning attempt to feminine jealousy. Babur had given the Sultan's mother a palace near Agra and is said to have visited her often; but then an embassy from the Shah of Persia arrived bringing, among other presents, two Circassian girls, with one of whom Babur became enamoured. However, it would be much more in the character of this Afghan lady simply to assume that at the moment when her relatives were collecting their forces against the invaders she attempted in her own way to get rid of him. She had an infant grandson and could hope to win his kingdom back for him.

In any case the timing of her attempt was correct; a month later Babur's position in India became critical, although she did not live to see the outcome of the new struggle. The cook, the taster and her maids were flayed alive or trampled to death by elephants; she herself, robbed of all her possessions, was sent under guard to Kabul, but while crossing the Indus she eluded her guards for a moment and threw herself into the river. Babur, describing his feelings when poisoned, says: 'Whenever they pass before my memory, I feel myself involuntarily turn faint'. And then the same joy of living which he had felt as a youth, when, fleeing from Samarkand, he reached the village where he could eat well and rest, breaks out again in the man of forty-three: 'I did not fully comprehend before that life was so sweet a thing. The poet says: Whoever comes to the gates of death, knows the value of life.'

The moment he felt recovered he started to prepare for the new contest. Up to now his adversaries had been Moslems, Afghans who, like himself, had invaded and conquered the North of India at different periods. Now he was to meet for the first time the original Indian warriors, the Rajputs, who were a military caste organized as an intricate feudal hierarchy of petty chiefs, lords and princes, often at loggerheads among themselves, isolated in their strong castles and mountain fortresses. They were vain about the glory of their arms, scornful of the common people and tradesmen, proud of their chivalrous courtesy. Never retreating and never surrendering, they were jealous of their privileges and their heroic code and had successfully resisted all the efforts of the various Moslem rulers to subdue their country. Their foremost Raja, Rana Sanga, had given encouragement to Babur when he was preparing for his campaign against Sultan Ibrahim, in the hope that when both adversaries had exhausted themselves he, Sanga, would be able to free Hindustan from the Moslem yoke. With Babur installed as his new neighbour he decided to secure the frontier of Rajputana by seizing the forts and towns on the approaches to Agra, and he called upon all the lords and princes to join him in his advance.

Babur also collected all his forces, called Humayun and his army back from the east, and, remembering the part that artillery had played in the battle against Sultan Ibrahim, ordered his 'rumi'-gunner to cast a new cannon, the balls of which carried 1600 paces. In this campaign he felt he could not rely on Hindu nobles who had joined him and sent them to the rear to strengthen various garrisons, but welcomed a reinforcement that had arrived from Kabul. It was mid-February when he marched from Agra against the advancing enemy; having to fight deep in India against non-Moslems he declared this war a 'Jihad'—a holy war against the infidels, but while he was bringing his train of artillery and his troops into shape and choosing the best sites for his camp, his reconnaissance troops were severely beaten by the heathens in various engagements. The routed detachments brought back stories of the bravery and the daring of the Rajputs, and alarm and despair spread in his camp.

5. Babur defeats the Rajputs at the battle of Khanua.

6. Babur receiving Uzbeg and Rajput embassies in a garden near Agra.

'There was not a single person who uttered a manly word nor delivered a courageous opinion'.

A spectacular gesture was needed to revive the courage of his troops, and when a camel caravan arrived with wine from Ghazni, Babur had an idea. He had often, as excuse for his excessive drinking bouts, declared that at the age of forty he would give up alcohol. Now, when he was forty-three, he was waging a holy war, and a solemn renunciation of this sinful habit would impress his troops. He sent for the gold and silver goblets and cups, and for all the other utensils used at drinking parties, and ordered them to be broken to pieces and the fragments distributed among dervishes and mendicants. He publicly renounced the drinking of wine; the supply which had been brought from Ghazni was poured on the ground, and he ordered that on this spot an alms-house should be erected.

This act of repentance by the Padishah was followed by the amirs and begs, courtiers and officers; 'nearly three hundred men made vows of reformation'. Then he sent out messengers to declare everywhere in his dominions that the poll-tax levied would no longer be exacted from Moslems. And finally, he assembled his officers in a council and addressed them, saying that 'whoever comes to the feast of life, must, before it is over, drink from the cup of death. How much better is it to die with honour than to live in infamy.' God had placed them in such a position that if they fell in battle, they would die the death of martyrs; if they survived, they would rise victorious as avengers of God's cause. He made them take an oath that none of them would desert the battle 'till his soul is separated from his body'. And he promised them that after the victory over the infidels anyone who wanted could return home.

His effort bore fruit. 'Master and servant, small and great, all with emulation, seizing the blessed Koran in their hands, swore in the form that I had given. My plan succeeded admirably, and its effects were instantly visible, far and near, on friend and foe'. He arranged and fortified his camp, only about sixteen miles from Agra, on the same pattern as for the battle against Sultan Ibrahim, with the gun-carriages connected by twisted bull-hides, with Mongol detachments stationed on the sides for out-flanking movements; but the breastworks protecting the matchlock-men were now on wheels, so that they could be moved forward and still give protection. The charges of the Rajput cavalry continued unabated, and, faced by gun- and matchlock-fire in front and a hail of arrows on both flanks, as well as from the rear, they fought on all sides. The battle lasted throughout the day, and the Rajput report of the battle ascribes their final defeat and flight to the betrayal of one of their chieftains. The pursuit went on for miles, and after the victory in this battle at Khanua, eleven months after the battle of Panipat which had given Babur the throne of Delhi, he assumed the title of 'Ghazi'—victor over the infidels. Rana Sanga, badly wounded, was carried away from the field only to die from his wounds within a year.

If Babur had hoped to follow up the victory with an immediate invasion of Rajputana, he had to abandon the plan. The war council held after the battle decided against it. It was March and the heat was becoming oppressive. Moreover, he had promised that all who wanted could depart after the battle, and the mountain warriors from Badakhshan who had come with Humayun demanded the right to return home. He had to let them go, and on the news that there were new and suspicious Uzbeg movements in the north, he took the precaution of sending Humayun with them, so that he might again take over the government in Badakhshan.

On his way, passing through Delhi, Humayun opened several treasure houses by force and took possession of their contents. When Babur received the news, he was shocked: 'I certainly never expected such conduct from him, and being extremely hurt, I wrote and sent him some letters containing the severest reprimand'.

This entry in the memoirs shows the first serious discord between the father and the son on whom he had heaped honours and riches on every occasion; and it is remarkable that Humayun, when he later copied the memoirs, let this condemnation of his behaviour stand. But when he copied them it was in the idle hours of exile, after he had been defeated and had fled from India; and by removing some of the treasures stored there he may have believed to have proved his early recognition of the fact, as it then appeared, that his father's empire was a transitory gain and that the treasures remaining there would in any case have been lost.

6

SAFEGUARDING THE EMPIRE

After Humayun's departure Babur apportioned various fiefs among his amirs and let them repair to their provinces and districts, with the order to keep their men and equipment trim and ready to join him, once the rains and the heat were over. He himself knew no respite. Throughout the rainy season he travelled from place to place. Twice he fell ill and developed a high fever, but as soon as this abated he was again on horseback, curious to see everything worth seeing—a fountain head, a lake, a garden, a wood of ebony-trees, and everywhere he ordered improvements, in particular the building of reservoirs and artificial water-courses. Seeing a rock of building stone, he ordered that a house should be cut in it all in one piece.

By the end of October he went down with malaria for nearly four weeks, but early in December he was ready to set out against Chanderi, one of the main strongholds of the Rajputs. To get there his troops had to cut their way through jungle and make it passable for guns and chariots. After six weeks' march, during which, as Babur reports, they often boarded a boat and ate 'Majun'—an intoxicating cake which now replaced the wine—they reached the fortress. The citadel was perched on a high rock above the walled town and the outer forts. In preparation for the assault the army was kept busy, during the hours of daylight, with making ladders, counterweights for catapults and various other devices; at night the engineers sank mines into the base of the ramparts. When the mines were exploded parts of the walls fell in, and through the breach and over the debris the assailants poured into the town. A merciless massacre followed. The Rajputs retreated into the citadel, and when Babur's men had found their way into the citadel through a hidden shaft, the Rajputs proved that they still maintained the valour of their ancient and glorious tradition. They killed their women and children to prevent their being taken into slavery, and then, naked, threw themselves upon the invaders, to kill and to be killed in order to escape being taken prisoner. At the end the remnant of the defenders gathered in the house of the governor; one man took a sword and the others came one by one, stretching out their necks, to receive a knightly stroke of death from a friend.

It is significant that Babur was unable to appreciate this suicidal heroism. He merely remarks: 'In this way many went to hell', and records that he ordered a pillar of pagan heads to be erected on a hill.

He had undertaken this campaign with the intention of following it up with a general assault on Rajputana to achieve the complete subjugation of the land, but already during the siege of Chanderi bad news had begun to arrive. Everywhere in the eastern part of the domain Afghan forces were pouring in and, since his main troops had been withdrawn, these forces had beaten his detachments. Driving out his garrisons, they occupied the towns and forts, and, instead of advancing against Rajputana, Babur had to hurry back to the Ganges. All boats found on the river were seized to build a pontoon bridge under protection of the guns and matchlocks, and when, after some skirmishing and fighting, his army crossed the river with the artillery, the enemy dispersed, retiring across the Gogra into the jungle or in the direction of Bengal and Bihar.

Now it was April again and the campaign had to be suspended. A hunting party was held, then Babur set off for Agra, his capital, visiting towns and forts on the way as usual, and inspecting the works and embellishments which he had ordered to be done. He stubbornly maintained his usual routines, left Agra again to see the Hindu palaces and pagodas around Gwalior, and, though acknowledging them as wonderful, had little liking for them, was scandalised by the enormous sculptures of 'idols' carved in the rock in all their nudity, and ordered them to be destroyed. They were mutilated at least.

But this restless life in the Indian climate impaired his health. Attacks of malaria lasted longer, and the fever grew worse; he contracted an inflammation of the ear which impaired his hearing, and to soothe the ear-ache he took opium, although it made him sick. Because the usual remedies did not help, he began to describe in verse the exploits of a certain Saint and then observed that within a few days 'by God's grace and the Saint's favour' he was freed of the fever 'except for a little depression'. He had no time for being ill. The campaign for the next winter had to be prepared; it had to be a profitable campaign as the spoils found in Delhi and Agra were now exhausted, and in order to be able to pay for war materials, equipment, gunners and matchlock-men, he had to raise the taxes by thirty per cent. But still more important to him was the news from outside his Indian realm, from Badakhshan.

The Uzbegs had again been very active of late. They had invaded Khorasan, had beaten various Persian armies and laid siege to Herat. Thereupon Shah Tahmasp, the son of Shah Ismail, had collected all his troops, had set out eastwards with all his artillery and had crushed the combined Uzbeg forces, killing their leaders. Babur's life-long dream of Transoxiana and Samarkand was revived at once. He ordered Humayun to march 'against Samarkand, Hissar, or wherever there seemed to be the best hope of success'. His half-brother Kamran, Babur's second son, together with the begs of Kabul, should join him. This letter to Humayun throws a very interesting light on Babur's views of the role of a ruler and on his wishes as to the disposition of his realm. It criticizes Humayun's style of writing as too elaborate and condemns his use of obscure words instead of plain and clear ones. It urges him not to seek retirement and sit alone, but to be sociable, as a ruler should be, because there is no greater bondage that that of sovereignty: 'Life in indolence and ease does not befit sovereign rulers.' It urges him that now is the time for him to expose himself to danger and hardship and to prove his valour in arms; but he should take counsel with prudent and experienced begs and act as they say. It particularly urges him to live in harmony with his younger brother Kamran; he as the elder must be magnanimous, for it had always been so that when he got six parts of anything Kamran received no more than five. If Samarkand should be won, it would become Humayun's seat, while Kamran would get the much smaller Balkh, with Babur making up his part out of other lands in the region. But Kabul he declared a crown-domain, and said: 'Let no one of you covet it'.

Kabul was still very dear to his heart; as all his victories and conquests had occurred since he took Kabul, its possession was his good omen, and in a letter to Khoja Kilan, whom he praised to Humayun, Babur deals particularly with Kabul. Khoja Kilan should see that the walls and forts were always in the best repair, that the provision stores were full, that the buildings which he had started were well finished, that the gardens which he had laid out were well watered and planted with sweet herbs and flowers. The country should be kept safe and prosperous; the manufacture of armoury and the corps of matchlock-men should be maintained and treasure accumulated.

Having given his instructions about the administration of the country, he finishes the letter with a definite order: as soon as it arrives, Khoja Kilan must call upon Babur's sister Khanzada, and his wives, get them out of Kabul and escort them to the Indus. When Babur had set out for India all the ladies of his household, his sister and his wives and aunts, had stayed behind in Kabul. Recently he had summoned them to join him in Agra, and whatever objections they might raise, Khoja Kilan should see that they started out within a week.

Babur knew from experience the family intrigues which were always going on, the conflicting interests and the jealousies, and the efforts with which all of them were trying to gain adherents among the begs and tribes for their special causes and to sow discord. He confesses that it affected him greatly to write about these matters, but the women were too interested in things which were none of their business, and no country could be strong and prosper where there are seven or eight chiefs. Therefore, he had decided to have them all with him in Agra, in his new capital, under his observation. It would be an enormous cavalcade. There were over ninety female relatives of his out there in Kabul, many married and with children, with a multitude of servants and adherents; but he was preparing comfortable accommodation for them, with palaces according to their status. He would visit the elderly aunts regularly when he was in Agra; and he would pay them the customary respect, but leave Kabul they must. He informed Khoja Kilan that a detachment of troops was being sent out and would be waiting for them, 'and any delay will expose it to difficulties, and the country, too, will suffer'.

In this letter to Khoja Kilan he also confessed the difficulties he was experiencing in reconciling himself 'to the desert of penitence'—his abstention from wine. 'Indeed last year my desire and longing for wine and conviviality were excessive beyond measure; so strong that I have found myself shedding tears of vexation and disappointment . . . But this year, thank God, these troubles are over, and this

I ascribe to my occupying my mind with poetry.' And he sent Khoja Kilan a quatrain which he had composed:

> Distraught I am since I gave up wine;
> Confused, to nothing does my soul incline.
> Regret did once my penitence beget;
> Now penitence induces worse regret.

Nevertheless, he even recommended his friend to follow his example. When his was tired, he took 'bhang'.

When this letter to Khoja Kilan was written, there was no longer any question of conquering Transoxiana and Samarkand. Humayun had set out and occupied Hissar, but then Shah Tahmasp, menaced by the Ottoman Turks in the west, had made peace with the Uzbegs and withdrawn from the east, and Humayun, not strong enough to face the Uzbegs alone, had come to an arrangement with them. Babur's possessions in the north were for the time being confined to the kingdom of Kabul and its northern barrier Badakhshan. Nevertheless he hoped that the affairs of Hindustan would soon be brought to order, and then, 'without losing a moment', he would go to Kabul. He wrote to Khoja Kilan that a little earlier a musk-melon from Kabul had been brought to him. 'As I cut it up, I felt a deep homesickness and a sense of exile from my native land, and I could not help shedding tears.' He had ordered the construction of a highway nine hundred miles long from Agra to Kabul; at every sixteen miles a post-house was to be built and maintained, fully provisioned and equipped with horses for the couriers, in order to speed up communications.

However, all future plans depended on his success in India. The council had decided that what was now needed was a profitable campaign; the provinces and towns in the east, occupied and plundered alternately by Babur's or Afghan troops, could not offer much, but quite near, in the west, were several countries and places still rich and untouched. From the east the amirs reported that Babur's personal presence was not necessary, as the contemplated operation would only amount to a punitive expedition against invading tribes; so Babur gave his third son, the twelve-year-old Askari, the rank of a royal commander with a horse-tail standard, kettle drums and other insignia, and sent him eastwards with a contingent of troops, led by experienced war chiefs who were instructed to discuss all military operations with him so that he could learn the art of war. The amirs of the eastern provinces beyond the Ganges were to join Askari with their retainers. Babur himself, with the main army, was still waiting in camp for the first reports before setting out westwards, when he received news that Sultan Mahmud, the brother of the late Sultan Ibrahim of Delhi, was advancing from Bihar with all his Afghan troops.

This information decided the issue. Babur abandoned the idea of a western campaign and again went east with his army. While he was marching down the right bank of the Ganges, with Askari marching down the left, the opposing troops began, as they usually did at his approach, to disperse. Some of the tribes hastened away, some of the Afghan chiefs came to him offering submission. Only at the confluence of the Gogra and the Ganges, where the kingdom of Bengal began, did he find an army occupying a strong position. It was a Bengal army, but it was sheltering the retreating Afghan troops; so Babur sent an envoy to the Shah of Bengal to stress that peace had prevailed until now between the two kingdoms but that he could not be deterred from pursuing his enemies. He started preparing for the assault at once. Under the protection of his artillery he made some of his troops cross the Ganges, while others crossed the Gogra; then he charged the Bengal army from three sides. The Bengalis were forced to retreat, and the Shah accepted the conditions dictated by Babur.

These conditions cannot have been very hard, because it was May and the rainy season was starting. One day such a storm broke out that most of the tents were brought down. Even the audience tent, where Babur sat writing, fell on him, and though he himself suffered no harm all his papers were drenched and only rescued with much difficulty; he and his attendants were all night 'without sleep, busy drying folios and sections'. On another day the whole camp was flooded. At last he got so impatient of the slow and difficult progress, with exhausted horses and cattle, that, ordering the troops to rest until they received fresh supplies, Babur left the army and set out for Agra with his companions 'in raid fashion', without encumbrance or baggage, riding over 150 miles in two and a half days.

In Agra he had the great satisfaction of tasting the first melons and grapes grown in his gardens by the gardener who had come at his behest from Khorasan. Then, just three days after his return, late in the evening, a messenger brought him the news that Maham, his best loved wife, the mother of his eldest son Humayun, was approaching. She had started out from Kabul earlier than the other ladies and seems to have made unexpected progress. Babur did not even wait for a horse to be saddled, but rushed out on foot to meet her, did not let her dismount for the conventional curtsy, but himself led her on her horse to his palace. Next day the relatives and attendants in her train arrived in a great cortege with the usual pomp and etiquette, and ten days later there is a note in the memoirs: 'The offerings made by Humayun and Maham were set out while I sat in the large Hall of Audience'.

From this point, the succession of events and their significance becomes unclear and the chroniclers describe and interpret them differently. The facts known and agreed on are that Humayun suddenly left Badakhshan, went to Kabul, where he met his brother Kamran, and then both sent Babur's youngest son Hindal, a ten year-old boy—naturally, with his begs—to Badakhshan as ruler, even though he had been summoned by his father to come to him in Hindustan. Then Humayun himself hurried post haste to Hindustan and arrived quite unexpected in Agra. The historians are in doubt about the precise time of Humayun's journey and his arrival; some of them, referring to the note in the memoirs, assume that at that date he must already have been in Agra, while others put his arrival later. About what happened on his sudden appearance in Agra an appendix to Babur's memoirs says: 'I was just talking with his mother about him when in he came. His presence opened our hearts like rosebuds, and made our eyes shine like torches. It was my rule to keep open table every day, but on this occasion I gave feasts in his honour, and showed him every kind of distinction. We lived together for some time in the greatest intimacy . . .'

Now, not only is the style of the appendix very different from Babur's usual style of writing, but the facts contradict it and a number of historians maintain that it is a forgery, put in at a much later date under one of Humayun's descendants. Humayun's desertion of such an important outpost, and the appointment in his place of the small boy Hindal, whom Babur had ordered to India, must have upset Babur. The consequence of the absence of Humayun and his guard was that the Mongol Khan of Kashgar, invited by some unruly chiefs, appeared in Badakhshan. Whether it was on Humayun's or Maham's advice that Babur was induced to ask his Chief Minister, the old Khalifa, if he would go to Badakhshan to restore order there, is not clear; reports only say that Khalifa 'delayed obeying'. But it was known that he was critical of Humayun and he may have made some allusion to his master, because Babur suddenly asked Humayun whether he would return to Badakhshan, to receive the answer that if this was an imperial order for him to go there on duty, he would not disobey, but he 'would not voluntarily exile himself'; whereupon he was banished to Sambhal, a smallish Indian fief allotted to him on the other side of the Ganges.

Babur seems to have understood the intrigues spun around him and the part Maham played in them; for in the book of reminiscences which his daughter Gul-Badan wrote some fifty years later, on the order of the Emperor Akbar, Humayun's son, there is a significant passage. At that time she was about six years old, but she remembered that during an excursion to one of his gardens in the neighbourhood Babur said to Maham that he had had enough of ruling and reigning and would retire to the garden as a dervish. Humayun could have his kingdom; whereupon Maham broke out in tears and said: 'God keep you in His own peace upon the throne for many, many years, and may all your children after you reach a good old age!'

In any case, he conferred Badakhshan on Suleiman Mirza, the son of his cousin Mirza Khan, who had ruled there before. Then he set out himself with an army northwards. Although it was given out as no more than a pleasure trip, at the first news that Babur was on his way the Mongol Khan preferred to retire quickly to Kashgar, and Badakhshan was safe again. Babur remained the winter in Lahore, leaving it at the beginning of spring, then spent two months hunting near Delhi and returned to Agra. From there, to avoid the approaching heat, he went with Maham and other Begams by boat to Dholpur, where he had laid out gardens and lakes. But they had scarcely arrived before a messenger came from Delhi with news that Humayun had been brought there dangerously ill.

Maham started for Delhi at once and took Humayun by boat to Agra. He seems to have been in a high fever, semi-conscious, and a strange story has been told to prove Babur's limitless and sacrificial love for his son. Maham is reported to have said to him that he need not grieve, since he had other sons but she had only this one—Babur's other sons were from other wives, while Maham's further children had all died in early childhood. According to the story, Babur answered that although he had other sons, he loved none as much as he loved Humayun, and he craved that Humayun should live long, and that he desired the kingdom to be for him and not for the others, because none was his equal in distinction. The doctors knew no remedy, but when a saintly man remarked that in old times, after all human efforts had failed, an offering was made to the Almighty of the most precious thing belonging to the sufferer; if it was accepted his health was restored. It was recommended that the Great Mogul diamond should be sold and the money devoted to pious uses, but Babur declared that not the diamond but he himself was his son's most precious possession. He went three times around Humayun's bed, praying that Humayun's suffering should be upon him and then cried out: 'I have taken the burden!' The story goes that Humayun immediately recovered while Babur fell ill.

This story was composed nearly half a century later when, on the order of Emperor Akbar, an official history of the dynasty was written; Humayun's ascent had to be presented as Babur's innermost wish, for the fulfilment of which he gave his life. In fact he fell seriously ill only a few months later, after Humayun had recovered and left or been sent away, probably to his fief. Again, Babur's illness lasted about three months, becoming progressively worse. It was a disorder of the bowels, and Gul-Badan adds that the doctors found the symptoms were the same as at the poisoning by Ibrahim's mother. But rumours of poisoning were always rife as soon as a sovereign fell ill.

The reports agree that all the time he was clamouring for his youngest son Hindal, whom he had summoned once more when sending Suleiman Mirza to Badakhshan, and that Hindal had started out as soon as Suleiman arrived. He got to Lahore shortly after his father had left it, but since then eight months had passed and the bed-ridden Babur kept asking continually, and in vain: 'Where is Hindal? When will he come?' Only when he was nearly dying did Hindal's preceptor arrive in advance to say that Hindal had reached Delhi. But still he was not coming. Instead, as soon as Babur's condition became hopeless, Humayun was called and arrived immediately, and Babur, feeling that death was approaching, summoned his dignitaries and, declaring Humayun his successor, requested them to acknowledge Humayun and be loyal to him. He again reminded Humayun to be munificent and just, and he particularly entreated him to do nought to his brothers, even if they deserved it. Three days later, on December 26, 1530 he died in his forty-eighth year.

The incidents of his last year, and the strange circumstances of his illness and the behaviour of the people concerned, present a good many problems which have troubled the historians, the solution of which would make the events and the attitudes of his heirs and their followers more understandable. The question which first spring to one's mind are: Why did Humayun suddenly leave Badakhshan? How did it come that he and Kamran, who were always at loggerheads, immediately agreed to send the young Hindal to this furthermost province, contrary to Babur's order that he should come to Hindustan? Why did Babur, after spending the following winter in Lahore, not continue his journey to Kabul in the spring, when he was so eager to see the city again? Why, after his miraculous recovery, did Humayun go away, leaving his father who, it is said, had sacrificed himself for him? How did it come that Hindal, already on the way from Lahore, was not immediately rushed to his father who was asking for him, but delayed even in Delhi, so that he appeared in Agra only the day after Humayun had been proclaimed emperor, to pay him homage? We shall probably never get satisfactory answers from the original sources, because either they were composed much later under Humayun's descendants, and were bound to exalt the rights of the dynasty, or they were written by people who were not immediate participants. However, some conclusions may perhaps be drawn from the known facts:

Babur's letter to Humayun, written in November 1528, with the strange remark that none of his sons should covet Kabul, must have reached its destination by the end of the year. Probably the order for Babur's wives and relatives to go to Hindustan arrived at the same time, as Maham departed from Kabul on January 21, 1529, the same day that Babur set out on his last eastern campaign. Some two weeks later the letter to Khoja Kilan went off, containing the order to accelerate the departure of the other wives and relatives and the summons to Hindal. While these letters were on the way, Maham, who had in the meantime crossed the Indus and was received and accompanied further by the escorts from Lahore, may have heard that Babur's health had lately been failing and naturally informed Humayun.

Babur's intention to make Kabul a crown-domain and his decision to order all the relatives out of a place where the families of the various clans had their own adherents, must have caused quite a stir. The summoning of Hindal appeared ominous. Humayun had Badakhshan, Kamran had Kandahar and was now also accorded

Multan, which until recently had been under Askari's governorship; and if Babur, getting old, were to make Kabul his capital and government centre, it was to be suspected that he intended to divide Hindustan between his two younger sons, Askari and Hindal. The delay in Hindal's southward journey was therefore in the interest of both the elder brothers, Humayun and Kamran, and they braved Babur's order by sending him to the furthermost northern province instead, while Humayun went southwards after Maham, relying on his mother's support. The notice that Babur and Maham were speaking of him when he suddenly appeared is an indication that she was well informed.

If Babur had the idea of dividing his empire among his sons, as his grand father Abu-Said had done with Transoxiana, Humayun's arrival and his refusal to return to Badakhshan upset all his plans. The sending of Suleiman Mirza to Badakhshan excluded this province from his heritage, making it at best a kind of vassal state, and his own position in Hindustan was quite clear. The kingdom of Delhi that he had won four years earlier and for parts of which he had since been fighting incessantly was a long and narrow intrusion into a foreign continent, with foreign people speaking a foreign language and hating the invaders, the accursed 'Moguls'.

Babur himself deeply disliked the Mongols for their predatory habits and their aversion to discipline. He had suffered often enough from their sudden uprisings, which more than once endangered his life, and he had aired his feelings in verses such as these:

> If the Mongol race were a race of angels, it is a bad race;
> And were the name of Mongol written in gold, it would be odious.
> Take care not to pluck one ear of corn from a Mongol's harvest;
> The Mongol seed is such that whatever is sowed with it is execrable.

He prided himself on being a Turk, and now, in the country which he had conquered, he and his troops were never called anything but 'Moguls'—a deformed pronunciation of the word Mongol, widely used by Turkish and Afghan people. He felt their hate and their detestation in that name and he knew that this country would be his only so long as he was able to use his military power at any spot where danger arose. Only the districts and towns in his direct possession and garrisoned by his troops were secure. The submission of the Afghan tribes in the mountain districts was no more than a formal gesture; in practice they were independent, and those Afghan amirs on whom he had bestowed fiefs in Hindustan would at the first opportunity change their allegiance and join his adversaries, the relatives of the earlier kings of Delhi. In Rajputana, the only Indian country he had fought which had not been under Afghan domination, he held no more than a few strong points. All his possessions were surrounded on all sides by enemies. His hold was only possible with absolute unity in his own camp, and he saw that with the transfer of all his relatives to Agra the formation of various group interests had started. In these circumstances it would have been unwise for him to leave with his army for far-off Kabul; he had to be near. And while he had not decided about the succession, Humayun had to be kept away. Even after Humayun's recovery he had to stay away so long as Babur's own illness was not considered dangerous.

However, why did Babur so eagerly await Hindal? The name Hindal meant 'of Hind', and Babur was superstitious. Hindal was now in his twelfth year, just about the age at which he himself, after his father's fatal accident, had become king, and he knew from his own experience how the begs preferred such boy kings, who could make no changes in the prevailing establishment. Did he want to secure Hindustan for his two younger sons, Askari and Hindal, while perhaps giving Humayun, as the eldest, the crown-domain of Kabul with the overlordship? We do not know.

In any case Babur must have been fully aware of the intrigues going on behind his back, as, when reproaching Hindal's preceptor for the boy's non-arrival, the nearly dying Babur called him 'Ill-fated fellow!' and added: 'I have heard that they have married your sister in Kabul and yourself in Lahore!' implying deliberate delay. But whatever Babur's intentions had been, in the end he had to acknowledge that they had been thwarted. He now had to prevent the throne from remaining empty for any space of time during which the usual rivalries and feuds at the death of a sovereign could start. Humayun was the only heir at hand, and in the last moment Babur named him his successor. Humayun certainly seemed to have the most efficient support at Court, and troubles and upheavals would probably be prevented. Nevertheless, while bidding the begs and amirs to acknowledge him, Babur made a point of publicly and in their presence enjoining upon Humayun: 'Do nought to your brothers!'

It was a strange heritage that he was leaving. He had conquered an empire which ostensibly stretched from the hills south of the Amu

Darya to the confluence of the Ganges and the Gogra; but its riches and its destiny lay in the south, and the chances of holding this southern part depended entirely on the adventurous mood of the men from the north within and without his domain, whether their desire for booty and fiefs was strong enough to make them migrate and endure the climate which they hated. Nothing here was safe, nothing consolidated, but it had been the will of God that, instead of his native Samarkand, he should gain possession of the remotest region into which Timur had ever come; if his own descendants, too, followed the will of God, they would succeed.

Babur's death was at first concealed, as Gul-Badan states, out of fear 'that the Moguls—at the time of her writing the name was generally adopted and had lost its sting—should come and loot the houses and dwelling places'. Then, on the advice of an amir, a herald, dressed in red and sitting on an elephant proclaimed, that the Emperor Babur had become a dervish and given his throne to the Emperor Humayun, and on December 29, 1530, the Khutba was read for the first time in Humayun's name.

7. A composite picture glorifying the dynasty. On the left Timur, in the centre Babur, and on the right Humayun with Bairam Khan.

8. The Emperor Humayun.

Hamida Banu Begam, the mother of Akbar

PART TWO

HUMAYUN

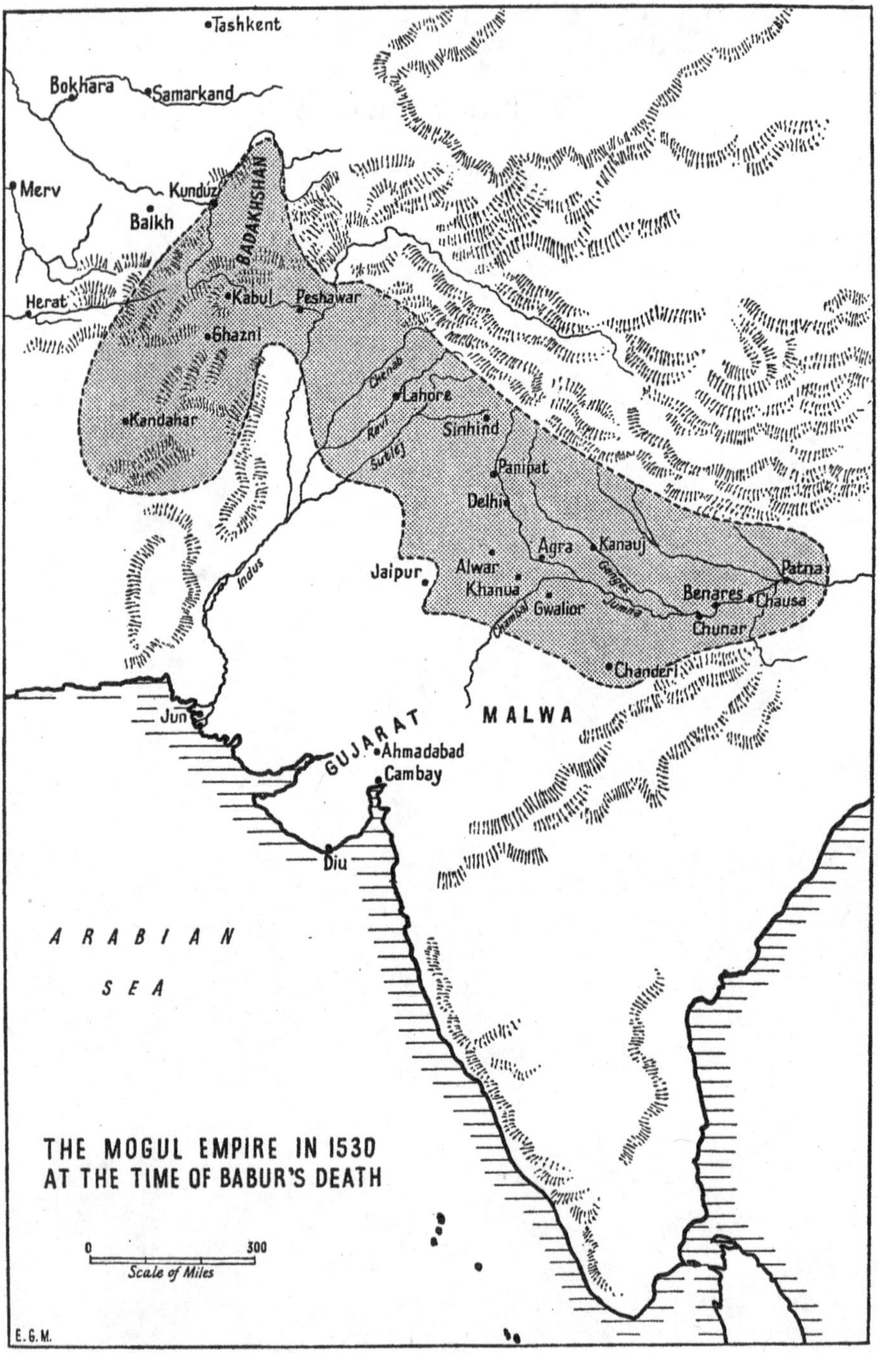

THE MOGUL EMPIRE IN 1530
AT THE TIME OF BABUR'S DEATH

1
THE FIRST YEARS

HUMAYUN was twenty-two years old when he acceeded to the throne of Babur. As the usual festivities proceeded the nobles came to wait upon him and to tender their allegiance, and he confirmed all the amirs, begs and chieftains in their positions and fiefs and asked the men at court to continue their service in the offices which they had occupied under his father.

Little Hindal, the youngest of Babur's sons, came to Agra to pay his homage and was granted the near-by province of Alwar as appanage. To his second youngest brother, Askari, Humayun gave the fief of Sambhal, to which he himself had been sent by Babur after he had left Badakhshan. But when he tried to restrict his brother Kamran to the possession of Kabul and Kandahar, which he had already governed at Babur's death, Kamran collected his troops and marched for Hindustan. Humayun immediately sent an envoy announcing that he was allotting to him also the frontier province of Peshawar, but Kamran pushed on, crossed the Indus, took Lahore by a stratagem and demanded the whole of the Punjab—and Humayun gave his assent.

Some historians ascribe this to his wish to maintain good relations with his brother, as the dying Babur had ordered; others consider that he could not at the time take any action against Kamran, as Babur's death had stirred the Afghans to renewed activity and they had invaded the provinces east of the Ganges. But there is the strange fact that, even while crossing the Indus, Kamran sent envoys to Humayun, assuring him of his fidelity and humbly petitioning for the confirmation of his rulership over the Punjab; and when the consent came, he composed an ode in praise of Humayun and sent it to him. We simply know nothing of the arrangements which were made between the two brothers in Kabul at the time when they had sent Hindal to Badakhshan while, instead of Hindal, Humayun had gone to Agra. It is also significant that Khoja Kilan, Babur's trusted friend, who wrote grief-stricken verses on his death:

Alas! and Alas! that time and the changeful heaven should exist
without thee;
Alas! and Alas! that time should remain and thou shouldst be
gone!

now stood clearly by Kamran. This can be accepted as a sign that he thought Kamran was acting within his rights.

In the meantime Humayun's campaign against the Afghans was crowned with success. He defeated them in a pitched battle in which some of his chief adversaries were killed; as usual the Afghan tribes dispersed and he returned victorious to Agra. A series of magnificent festivals and entertainments followed to celebrate his victory and also the anniversary of his succession to the throne, in the course of which he is said to have distributed 12,000 honorary dresses, many embroidered and covered with jewels, among the officers and officials. It looked as if all could expect profitable service and rich rewards under the reign of Humayun. To increase the glory of his court he made its ceremonial and manners very different from those of Babur's time.

As an enthusiastic adept of astrology Humayun fitted up seven houses of audience named after the seven planets, and no other business might be effected except that appropriate to the day of the planet. On Sunday (the day of the Sun) and on Tuesday (the day of the planet Mars) all government business was transacted. Thursday (Jupiter day) and Saturday (the day of Saturn) were the days for receiving pious and learned men. Monday (the day of the Moon) and Wednesday (the day of Mercury) were put aside for pleasure and parties, attended by singers, musicians and dancers. On Friday councils and assemblies were held.

In addition Humayun introduced a special grading at his court, dividing the people into three classes: 'Officers of State', to which his relatives, nobles, officials and military men belonged; 'Good Men'—religious leaders, scientists, philosophers and 'other great and respectable men'; 'Officers of Pleasure'—poets, singers, musicians, dancers, painters and architects, and other 'men of beauty and elegance'. Each of the three classes was divided into twelve ranks, and each rank had three grades: high, middle and low.

Each class was accorded a particular type of arrow, and for each type of arrow there were twelve different grades. The highest, the twelfth grade of each division, was an arrow of pure gold which belonged to Humayun as the apex of the whole pyramid. The eleventh grade was held by his relatives and the highest dignitaries, and then it went down to the first grade for gate-keepers, camel-drivers and so on. The government departments were divided according to the four elements: the military departments came under 'fire'; kitchen, wardrobe, stable under 'air'; canals and irrigation, but also cellars under 'water'; while 'earth' combined buildings, agriculture and land grants. The officers of each department were to wear a prescribed form of dress; moreover, Humayun himself wore clothes in the colour of the planet of the day, and he recommended the same practice to his entourage.

When on the reception day he went to occupy the throne, drums were beaten; when he left court, guns were fired. Keepers of the wardrobe with fine apparel and treasurers with purses were in the court to give the rewards without delay; guards in coats of mail, sword in hand, stood before the throne to seize and punish culprits on the spot. A special drum was placed near the audience hall, so that aggrieved persons could beat it; they were then allowed to lay their complaints before the king.

These improvements in court ceremonial and the display of the monarchical magnificence were meant to become known in adjacent countries and to attract learned and pious men, poets and other writers to Humayun's court. Humayun cherished his discussions with them. Persian had become the language of the court, but when he did not want to be understood by the majority of those present he spoke his native Turki, and he also knew Arabic. He himself wrote verses and liked to suggest improvements to the poets surrounding him; but his main concern was that every undertaking should start at the most propitious hour, whether it was building a palace, setting out for a campaign, or engaging in a battle, and he always had astrologers in attendance around him. It was a most magnificent life, worthy of a great Timurid sovereign, and Humayun in his opium-enriched imagination never failed to invent new refinements.

But the empire which he had inherited was not yet safely enough established for such leisurely pursuits. It was only a long protrusion into Hindustan, about a thousand miles deep from the Khaibar Pass which led from the northern countries into India. This strip, in places no more than about two hundred miles in width but widening towards the end, was held in obedience by military force and was faced in east and west by hostile states or territories. It was only their lack of power and unity which deterred their rulers from seizing Humayun's possessions.

As the Afghan intrusions always came from the eastern parts of North India, Humayun regarded it as his most important task to seize the strongest fortress on the river Ganges, Chunar. Chunar was at that time in the possession of one of the most remarkable Afghan leaders in Hindustan, Sher Khan, who had risen to the position of actual ruler of Bihar, although nominally he was a vassal of Humayun. Humayun demanded from him the surrender of this key fortress. Sher Khan refused.

He had an extraordinary career behind him. As a youth he had distinguished himself as a scholar, learning Arabic and Persian, studying religious and philosophical works and delighting in poetry. He devoted much attention to the history of Hindustan, reading in particular the biographies of ancient kings and their deeds. Entrusted later on with the administration of his father's fiefs, he made them prosper by checking the oppressions and extortions of tax-collectors and other officers, and on the other hand severely punishing tax-evaders or rebellious villages. However, his father, infatuated with a Hindu slave woman, transferred the fiefs to her sons, and Sher Khan went to Daulat Khan of Lahore and rose in his service. When Babur invaded India and slew Sultan Ibrahim in the battle of Panipat, Sher Kahn entered the service of Sultan Muhammad of Bihar, the far-off province in the east, and there again rose to highest rank.

From the Sultan he received the title of Sher (tiger) Khan, when hunting with him one day, he killed, with a stroke of his sabre, an enormous tiger that had attacked them. The patronage which he enjoyed awakened the jealousy of other favourites, and as the result of various intrigues he left Bihar after his fiefs had been taken by force by a mighty vassal of the Sultan. He then applied to one of Babur's generals, who accepted his services and gave him some troops with which he regained possession of his lands. Later he accompanied the general to Babur's court and took part in Babur's expedition against the Rajput fortress of Chanderi. Having had the opportunity to observe the ruling and fighting methods of the new lords of the country, he is said to have remarked to a friend that the Moguls were not superior to the Afghans either in battle or in single combat. The Afghans had let the empire slip from their hands through their disunity. The Mogul king, too proud to apply himself to the government of the country, left all the affairs of state to his ministers, who were greedy and corrupt. If fortune favoured him, he would bring the Afghans under his control and drive the Moguls out of India.

His remarks seem to have become known, for he suddenly fled at night, joined Sultan Muhammad of Bihar again, was welcomed and appointed instructor and lieutenant of the Sultan's son Jelal. Shortly afterwards, the Sultan died and Sher Khan became the actual governor of Bihar in Jelal's name. He succeeded in defeating a Bengal army which invaded Bihar, but he kept the booty for himself and his troops and thus made enemies of the relatives of the young Jelal, who was already chafing under his deputy's rule. They induced Jelal to flee to Bengal and to ask the Shah for help against the overbearing regent. The Shah sent a large army with elephants and artillery to conquer Bihar. Sher Khan engaged the much superior army, feigned retreat, and when the Bengali cavalry pursued the seemingly beaten enemy, Sher Khan with the main force, which he had held in reserve, fell upon the Bengali artillery and foot troops, and after beating them attacked the cavalry from the rear. The victory was his and with it all the artillery, elephants and baggage.

Now he could, unhindered, occupy himself with the improvement of the administration of the country, stamping out the abuses of some fief holders and ensuring that every man in his service received his due. Soon it was known everywhere that Sher Khan paid his troops regularly and did not oppress anyone, and the Afghans flocked to his service from all directions. His forces grew, and his reputation unexpectedly brought the important fortress of Chunar into his possession.

The widow of the lord of Chunar was in an intense struggle with his sons by another wife, and Sher Khan won the beautiful lady and the fortress. He was already in a position to look for an opportunity to declare Bihar independent and himself its ruler, when, following Babur's death, the Afghan leaders once again rallied around Sultan Mahmud, the brother of Sultan Ibrahim, proclaiming him King of Delhi. When Sher Khan hesitated to follow their example, they took their way through Bihar, and, unable to resist, Sher Khan waited upon Sultan Mahmud and acknowledged him. Powerless he had to look on while the Sultan distributed the districts and lands of Bihar among his followers, promising to Sher Khan only that after the reconquest of the empire he would give him the whole of Bihar. Sher Khan had to join the Sultan's army with his troops; but when this army was at grips with the army of Humayun, he suddenly withdrew his troops after having informed the enemy of his intention. This defection gave Humayun his decisive victory over the Afghans.

It must have been a very difficult decision for Sher Khan to make, for he was an Afghan of the Sur tribe and had always been devoted to the Afghan cause and the re-establishment of their rule over Hindustan, but he may have doubted the ability of Mahmud and his adherents. In any case, their defeat enabled him to lay his hand once more on the whole of Bihar, and when Humayun, instead of being grateful to him, demanded the surrender of his key-fortress of Chunar, he decided to resist. And so, shortly after the victory over the Afghans, Humayun took the field against Sher Khan and laid siege to Chunar. But the siege did not develop as he had expected. Sher Khan had left his son Jelal in the fortress and himself had retired to the hills with a strong force which harried the besieging army with raids and night attacks. After a blockade of four months, as Sher Khan had foreseen, disquieting news began to arrive in Humayun's camp.

In the south-west the might of Bahadur Shah of Gujarat was rising. He was subduing the neighbouring principalities one by one, encroaching upon land nearer and nearer to Humayun's dominions, and within the domain itself there was unrest. Some of Humayun's Timurid relatives, descendants of the late Sultan Husain Baikara of Khorasan, challenged Humayun's supremacy. They did not see why they should be satisfied with an Indian fief when they might make the province where they sat an independent kingdom; by their promises they were gaining more and more followers among the chieftains who expected more favours and greater importance at a smaller court. It became obvious to Humayun that he could not tarry any longer with his army far away at the Ganges, and when Sher Khan proposed peace terms he had to accept them, although all that Sher Khan offered was formal submission and a profession of allegiance. Chunar was to remain in Sher Khan's possession.

Humayun returned to Agra and sent troops against the rebellious Timurids. They were surprised and taken prisoner. But when he ordered that they should be blinded, their warders fled instead with them to Bahadur Shah in Gujarat. The kingdom of Gujarat lay far away, some three hundred miles to the south-west, beyond Rajputana. It had a long coast-line with the best north-Indian ports and drew rich benefits from trade not only with Persia, Arabia and the Turks, but even with Europe through the Portuguese trading post at Diu. Although relations with the Portuguese were not always amicable and often led to armed conflict, the armies of the young and ambitious Bahadur Shah naturally possessed artillery and had matchlock-men and a large number of mercenary troops. His attacks were mainly directed against Rajput fortresses, but he was extending his domains nearer and nearer to the kingdom of Delhi, and the court of Gujarat became a plotting centre for all the enemies of the Emperor. Bahadur Shah not only harboured such people but he provided them with money to hire mercenaries for the invasion of Humayun's dominions, without taking up arms himself. When Humayun at last decided to march against Gujarat, Bahadur Shah, who was besieging the Rajput fortress of Chitor, lying about halfway between Gujarat and Humayun's territory, wrote to him that he was engaged in a 'Jihad', a holy war to the glory of Islam, and Humayun as a faithful believer would not want to help the infidel. He knew the Emperor. Humayun immediately stopped his advance and waited. He had no wish to be accused of having interfered in a holy war on the side of a disbeliever.

Only after the fortress had fallen did he rush with all speed to engage the Shah, and now it was the Gujarat army which, relying on its artillery, settled down in an entrenched camp, waiting for the Moguls to attack them and be taken under the fire of their guns. However, Humayun's men knew the effects of artillery and kept well outside the range of the guns, satisfied with daily skirmishes in which they proved themselves vastly superior, and attacking any foraging detachment which dared to venture outside the camp. Soon famine reigned in the impregnable camp and the Gujarats lost all courage. The Shah did not dare to offer a battle and decided to break camp. He ordered the guns which had been his pride to be destroyed, and one night Humayun, hearing continuous uproar in the enemy camp, let all his cavalry mount and prepare for battle in the expectation of a general attack. Instead, the morning brought the news that the Shah had fled, covered in his flight by the best Gujarat cavalry, and that the remaining troops were dispersing. Some of them entered Humayun's service and were welcomed, particularly the gunners.

Humayun's main care was now not to let the Shah escape, and he pursued him from stronghold to stronghold as far as the port of Cambay, which he reached just as the Shah, having set on fire a fleet of small warships built by him to harass the Portuguese, embarked for the island of Diu. Humayun was the first Mogul emperor to have reached the coast of India, and he encamped on the shore of the Gulf of Cambay. His dash to the coast in pursuit of the Shah had been made with only a thousand horsemen. The main army had been left engaged in the siege of Champanir, one of the chief fortresses of Gujarat, and as he had only this small force with him, some of the tribes in the neighbourhood felt induced to make a night attack on his camp in the hope of plunder. However, he was forewarned and managed to drive them off, but as retaliation the unfortunate town of Cambay was plundered and burned by his men. Then he joined his army before Champanir and took the fortress by a feat of outstanding personal bravery, climbing with his best warriors a sheer rock into which iron spikes had been driven by night to serve as steps, while the attention of the garrison was diverted by furious assaults on the other sides. The achievement was commemorated by striking coins.

The treasure found in Champanir was immense. The fortress had been considered impregnable and served to store the enormous wealth of the kings of Gujarat, assembled in rich trade with Turkey, Persia and Portugal, and it is said that Humayun gave to his officers and men so much gold, silver and jewels as could be heaped on their shields, naturally corresponding in value to their ranks. Then the court and the army celebrated their luck by indulging for months in revelry and debauches.

The whole campaign had been conducted in a strange fashion. Sudden outbursts of hectic activity and dashing exploits were always followed by long spells of demoralizing inactivity and indecision, when Humayun indulged in opium, discipline loosened and all the jealousies and the usual bickering among his nobles came to the fore. Sometimes, when a well-defended stronghold surrendered, the commander was congratulated on his gallantry and taken by Humayun into his service; at other times, Humayun clad himself in red garments, and then streams of blood flowed. When Humayun had to administer justice for disciplinary offences and it was Tuesday, the day of Mars, the punishments were terrible: the culprits were mutilated or trampled to death by elephants. At other times he proved himself generous and lenient.

But now the campaign had lasted over a year and the news arriving from home was of the usual unrest and sedition not only in the eastern provinces but also in nearby Malwa, the kingdom which Humayun had taken from Badahur Shah's occupation. The local chiefs were driving out his governors. He could no longer afford to dally with his army in Gujarat, so he decided to turn back, leaving Askari as viceroy in the capital city of Ahmadabad, and posting experienced officers with strong garrisons in the conquered strongholds. But wide tracts of the country were not subdued, no provision was made for a regular administration of the land, and the people hated the invaders who were strangers and marauders. They liked Bahadur Shah, under whom they had lived in comfort, and scarcely was Humayun out of the country when everywhere the followers of the Shah rose in arms. In return for conceding to the Portuguese the right to build fortifications at Diu, Bahadur Shah received from them artillery and auxiliary troops, and he soon marched with an ever increasing army against Ahmadabad. Askari drew all the dispersed forces together, and each town from which the garrison had to be withdrawn was immediately occupied by one of the Shah's followers.

All appeals to Humayun for reinforcement or for definite orders remained unanswered and the amirs, disgusted with the indifference of the Emperor who was pleasurably lingering in the hills of Malwa, persuaded the twenty year-old Askari, who in any case was not strong enough to face the army of the Shah with the forces at his disposal, to march to Agra where they would proclaim him Emperor. He, too, was Babur's son, and he had just as much right to the throne; they trusted him while they no longer trusted Humayun. Thus, without even a battle, the Moguls evacuated Gujarat, which they had so recently regarded as conquered.

Humayun, who was delaying in Malwa, the land between the two countries which Bahadur Shah had been in the process of subduing before Humayun's onslaught, had the usual experience there that when he appeared with his army all the petty rulers hastened to pay homage, assuring him of their loyalty, while those who had compromised themselves too much left the districts they had seditiously seized and disappeared to some inaccessible retreat. Considering himself the conqueror of Gujarat, he played with the idea of establishing his permanent headquarters in Malwa as the central point from which he could quickly reach any seat of unrest. However, at the disastrous news of the loss of Gujarat and of Askari's march to Agra by the shortest route, he broke up his pleasure camp in all haste and managed to intercept Askari with his disloyal officers. But they all pledged submission. They had retreated because they saw no possibility of resisting the Shah, and by returning with all their forces had saved the army from dispersal.

Humayun needed every fighting man and preferred not to delve too deeply. Instead, he distributed some clothes of honour and they proceeded together to Agra. But even before they reached the capital the news came that, immediately after Humayun's departure from Malwa, the various Rajas and Khans had taken possession of the whole territory. Without a single battle Humayun had lost all the gains he had made in the victorious campaign of one and a half years' duration.

However, shortly afterwards the information reached Agra that Bahadur Shah was dead. While the Moguls still held the fortresses in Gujarat he had applied to the Portuguese viceroy of Goa to come to his aid, but before the viceroy arrived in Diu from Goa with a fleet and an army the Mogul troops had left the country; his help was no longer necessary and both partners were scheming how to gain the greatest advantage by kidnapping the other. The Portuguese aimed at the control of the Gujarat coast in order to cut off the Persian and Arabian traders, while the Shah wanted to lay hands on their ships and arms. Bahadur Shah invited the viceroy to visit him for a hunting party, but the viceroy excused himself as being ill. Politeness demanded a counter-visit to enquire after his health, and the Shah came on a barge to the Admiral's ship; but feeling that he was in a trap he hastened away. There was a scuffle, his barge was attacked, and whether he fell overboard or jumped into the sea to escape, he was drowned.

His death freed the Moguls from the most dangerous enemy in the west. As usual, there were various pretenders to Bahadur Shah's throne and soon Gujarat was in disorder and internal confusion. Humayun, enjoying his leisure and opium in Agra, could dream of the reconquest of the western kingdoms and the re-establishment of his glory. But when after long months of pleasure and time-wasting he at last assembled his army for a new campaign, it was not for the reconquest of the west but in order to break the continually rising power and the dangerous ambitions of Sher Khan in the east.

2

LOSS OF THE EMPIRE

SHER Khan had put the time of Humayun's absence with his army in the south-west, followed by his sojourn in Agra, to good use by establishing and securing his own supremacy in the east. Having consolidated his hold on Bihar, he started with inroads into the country north of the Ganges, collecting booty and plundering towns. Each expedition made him richer, allowed him to enlist more and more mercenaries, so that he gradually became the recognized national leader of all Afghans. The proudest Afghan chiefs now served as his retainers. At last, feeling strong enough, he attacked the neighbouring kingdom of Bengal, defeated the Bengal army and laid siege to its capital Gaur.

This news forced Humayun to act. Gaur contained the accumulated treasures of Bengal and if they fell into Sher Khan's hands, they would vastly increase his resources. If he were left undisturbed to subdue Bengal, he would become too dangerous. He had to be crushed now, and Humayun assembled all his forces. With his vastly superior army he did not consider the task too difficult. He proceeded comfortably down the Jumna and the Ganges, partly by boat, partly by land. He was accompanied by both his younger brothers, Askari and Hindal, and he even took part of his harem with him.

The first decision to be taken was where the blow should be struck. The old warriors of Babur's time wanted to push through to Bengal and face Sher Khan's main army at once before Gaur, but Humayun considered it unwise to leave the fortress of Chunar in his rear; also he was eager to erase the stain left on his honour four years ago, when he had been forced to leave the stronghold in Sher Khan's possession. Thus it was in vain that one of his old advisers remonstrated: 'The luck of Sher Khan is great. Before we take this fortress the Afghans will have conquered Gaur, and all its treasures will fall into their hands.' Humayun stuck to his plan. Chunar was besieged, and it took six months until the siege guns, placed on boats, on specially built platforms, could breach the wall from the river side, and the fortress was taken. When Humayun was ready to set out again, Gaur with all its treasures had in fact fallen to Sher Khan and the wounded Shah of Bengal came to Humayun pleading for help. The rainy season had already started and Humayun's officers maintained that during the rains the movement of troops, and particularly of the artillery, would be extremely difficult in the low-lying land of Bengal; but the Shah insisted that it was most important not to let Sher Khan get his grip on the country itself, that the granaries there had enough food for the whole army, and so Humayun pushed on.

Sher Khan detached a large contingent of his troops to block the passes to Bengal and delay the Mogul army, while he himself was moving the treasures and the artillery on round-about ways to a hill fortress in South Bihar. As soon as he reached his destination his Afghans withdrew everywhere and Humayun marched into Bengal without meeting any resistance. He was enchanted with the richness and the fertility of the country. Gaur itself was in ruins, with dead bodies lying in the streets and bazaars, but it did not take long to restore it to some kind of order, and he liked the place so much that he called it 'the paradisial city'. Here he commemorated his success by striking coins and spent three months in festivities and pleasure, and when the heat and the extreme humidity made him and his court ill, he merely moved to another district. It was a life of enjoyment and dissipation, and the alarming news that came from the rear were either concealed as 'too disagreeable for royal ears' or did not penetrate the Emperor's opium dreams. Moreover, messages from Hindustan arrived less and less frequently as one after the other the routes of communication became blocked.

As soon as Humayun had moved into Bengal, Sher Khan emerged from his hills in South Bihar, invading the northern part of the province through which Humayun had moved, defeating and killing his garrisons and seizing the roads and passes. Then he crossed the Ganges and succeeded in occupying various towns and strongholds. And then the events of Gujarat repeated themselves: Humayun had allotted certain districts to Hindal to secure the communications between Agra and Bengal, but Hindal, feeling that he would not be able to withstand Sher Khan and receiving neither answers nor instructions from Humayan, left his post. His begs and amirs, dissatisfied with Humayun's dilatoriness, persuaded Hindal to march to Agra and there to assume royal power.

When Humayun at last, after five months, started on the way

home, the monsoon happened to set in early and torrential rains made the roads nearly impassable. The carriages sank in the mud, the horses were soon exhausted and many perished, much of the baggage had to be left behind, and the troops became dispirited. Moreover the news came that Sher Khan was gathering his troops and following Humayun's movements at a distance. The safest way would have been to proceed westward along the left bank of the Ganges, but told that Sher Khan would boast that he did not dare to return the way he had come, Humayun let the army cross the Ganges and resumed his march up the river on the right bank, exactly as he had come down. And there, one day, at the village of Chausa, he was faced by the Afghan army. Between the armies there flowed a small river with extremely steep banks, the bed of which was full of clay and mud, so that it could only be crossed by a ferry, or by a ford higher up. Sher Khan had immediately entrenched his camp and secured it with strong earthworks; Humayun sent messenger after messenger to Agra demanding supplies and reinforcements, but nothing arrived.

In the meantime Hindal, now nineteen years old, had been joined by all the malcontent officers and chiefs who were telling him that if he did not accept the throne they would offer it to Kamran, Babur's second son; for at the news of the disorders in Hindustan Kamran had left his own domain of Kabul and had set out for Delhi with 10,000 horses. Delhi was held by one of Babur's faithful old officers who, recognizing that Kamran had not come to protect the interests of Humayun but to gain the throne for himself, persuaded him to go first to Agra and settle affairs with Hindal. Hindal was forced to submit, and the two brothers first assembled troops in order to move under Kamran's command against Sher Khan, but then some of the amirs argued that it would be better to husband their resources. If Humayun should defeat Sher Khan, he would not undertake anything against them so long as the brothers were well armed. If Sher Khan was victorious, Kamran would take over the empire and strike at him with all its might. And so they waited.

After their armies had faced each other for two months, Humayun and Sher Khan started peace negotiations. The treaty provided that Sher Khan should keep Bengal and Bihar and that Chunar would be restored to him, but that the Khutba would be read in Humayun's name, thus acknowledging him officially as overlord. While the negotiations went on a kind of armistice prevailed. Parties from opposing camps visited and entertained each other. Sher Khan constructed a bridge over the river that divided the armies and sent his best troops off in the direction of Bengal. Humayun's troops in the meantime were occupied with constructing a bridge of boats over the Ganges for his return home along the left bank. But then Sher Khan ordered the troops who had been sent away to march back with all speed, crossed the river at night with the rest of his army and at dawn thrust at Humayun's camp from three sides. The Moguls were caught completely by surprise .The slaughter was terrible. Humayun, wounded by an arrow in the arm, plunged with his horse into the Ganges, but his horse was carried away by the current and he was saved by a water-carrier who made him hold on to his inflated leather bag. The story goes that after reaching the opposite bank, Humayun promised the water-carrier that when he came to Agra he would let him sit for two hours on the throne and issue orders—a promise which Humayun is said to have kept.

The defeat was complete. Many thousands of soldiers and officers were slain or drowned, and everything in the camp, the tents, the baggage, the artillery and all the stores fell into the hands of the Afghans, including the whole harem. Though some of the ladies had perished, Sher Khan gave orders that none of the surviving women should be held captive, sent to Humayun's queen a condoling letter, and later arranged for her and all the other ladies to be escorted to Agra. He celebrated the victory with a magnificent festival at which he officially arrogated to himself royal rank and had the Khutba read in his name, though he had already assumed the title of Sher Shah. Now the whole eastern part of Hindustan was his. He sent an army to Bengal which defeated or drove out the troops left there by Humayun; another army conquered the lands north of the Ganges as far as Kanauj, and Sher Shah was already preparing to drive the northern invaders out of Agra and Delhi as well.

After the battle Humayun had waited for a short time on the left bank of the Ganges to collect the men who had managed to escape across the river and then hastened to Agra. When he arrived there, the danger to all Mogul possessions in Hindustan was so obvious that the brothers forgot their separate interests. The amirs from the provinces, too, hurried from all sides to Agra. Daily consultations took place, but there was no real trust and no agreement between the brothers. Kamran had now about twenty thousand men from Kabul and the Punjab with him. He wanted to march at once and strike at the Afghans, but that would only be one more blot on Humayun's honour, for it was he whom the Shah had overcome by a treacherous attack, and it was he who must punish him. Kamran should wait until the new army was levied.

Kamran waited, but he fell ill. The illness grew worse and worse. The fever emaciated him, his body was covered with eruptions, and he became so weak that he partially lost the use of his hands and feet. The doctors knew no remedy and suspected poison. Kamran believed that the poison had been given him on Humayun's orders by one of the royal ladies where the dishes were not tasted before offering them to a guest. On hearing this, Humayun came to see him and swore that he had never had such a thought nor given any such order. Slowly Kamran recovered, but he could not be persuaded to stay on. He set out with most of his amirs and begs for Lahore, leaving only a couple of thousand men with Humayun. Some historians try to put the blame for all that followed on Kamran's defection, but the army which finally marched aginst the Afghans was double the size of Sher Shah's, with sixty heavy and hundreds of small guns, and nearly five thousand matchlock-men. It encamped at Kanauj, on the one side of the Ganges, while Sher Shah's troops were on the other bank.

In this position both armies remained facing each other for a month, without moving, and on Humayun's side desertions began. The mood of many begs and amirs was, as a chronicler puts it: 'Let us go and rest in our own homes'. At last, Sher Shah sent a message to Humayun asking him to withdraw a few miles, then he would cross the Ganges and accept battle, or he was prepared to withdraw himself so that Humayun could cross the river. Humayun was afraid that even a short retreat would lead to the dissolution of his army; on the other hand, with the river behind them, the soldiers would not be able to desert. Consequently Sher Shah withdrew some six miles, letting Humayun cross the Ganges with all artillery and baggage and establish a new camp, which was of course on low-lying ground and became swamped by the first rain. At that moment Sher Shah attacked.

This time it was the Afghans who employed the enveloping tactics. While the mail-clad riders engaged each other in direct combat, two Afghan divisions fell upon the camp and the rear. In Humayun's army every amir and every chief had, besides his regular retainers, a multitude of servants and followers, who, finding themselves suddenly attacked, became unmanageable. They pressed from behind against the troops, pushed the soldiers over the chains holding the gun-carriages together, until everything was in disorder and confusion. 'It was not a fight but a rout', with everybody fleeing in panic, pursued and slain by the Afghan riders, who drove those who had escaped into the river, where most of them were drowned. Humayun succeeded in crossing the river on an elephant, was hauled up the steep further bank and fled in the direction of Agra with the few retainers whom he managed to collect.

This was more than a lost battle, this was a total defeat from which no quick recovery was possible. With all his artillery and war equipment in the hands of Sher Shah, Humayun could not even think of defending his capitals or forts. He did not dare to delay in Agra, as Sher Shah had immediately despatched a strong detachment in pursuit of him. He avoided entering the town itself and sent Hindal in to collect the valuables and the royal family. The story goes that, remembering how his little daughter Aqiqa had vanished after the defeat at Chausa, Humayun said to Hindal: 'I was filled with remorse and asked myself, would it not have been better to kill her in my own presence? Now again, it is difficult to take the women with us'. Hindal is said to have answered: 'What it would mean to your Majesty to kill mothers and sisters, speaks for itself! So long as there is life in me, I will fight in their service. I have hope in almighty God that—poor fellow that I am—I may pour out my life's blood for my mother and my sisters.'

He assembled the ladies and conveyed them through the dangerous areas where he had to beat off the attacks of robber-tribes, before letting them continue their journey to Lahore under a safe escort. Then he joined Humayun, who in the meantime had first reached Delhi, where some chiefs with their retainers, who could only expect trouble from the Afghans, came to him, and then resumed his march northward. Though his following increased all the way, he did not dare to delay, as at each stop there came further news of the pursuing Afghans. In reality, Sher Shah, having occupied Agra and Delhi without resistance, had remained in Delhi to settle the immediate problems of the government of the country, distributing fiefs and nominating governors and various officials. He sent only sufficient men in pursuit with the strict orders to follow the refugees closely enough to keep them on the move but not to engage in fighting. He had promised to drive the Moguls out of Hindustan, and that was the way he preferred to do it.

When Humayun arrived in Lahore, he was received by Kamran with all due honour, but that was all. All the Mogul nobles and chieftains came together in Lahore and every day there were consultations, but no agreement could be reached about the next move. Sher Shah, apprehensive of the assembly in Lahore, invaded the Punjab, but except for Humayun himself no one was prepared to risk another battle against him. The Indian Empire won by Babur was lost less than ten years after his death, and each of his sons had different plans for the future.

Kamran had lost the Punjab through no fault of his own, but he still possessed Kabul. Humayun declared that he wanted to go to Badakhshan, where he was well known, as he had been the governor of Badakhshan until shortly before Babur's death. But after he had abandoned it Babur had conferred it on Suleiman Mirza, and Suleiman would not cede it without war. Moreover, the way to Badakhshan led through Kabul, and Humayun's appearance there, with the attitude of the Emperor and liege lord which he maintained, would reduce Kamran's own status in his land to that of a fief-holder and weaken his grip on the country. So Kamran refused to give him passage through the domain, declaring that he would resist it by force. He was prepared only to give refuge to those who wished to seek asylum in his domain, and taking his brother Askari, like himself the son of Gul-rukh, Babur's second wife, with him, he left India and retired with his troops to Kabul.

Hindal, with his own retainers, decided to go down the Indus to try either to establish himself in the country of Sind or to get through it to Gujarat, where, since the death of Bahadur Shah, no stable government existed. The conquest of Gujarat would provide sufficient population and money for future action against the Afghans. He would try his fortune as a roving adventurer, trusting in his luck, and Humayun decided to follow him.

He had lost his empire, he was excluded from the country from which his father had drawn his forces, he had become a homeless vagabond. All he possessed was the empty title of Emperor. On the one hand, this title was dangerous because it was an inducement to some petty ruler, through whose domain he had to move, to lay a trap for him in expectation of a reward from Sher Shah. On the other hand, it gave him a prestige which might be of great value. When he approached the territory of a chieftain of the Baluchi tribe, he sent him a dress of honour, conferring on him a high title and accompanying it with the corresponding insignia: kettle-drum, horse-tail standard and so forth. In order not to antagonize the Afghans the chieftain thought it wiser not to wait on him, but supplied a large amount of grain and a number of boats so that Humayun could continue his march. Nevertheless, great scarcity reigned in his camp, and as more refugees joined him the worse the scarcity became. The soldiers had to kill horses and camels and eat their flesh. The ruler of Sind, Shah Husain, in spite of Humayun's reassuring messages that he was only passing through the country on the way to Gujarat, ordered his governors to lay waste the land through which Humayun had to move and to strengthen their fortifications, and all attempts to seize any of the forts were in vain.

Hindal was by now thoroughly dissatisfied with the way Humayun was conducting the new campaign, and rumours became rife that he wanted to abandon it, leave India and go to Kandahar, which was in Kamran's domain. Humayun travelled to Hindal's camp and was assured that there was no truth in the allegation. Here, at the reception provided for him, he was struck by the appearance of a fourteen year-old girl whom he had not seen before and heard that she was Hamida, the daughter of a Sheikh, Hindal's preceptor. He demanded her in marriage, but Hindal objected, declaring that he looked on her as a sister or as a child of his own; moreover, there was no adequate dowry to bestow on her. A quarrel between the brothers was about to break out which was patched up by Hindal's mother, Dildar. She approached the girl, but Hamida refused the offer of marriage. To Dildar's prompting that one day she would want to marry and who could be better than an emperor, Hamida replied that she would marry a man whose collar her hand could reach and not one whose skirt it did not even reach. This wooing went on for forty days until Hamida finally gave in and became, in an astrologically propitious hour, the exiled emperor's wife. However, Hindal was not appeased and, leaving Humayun's cause, went with his troops to Kandahar.

With Hindal's defection Humayun was now the last of Babur's sons still on Indian soil. About a year had passed since he had fled from Lahore, but instead of improving, his position was growing worse and worse. Seeing no chance of recovery in his fortunes his men started to drift away. When the ruler of Sind realized his weakness his attitude became still more hostile, and Humayun decided to accept the invitation of the Raja of Merwar, a Rajput prince, who some time earlier had promised him assistance, and Humayun left the Indus valley for his territory. It was a strenuous march through a desert and many in his train perished from hunger and thirst. When they approached the Raja's territory, the Raja sent food and presents but failed to appear himself and, suspicious of his true intentions, Humayun despatched envoys and also spies to the Raja's court. Their report was that emissaries from Sher Shah had been visiting the Raja with promises of high rewards if he captured Humayun. When the Raja had invited the Emperor, he may have thought of conquering some adjoining principalities with the help of the Mogul army, but recognizing its wretched condition he found it dangerous to antagonize Sher Shah on their behalf. Nothing would have been easier for him than to capture Humayun, but that was something which the Rajput code of honour would never have allowed, and so he was frankly relieved when Humayun hastened to quit his territory.

The direction he now took, was south-west, through the desert again, to the domain of the Rana of Umarkot, another Rajput prince. This journey was even worse than the last. It was full summer and the heat was deathly, the horses sank at every step into the sand. They had so few horses in any case that Humayun had none for Hamida, who was pregnant. He asked for one from a beg who flatly refused to give it; so he put Hamida on his own riding horse and himself rode on a camel, until another officer gave him the horse on which his mother was riding, putting her on the camel. Most of the party were on foot, men and women struggling along somehow, hungry and thirsty. When they reached a tank or a well, there were terrible scenes. However, on reaching Umarkot they were received with all due honour and hospitality, supplied with food, and, although the principality was a small one and possessed of scant resources, the Rana had a few thousand horsemen of his own tribe and declared that they were at the service of the Emperor.

Etiquette required that Humayun should send presents to the Rana and, as his means were exhausted, some of his courtiers drew his attention to the fact that many of the amirs still had money and valuables and costly apparel. Humayun called all his amirs to a meeting and while they took counsel their tents were searched and all valuables were brought before the Emperor. He restored half of the money and valuables and two thirds of the costly clothes to the owners and 'borrowed' the rest. The clothes were kept for the needs of the imperial household, the money and valuables he gave to his servants and followers, so that they could equip themselves again with horses and protective armour, and the Rana got his presents.

Humayun remained in Umarkot for seven weeks, in which time all the stragglers arrived and all his forces had collected, and then, accompanied by the Rana's men and some other Rajput troops he set out towards Jun at the delta of the Indus, a rich and fertile district near the Arabian Sea, belonging to the ruler of Sind, against whom the Rana was eager to fight since he had killed the Rana's father. The Sind forces in the district were quickly overcome, the town was taken, and in the near-by gardens Humayun established a strongly secured camp where he received the submission of various local chieftains, so that his forces were continually growing. For the first time since his wanderings began, his luck seemed to be turning. Two months after the fall of Jun, Hamida arrived in the camp with her little son, born to her in the castle of Umarkot a few days after Humayun had left the town. The boy was named Jallal-ud Din Muhammad Akbar, who was destined to become the real founder of the Mogul Empire, the Emperor Akbar.

In the meantime Shah Husain, the ruler of Sind, came down the Indus with a large army and pitched camp on the opposite bank. Daily skirmishes took place, but Humayun would have had a good chance of successfully prosecuting the war had not certain of his officers insulted the Rana of Umarkot. Humayun did nothing to redress the insult and the disgusted Rana left the camp with all his men, declaring that it was a mistake to do anything good for the Moguls. The other Rajputs followed his example, and Humayun was left with only his own adherents. His position was strong enough to beat off Shah Husain's attempt to storm his camp, but now, as the local tribes had become hostile, supplies ceased to arrive. Famine threatened his camp, desertions began, and Humayun was only too glad when Shah Husain offered grain, horses and camels if Humayun would leave Sind.

But now he had nowhere to go. No Indian prince would welcome him, and he could no longer think of conquests; and so, two and a half years after his flight from Lahore, he had to leave the soil of India and begin the long trek to Kandahar. Hindal, who nearly two years earlier had gone the same way and occupied Kandahar, was soon afterwards forced by Kamran to surrender the city but had received, after a short imprisonment in Kabul, Jallalabad as a fief.

Jallalabad was near the Khaibar Pass, leading to the Punjab, and Hindal could act as a shield if Sher Shah's Afghans should try to invade Kamran's dominion. With Humayun the position was different, because nominally he was still the liege-lord, and as soon as he had crossed the mountain passes of Baluchistan and entered the territory of Kandahar he received intelligence that on Kamran's orders Askari was about to waylay and capture him. The danger was so imminent that he had to leave camp at once and flee, accompanied only by Hamida, a lady in waiting, and about forty persons, most of whom were his high dignitaries. The camp and all possessions were seized by Askari. The one-year-old Akbar was brought to Kandahar, where Askari gave him into the keeping of his own wife.

Humayun's flight into the desert parts of the country in the midst of an icy winter without equipment and without food naturally meant more suffering and privation for the small party. Fortunately, the woman attending Hamida, the wife of one of his officers, was a Baluchi, of the local race, speaking their language, and the tribesmen received the refugees hospitably and accompanied them through their territory. In another district they were given tents, provisions and even money, in spite of the fact that the chief officer who provided the equipment was a tax-collector in Kamran's service. However, they had to move on and in his distress Humayun finally sent a letter to Shah Tahmasp of Persia, asking for a refuge in his country, for he was now near its border. He was waiting for an answer to his letter when he heard that some troops sent by Kamran were approaching, and so he crossed the border of Seistan without permission and encamped on Persian territory.

The governor of the province, waiting for orders from the Shah, received the unexpected guests with hospitality, though without engaging himself too deeply, and looking with a certain amount of apprehension on the increasing number of refugees arriving from Kandahar. Among the new arrivals were two foster-brothers of Kamran who, dissatisfied with his despotic rule, urged Humayun to invade some other districts which they assured him were ripe for defection. But this the Persian governor, not knowing the intentions of the Shah, could not allow and he invited the Emperor to accompany him to Herat, which Humayun was curious to see.

On the way to Herat, orders from the court of Persia arrived. Shah Tahmasp, the son of Shah Ismail, found that for the Emperor of India to seek refuge at his court was an historic event which gave additional glory to his reign and had to be celebrated with corresponding splendour. Together with the letter of invitation to Humayun edicts were sent to all governors and chiefs of the provinces and cities through which he was likely to pass, prescribing in every detail how he and his retinue were to be received, entertained and provided with food and comforts. The minutest directions were given: loaves of white bread baked with milk and butter, five hundred trays of different kinds of meat, sherbets cooled in ice, sweetmeats of different kinds, grapes and other fruits, rose water, amber and perfumes had to be offered to the guests. They were to be supplied with table linen, sheets, plate, changes of wearing apparel, and ornamental clothes of gold tissue and brocades. A thousand men on horseback were to attend him, and never less than fifteen hundred trays with food were to be served daily to him and his suite.

From this moment Humayun's journey resembled a triumphal procession. After the privations and humiliations of the last three years, luxury and honours were showered upon him and his party. The inhabitants of the towns and villages along his route were commanded to line the road. Everywhere the dignitaries received him at the approaches to a town, everywhere magnificent entertainments were arranged. He visited the mausoleums and the holy places. It was January when he reached Seistan, and it was July when he approached Kazvin, Shah Tahmasp's residence. At the Shah's request, he sent Bairam Beg in advance as an ambassador. Bairam was a Turkoman, originally in Persian service, who had gone to Transoxiana with the army which Shah Ismail had once sent to Babur, and remaining in Babur's service had risen to high positon. After Humayun's defeat, he had found refuge with a sheikh but was finally captured and handed over to Sher Shah who, however, set him free because he had been harboured by a holy man, and a refugee protected by a holy man should be pardoned. He was assigned a place of residence but managed to flee and ultimately joined Humayun in his camp at Jun during the invasion of Sind, to become henceforth the Emperor's chief adviser.

As a Shiite and still owing partial allegiance to the Shah, he was the very man to plead with Shah Tahmasp for his new lord, to arrange the complicated details of etiquette as to how the two sovereigns should meet, and then to bring Humayun to the Shah's summer residence. There at once arose the great difficulty that Tahmasp demanded from Humayun, precisely as his father Ismail had done from Babur, the acceptance of the Shiite creed. At first Humayun resisted, but when told that he was endangering not only his own life but also the lives of all his followers, whose numbers had risen to seven hundred, he submitted.

Now the Shah, proud to have achieved the conversion, arranged magnificent feasts and splendid hunting parties, which even that far west were held in the Mongol fashion of the times of the Il-Khans The army surrounded a large area and drove the deer in ever contracting circles to the prearranged place, where first the Shah and the Emperor, then the highest dignitaries and then persons of lower ranks proved their valour and hunting abilities. During these festivities Humayun presented to the Shah, through the intermediary of Bairam Beg, the 'Great Mogul' diamond which he still had from the time of the conquest of Agra, together with hundreds of Badakhshan rubies, and the Shah, gratified, bestowed on Bairam Beg the title of Khan with standard and kettle-drum. Then for a while the good relations of the monarchs were disturbed by the intrigues of jealous Persian courtiers, but in the end harmony was restored.

The ultimate purpose of the meeting was not just to exchange pleasantries but to come to an agreement on far-reaching political and military plans. Humayun needed help, and the Shah agreed to supply him with 12,000 men of the Persian cavalry, not to regain the Mogul possessions in India but to recover Babur's old heartland, the kingdom of Kabul, from his brother Kamran. Some time after Babur's death, Shah Tahmasp had captured Kandahar, previously a fief of Khorasan which had become a Persian domain after the defeat of the Uzbegs. But no sooner had he left Kandahar than Kamran defeated the Persian governor and recovered the fortress. So Tahmasp demanded that, in return for his help, Humayun would cede to him the province of Kandahar as soon as Kamran was defeated. Humayun agreed, and an infant son of the Shah was sent with the army to become the nominal governor of Kandahar under the protection and guidance of the Persian commander Bidagh Khan Kajar.

3

THE RECONQUEST OF KABUL

JUST one year after Humayun had fled, poor and destitute, over the border to Seistan, he again crossed the frontier into Kamran's territory, this time at the head of a strong invading army. At first, the governors in the frontier areas surrendered their districts and the garrisons joined him. But when he pushed through to Kandahar he found the fortress well garrisoned and strongly defended by Askari. He was forced to lay siege to it, and his Persian allies, accustomed as they were to speedy movements and decisive battles in the field, grew restless. In the meantime, Humayun had sent Bairam Khan to Kabul to find out what Kamran's plans were or whether he could come to some agreement with him; but it soon became clear that Kamran had no intention either of surrendering Kandahar or of giving up any of his rights in the realm which he held with absolute authority.

The position was a curious one: Bairam Khan was received with all due respect, he was allowed to see the nearly three-year-old boy-prince Akbar who had been brought to Kabul the moment Humayun's invasion was expected, and was even allowed to visit Hindal, who was now confined to Kabul in the custody of his mother, Dildar Begam. He visited all the royal ladies, and although naturally closely watched, managed to deliver presents and messages from Humayun to all the chief nobles in order to remove any apprehension that a change of sovereignty might adversely affect them. However, he had to return without any hope of an agreement, and on his return journey he was accompanied by Khanzada Begam, Babur's elder sister. It was a remarkable sign of the important part the royal ladies played at the Mogul courts that this sixty-seven-year-old aunt of the contending brothers went to Kandahar in order to investigate the position there and to advise Askari in his beleaguered fortress. She first saw Humayun, she went into the besieged citadel, and when it became obvious that no relief was to be expected and the usual desertions began, she again went to Humayun to negotiate the terms of surrender.

When the fortress finally surrendered after a siege of five months, disagreement between the victorious allies broke out immediately. The Persian commander demanded the possession of the citadel, the treasure it contained and Askari as his prisoner. Humayun ceded the fort, but denied the Persians' right to the treasure. He declared, however, that he was ready to present it to the Shah and sealed the chests with his own seal. To hand over Askari he absolutely refused, and when the commandant threatened to take him by force, Humayun collected all his followers and the new adherents who were now joining him every day from the neighbouring districts, even from as far as Kabul, and reviewed them ostentatiously under arms. Bidagh Khan dropped his demand but declared the campaign finished, refusing further help for the conquest of Kabul. The Persian auxiliaries, the Turkoman tribes, went home, while Bidagh Khan, with the remaining Persian garrison, started to establish a stern rule in the city of Kandahar. The inhabitants of the town naturally hated the foreign oppressors and complaints came daily to Humayun's camp. The spirit among his own troops became bitter. With winter approaching and the cold weather having already set in, there could be no question of marching over the mountains and through the deserts to Kabul, and there was no safe place where they could leave their families and possessions. When Humayun asked for a few houses in the town to be set apart for them, Bidagh Khan refused. At that moment the infant son of the Shah, in whose name Kandahar was being held, died, and Humayun accepted the advice of his amirs to take Kandahar by surprise. The plan succeeded; Bidagh Khan was not prepared to sustain a siege in the fort and departed. Humayun sent a message to Shah Tahmasp that the Khan had been acting contrary to the orders of the Shah and had therefore been dismissed, but that Bairam Khan, who had been appointed in his place, was ready to obey all the Shah's orders. Shah Tahmasp, appeased by the treasure sent to him as well as by the tone of the message, and seeing no alternative, acquiesced and even allowed the remaining Persian troops to continue in Humayun's service.

The possession of Kandahar completely changed Humayun's position. He now had a safe base from which to operate, and leaving his and his officers' families in the citadel of Kandahar, he set out for

Kabul in spite of the onset of winter. On the way he was joined by Hindal, who had managed to escape from Kabul, and by some amirs, and although the troops which Kamran had assembled to meet him were much more numerous, he was joined every day by officers and men who had deserted from Kamran. In the end, doubting the loyalty of his troops, Kamran left his army, sped to Kabul and, collecting his family and the last of his adherents, fled to Sind to Shah Husain, whose daughter he had married, leaving Humayun in possession of the country.

Humayun at once sent a few trusty men to occupy the gates of Kabul to save the town from pillage, and then made a ceremonial entry to the acclamation of the populace. Thus, without even a battle, he had regained the kingdom which had formed the base from which Babur had made his conquests. The usual festivities followed, with the distribution of presents, with allotments of fiefs, with the arrival of chieftains professing their allegiance, and congratulatory embassies from neighbouring princes. Even an embassy from Shah Tahmasp arrived and was magnificently received and entertained, although the main purpose of their visit, the restoration to the Shah of Kandahar, was naturally shelved.

Suleiman Mirza, to whom Babur had given Badakhshan, had sent an embassy but failed to come himself to wait upon the Emperor, which meant that he regarded himself as an independent ruler and did not recognize the Emperor as his liege-lord. So, when spring came, Humayun set out for Badakhshan. Suleiman also collected his troops but was defeated in a pitched battle and was forced to flee. The country submitted, Hindal was made ruler of Badakhshan, and officers were appointed to various provinces and districts, when Humayun suddenly fell gravely ill. He remained unconscious for several days, rumours spread that he was dying, and at once chaos broke out everywhere. The followers of Suleiman, who had fled into the mountains, started to overrun the lowlands. Humayun's officers left their posts to discuss what to do and the jockeying for the succession began. Askari was still with the army as prisoner, Hindal rushed to the camp to be on the spot, and the question whether the amirs would proclaim the four-year-old Akbar as successor in Kabul was mooted.

When Humayun at last regained consciousness, he immediately issued a proclamation that he was convalescent and sent a messenger to Kabul with the same news. However, it was months before he was in a condition to be moved, and in the meantime a new threat arose: Kamran, supplied with troops and money by his father-in-law in Sind and thinking the chance had come to turn the tables on his brother, advanced from the south and managed to penetrate into the city of Kabul, where he put Humayun's governor to death with some of the chief officers, imprisoning others and taking cruel vengeance on everyone who had turned from him to Humayun.

Anxiety rose in Humayun's camp. Some of the officers whose families were in Kabul deserted, and it cost Humayun himself and his chief amirs a great deal of effort to keep the troops loyal by promising rewards and quick retaliation. Humayun also made his peace with Suleiman Mirza; he called for him, restored him as ruler of Badakhshan as he had been under Babur, and marched with his whole army back to Kabul over the snow-clad mountain passes of the Hindukush. When he had at last crossed them with great difficulty, he was met by a selected force of Kamran's best fighters, and the battle was long in the balance until he succeeded in defeating them. He also gave no quarter; the prisoners were executed, and in pursuit of the fugitives the outer enclosure of the city was taken. Yet the town and the citadel were too extensive to be effectively besieged by his small army, and desperate encounters took place daily, with both parties acting with the utmost brutality and cruelty. It is said that when the bastion was shelled Kamran placed the little Akbar on the exposed wall and that Humayun ordered the shelling to stop, but he informed Kamran that if anything should happen to Akbar full revenge would be taken on him and his family.

As the siege continued and more and more chiefs with their followers swelled Humayun's forces, Kamran's position became increasingly precarious and he was prepared to offer his submission. Reports have it that Humayun's own trusted advisers recommended to Kamran that it was better for him to escape and even arranged to help him. When Humayun sent Hindal in pursuit, Hindal also allowed him to get away. That was the persisting policy. They fought against Kamran and dreaded the thought of his regaining power, but the importance of their position with Humayun depended on his being somewhere, free and prepared to strike at any moment. It was their insurance that Humayun would not develop into a despot.

As Humayun earlier, at the time of his misfortune, had gone to seek help from the Persians, so now Kamran went to the Uzbegs.

The Uzbeg governor of Balkh was only too pleased to invade the country of his neighbour. Together they invaded Badakhshan, drove Suleiman Mirza and his begs into the mountains and beat the army which Humayun sent against them. Then, satisfied with the booty gained, the Uzbegs returned home; but the news of Kamran's success was sufficient not only to induce adventurous tribes to join him, but thousands of Humayun's soldiers, who had earlier been in Kamran's service, now went over to him again. They did not care for whom they fought. All they wanted was to be on the winning side where they could expect further spoils and higher rewards. Thus Humayun himself, after the second capture of Kabul, had for one day allowed them to plunder the city, under the pretext that this was to punish the inhabitants who had let Kamran in, though in reality it was the only way he could repay his troops for their long privations. Now, when Kamran seemed to be gaining the upper hand, it was better to be with him. There was no question of who was in the right; both were descendants of Timur, both were Babur's sons, and if an amir felt that his prince did not give him his due, he simply changed sides, assured that, provided he proved himself in action, the first prince, if success turned his way, would again accept his service.

When Humayun at last decided to march against Kamran in Badakhshan, he sent messages calling the amirs throughout the country to join him, and had the pleasure of seeing that, while some of the chiefs in his immediate neighbourhood had left him, others in far-off provinces on whom he had scarcely counted followed his call, so that his army was far stronger than Kamran's. He managed to enclose his brother in a fort, and once Kamran saw that the Uzbegs did not come to his relief he had to capitulate for the third time. The terms were harsh. He had to renounce his claim to independence and to retire to Mecca. The amirs who had revolted were to be delivered to the Emperor in chains and he himself escorted out of Humayun's territory. After that was done, and the amirs, having been humiliated, were pardoned, Kamran suddenly turned back and petitioned to be allowed to pay homage in person.

Humayun felt he could not deny this to his own brother; he also freed Askari, whom he was still holding prisoner, and a great feast of reconciliation between the four brothers was held. It so happened that they were near the place where Babur, having received the submission of his brother Jahangir and his cousin Mirza Khan, had commemorated the event by an inscription in the rock; together they went thither, and Humayun ordered the date and his and his brothers' names also to be inscribed. But despite the show of feeling the concord between the brothers was more apparent than real. When Humayun bestowed on Kamran a minor fief, the province of Kuljab near the Amu Darya, Kamran burst out: 'I have possessed Kabul and Badakhshan and that is only a dependency of Badakhshan. And now I am to accept service for this fief!' Askari, who had asked for permission to go with Kamran, received an adjoining district. Hindal was confirmed in the government of Kunduz and the land leading to the chain of the Hindukush, and Humayun, feeling himself at last secure in the possession of the whole of Babur's kingdom of Kabul, at once began to think, like his father, of fresh conquests to satisfy the needs of his followers and to acquire the means to pay his dependents.

His aim was the Uzbeg province of Balkh, lying to the south of the Amu Darya, whence Kamran had received the help for his last revolt. The possession of this rich and fertile valley would provide much-needed booty and would secure, moreover, the northern frontier of his domain. He set out from Kabul and proceeded northwards with all the troops he could collect, and was joined by Hindal and by Suleiman Mirza from Badakhshan with their troops. Only Kamran did not arrive, but sent instead a letter assuring Humayun of his loyalty and co-operation. Humayun pushed on to Balkh, had a few more or less successful encounters with the Uzbegs on the way, but as there was still no trace of Kamran, Humayun's councillors became alarmed. The general opinion was that Kamran was quietly waiting somewhere until the army became engaged before Balkh and then would march to seize Kabul; the War Council decided that, in order to prevent this, the army should return at once.

The retreat began, and soon there was complete disorder everywhere. The soldiers who had families in Kabul, assuming that Kamran was already there, separated from the army and rushed home in small bands; while those who came from other districts did not see why they should go all the way to Kabul and simply returned to their own homes. Further, when the Uzbegs heard that the army had suddenly retreated, they pursued the troops, beat the rearguard, and amidst the general rout and panic every leader tried to take a different route with his detachment, crossing the mountains by little-frequented roads. Finally reaching Kabul, hungry and exhausted, the troops found that everything there was quiet and safe, and that Kamran had in fact never moved or tried to cross the mountains.

Nevertheless, seeing the general disorder, Kamran could not now resist the temptation to improve his position and marched into Badakhshan. After initial successes, he had to recognize that he did not possess forces sufficient to subdue Suleiman Mirza and tried to win over Hindal. When Hindal refused to make common cause with him, he laid siege to Kunduz, but that too was in vain. However, at this time various amirs who were dissatisfied with the lack of stability in Humayun's regime and with his irresolution and unreliability, sent a message to Kamran that if he would come they would revolt. That was all that Kamran needed. In spite of the recent reconciliation, he hated Humayun's overlordship; he had nothing but contempt for his brother's qualities as ruler, and for the third time after his original defeat he made the attempt, the most dangerous of all, to regain the kingdom. He started by marching on Kabul. Humayun, having got the news, set out to meet him. To cover the different approaches he divided his troops, and saw himself suddenly faced by Kamran's army. The battle was engaged, but many of the Emperor's troops seem to have avoided the fight; the groups which did engage the enemy were forced into flight, and Humayun himself was severely wounded by a sabre stroke on the head. He was borne away on horseback by some faithful adherents, but he threw away his bloodstained padded coat as he fled. When this quilted cuirass was found and brought to Kamran, he hastened on to Kabul, and as the Khan who commanded the place refused to open the gates, he sent him Humayun's blood-covered coat. Resistance had now become pointless, and for the third time Kamran entered Kabul, ruthlessly taking revenge on everyone who had foresaken him for Humayun. He at once seized all the treasures he could find and began the distribution of fiefs among his partisans.

Not until about three months after he had gained possession of Kabul did the information come that Humayun was alive and preparing to retake the city. He had been carried by his friends to the country of Kunduz, where Hindal met him and where he slowly recovered from his wound. As soon as he was able to campaign again he issued another call to arms to everybody he could reach in the north, and he sent a special plea to Haram Begam, the wife of

Suleiman Mirza of Badakhshan. In a very few days she provided horses and arms for thousands of men, superintended their recruiting personally, and led them to the mountain pass on the way to Humayun's army.

Another equally important development took place in Humayun's own camp, which went far to tilt the balance in his favour. He was so apprehensive of being deserted at the critical moment that, just as Babur before the battle against the Rajputs had bound his officers by oath to fight to the death, Humayun demanded that each of his nobles should swear a solemn oath to follow and obey him faithfully and honestly. They were prepared to do so, but in return demanded from him also an oath that whatever they, his well-wishers, recommended and deemed indispensable he would consent to and carry out.

That was an incredible departure from all precedent, an imposition upon the royal prestige. It was quite usual for some chieftain actually to wield the power and to make all decisions for a puppet monarch, but that had always been done with due deference. An open undertaking on the Emperor's part that he would carry out the decisions made by his advisers was unheard-of and constituted a complete change in the relations between the Emperor and his great nobles. Humayun's immediate acceptance of this demand showed that he must have recognized how little trust there was in his ability to rule, despite his occasional dashes of reckless bravery. Perhaps with his easy-going disposition, his love for leisure and his addiction to opium he did not mind having a standing council in which his chiefs, with their contradictory interests, would soon be at loggerheads without being able to blame him for any obstruction to their wishes. On the other hand the increase in the chieftains' power, together with the assurance that they need not fear arbitrary decisions on the Emperor's part, had the result that desertions now began in Kamran's camp and Humayun's army gained a complete and decisive victory in the ensuing battle. Kamran's commander was killed and his head brought to the Emperor, Askari was once more taken prisoner, and Kamran himself fled, taking his way to the independent Afghan hill tribes. From there he still fought on, plaguing the eastern parts of Kabul with raids and skirmishes, but never again was he able to challenge Humayun's authority on a serious scale.

To a great extent Humayun owed his victory to the troops from

Badakhshan who had been recruited thanks to the efforts of Haram Begam, Suleiman Mirza's wife. To show how grateful he was Humayun betrothed his ten-year-old daughter to her young son Ibrahim; however, Haram Begam does not seem to have regarded this as sufficient reward, because, when he allotted Kunduz, which adjoined the territory of Badakhshan, to Hindal, she collected her troops, went with her son Ibrahim to Kunduz, occupied it and installed him there before Hindal had even arrived. Humayun yielded and gave Hindal another fief, and in order to strengthen the ties with Badakhshan still more, he sent presents there and asked for the hand of the daughter of Suleiman Mirza and Haram Begam To his astonishment he received a letter from Suleiman Mirza, begging to be excused because this matter was entirely in the hands of his wife. First of all, Haram Begam strongly upbraided the wife of the ambassador who had brought the presents for conniving at the seduction of other peoples' daughters and told her that if the Emperor was serious in his intentions he must send some of the Royal Begams to arrange the match. And to Humayun she wrote: 'Suleiman Khan is your slave and I am your slave. Thus my son and daughter are the offspring of your slaves. We happen to be near the Uzbegs, and command some respect. You are a great king. If you want to marry my daughter, please come over the hills of the Hindukush, accompanied by the Begams and amirs of Kabul. I shall arrange to provide every one of them with a good Badakhshan steed and with goats and silk for their dresses. I shall give my daughter in marriage to you, which will be a source of honour to us; and the enemies, who are near us, will know that you have done us this favour.' Though Humayun did not go to Badakhshan in person, he must have satisfied Haram Begam's wishes, for his betrothal to her daughter took place. He could now feel that the northern part of his dominion was safe.

His system of making the amirs and chieftains sit in judgment over offenders against the interests of his State also proved to his advantage in many ways. The men in the council were not afraid of pronouncing stern sentences, as the fiefs of the condemned nobles were apportioned among the loyal followers. They condemned two mighty begs of doubtful loyalty who might have been able to stir up discontent, and they were executed. In no case could Humayun himself be accused of arbitrary action.

One continuous source of trouble remained—and that was Kamran. Since his flight into the Afghan hills he had lived the life of a knight-errant, collecting adventurers around him and invading the eastern marches of Kabul, fighting the troops sent against him and retiring again into the mountains when faced with superior strength. In one such skirmish Hindal, who led the opposing forces, was killed. Humayun retaliated by invading the land of the tribes, devastating them and driving away their cattle. In the end they realized that sheltering and helping Kamran was to their disadvantage, and he left the hills and went to the Punjab. But finding that, instead of getting help there, he was only to be kept as a hostage by the son of Sher Shah, he fled, disguised as a woman with a veil over face and body, and continued wandering from one chieftain to another, until at last he was seized and handed over to Humayun. This existence as a roving adventurer had lasted for three years.

Humayun's amirs and councillors demanded Kamran's death. Humayun made them write down their verdict and sign and seal it, and then sent it to Kamran. Kamran returned it with the remark that those whose seals were affixed to the paper asking for his death were the same men who had urged him on to his deeds. Humayun, knowing how much truth there was in this remark and shunning the idea of killing his own brother, nevertheless understood that he had to render him incapable of causing further trouble and sedition, and so he ordered Kamran to be blinded and escorted to Mecca.

Very few servants could be found prepared to make the pilgrimage with the blinded man. When at last he came to Sind, Shah Husain, his father-in-law, allotted him a palace and an estate for his support, but Kamran himself insisted on continuing his pilgrimage. He went to the ship which was to take him on his journey, and there he found that the Shah's daughter, his wife, was waiting for him. When the Shah heard of this, he came and tried to dissuade her, but she replied: 'You gave me to him when he was a king and happy, and you want to take me from him now that he is blind and miserable. No, I will attend him and watch over him wherever he goes'. And she went with him to Mecca and cared for him until his death four years later, surviving him by only a few months.

Now that Kamran had been blinded and despatched to Mecca, and Askari, immediately after his having been taken prisoner, deported to Badakhshan and then likewise sent to Mecca, and with Hindal killed in combat, Humayun was the only male descendant of

Babur ruling over the territory which had been Babur's kingdom when he started on the conquest of Hindustan. Therefore Humayun decided that the time had come for the reconquest of the Empire. Fourteen years had passed since his expulsion, and all the information which he received from Hindustan indicated that it was ripe to fall into his hands once more.

4

RETURN TO INDIA

SHER Shar's assurance that he would drive the Moguls out and re-establish Afghan rule in Hindustan had proved to be no idle boast. His victory had been complete. But he soon found that the second part of his task, that of giving the reconquered lands a just and orderly adminstration, required a still more formidable effort, and it is as an administrator and organizer that Sher Shah laid the practical foundations on which Akbar was later to build the Empire of the Great Moguls.

Sher Shah's main care was naturally the military organization for the safeguard of his kingdom against invasion or internal disorder. His army amounted to 150,000 horses and 25,000 foot armed with matchlocks or bows, besides the troops of the provincial governors and the garrisons in the many forts which he continued to build on every suitable spot. The nobles, to whom assignments were granted or monthly salaries paid, had to provide exactly prescribed numbers of troops, and their horses were branded to prevent the same horse being fraudulently presented with another man riding it. To avoid corruption and favouritism, the troops were paid individually and not through the commanding officers or nobles.

The soldiers had to watch that no damage was done to fields or crops and to suppress ruthlessly the highway robbery that prevailed. The headman of the village where a crime was committed had to produce the thieves or robbers, or else make good the loss himself. If there was a murder and he did not find the culprit, he himself was put to death. Particular care was given to roads, which were being built throughout the length and breadth of the Empire, from Bengal to the Indus, from Malwa to Agra, and many others that connected important towns, and everywhere along these roads hostelries were erected with separate quarters for Moslems and Hindus, where servants provided the travellers with water and victuals at state expense. Along the roads fruit trees were planted to give shelter and refreshment, and merchants were patronized. When a traveller died on the road, his goods were restored to his heirs. Customs were levied only at the frontier and at the place of sale. No dues were imposed on the roads, at the ferries or in any towns or villages. The officials were not allowed to buy any goods except at market prices.

The cultivated land was measured every year and the taxes assessed according to the produce. In every district, while one official had to effect the collection, another had to see that the cultivators were not oppressed. Two clerks kept the accounts in Hindi and in Persian, and to prevent abuses the officials were changed every year or two. Naturally that only encouraged them to make as much as they could in that short time, but they did so at great risk, for Sher Shah maintained spies everywhere, who provided daily reports which were immediately sent to the central government, and the punishment was ruthless.

He did not believe in delegating too much power; on the contrary, he watched with particular attention that none of his amirs created for himself a preponderant position which could make him feel independent. When he heard that his governor of Bengal had married the daughter of the late Shah and was behaving like a sovereign prince, he marched into Bengal and, in spite of a magnificent reception and a profession of loyalty, he rebuked the governor, saying that a noble of the state must 'not do a single act without the king's permission'. He put the man into chains and divided Bengal into different provinces under different rulers, appointing a civilian as supervisor, not governor, of the whole. He was constantly reminding his Afghans that it had been their feuds and quarrels which had brought about their downfall, and really did succeed in arranging that, when they had a quarrel, they did not start a private war, as they used to do, but applied to him for a settlement of the disagreement.

Maintaining his sovereignty and the unity of his Empire in this way, through a strictly centralized administration, he employed his forces for further conquests, everywhere extending his possessions. But his main target was Rajputana, where he felt at liberty to break the most solemn promises and to slaughter men, women and children, because he was dealing with unbelievers. And it was here, while he was preparing for the assault on a fortress, that a rocket with gunpowder, thrown against the wall, rebounded and burst when falling back on an ammunition dump. The whole dump blew up, and the Shah, together with his nobles and divines, was dreadfully burnt and lost his life. Sher Shah's rule over Hindustan had lasted five years, only a few months longer than that of Babur. Under him, and thanks to his qualities in the military and political, as well as administrative fields, the country had enjoyed a period of unusual stability.

At the moment of his death all that he had taught during his reign was brushed aside. The chiefs in the camp assembled to elect his successor. Sher Shah's elder son Adil was an easy-going type, with a love for comfort and strong drink, and when his name was mentioned the leading Afghans said: 'No one obtains a kingdom by inheritance; it belongs to whoever can govern it by the sword', and elected the younger son Jelal who, as they maintained, 'resembled his father in his pomp and splendour, and in his desire of dominion and conquest'. He was proclaimed king under the title Islam Shah, and the nobles soon had occasion to regret their choice. First he took care to get rid of his brother, in spite of the fact that Adil acknowledged him as sovereign. Then he began to curb his nobles. He demanded absolute obedience to his will, seized their war elephants, and issued precise regulations; in each province the officials had to assemble every week under a canopy, where the Shah's quiver and shoes were placed on the throne, and the secretary read his ordinances aloud. He enforced the strictest discipline in the army, introducing regular service grades, and stationed large bodies of troops in permanent camps throughout his Empire. The espionage system became even more thorough than his father's had been, so that he was continually informed of all happenings even in the remotest corners of his Empire.

But the Afghans were not a people to suffer a despot. Every chieftain regarded himself as the traditional ruler of his clan and his territory, and revolts broke out. As the rebels failed to combine, everyone pursuing his separate interests, they were beaten, killed or imprisoned one after the other, and because they had connections with the Khans and amirs around the Shah and his court the persecutions increased. New conspiracies were hatched, new revolts started. They were again cruelly beaten down, and everywhere terror reigned. In spite of severe illness and continuous bodily pain, the Shah dominated the whole irascible mass, holding them in iron bonds. Shortly before his death, after a reign of eight years, he wanted to kill Mubariz Khan, his wife's brother; but she pleaded for his life in spite of her husband's warning that she was endangering the life of their own son. Three days after Islam Shah's death, when the amirs elected this twelve-year-old son of the Shah as his successor, Mubariz Khan penetrated into the harem and murdered his nephew in the arms of his mother. Then he ascended the throne as Adil Shah.

It was not long before three of his relatives declared themselves independent Shahs in the provinces which they governed and moved against each other. The first to move was Sikandar Shah from the Punjab and he marched against Ibrahim Shah who held Agra and Delhi.

This was the time when Humayun appeared again in India and invaded the Punjab. He found it empty of troops except for insignificant garrisons, and their commanders preferred to abandon even the strongest forts at the approach of the Moguls, and to retreat rather than stand a siege. Unopposed, Humayun crossed the Indus, the Jhelum and the Chenab and marched to Lahore. Even Lahore was abandoned without resistance, and as Humayun had sent an advance party to protect the town from being plundered he was received by the townspeople with joy. The rule of the Afghan lords must have become thoroughly oppressive, for all along the way Humayun was waited upon and congratulated by local sheikhs and other dignitaries. From Lahore Humayun let his troops proceed to wherever he was informed there was an Afghan army.

At the news of the Mogul successes, Sikandar Shah, having defeated Ibrahim Shah near Agra, sent several detachments against them, but at every encounter the Afghans were beaten. According to Mogul historians the Afghan armies were every time much more numerous than the Moguls, but it seems that the composition of the troops was quite different. The Afghans had their women and children with them, for the reports state that after the victory Humayun ordered that they should not be captured but escorted to the Afghan camp.

Yet even now the Afghan rivals, in their separatistic tendencies, continued with their private wars. The defeated Ibrahim Shah collected a new army to take revenge on Sikandar Shah, but on the way to Agra he encountered another army sent out by Adil Shah, also against Agra, which saw in him another rival and beat him. However, Adil Shah's army could not proceed to Agra, as the fourth pretender, the Shah of Bengal, was now marching against Adil. Thus Sikandar Shah, freed for the moment from all three competitors, was able to move with his main force against Humayun.

Humayun's troops also had little resemblance to the army that had conquered Hindustan for his father Babur. Before setting out for the Punjab he not only collected all the forces he could muster in his own realm but sent messengers to the tribes and adventurers in neighbouring countries, even as far as Samarkand and Bokhara, while his principal generals were a Persian Turkoman, an Afghan, a Turk from Central Asia, and an Uzbeg. The generals always held conflicting views on how the campaign should best be pursued: if one was for rapid advance, the other recommended caution. When the rainy season started, many wanted to delay the offensive until the autumn, but Bairam Khan, who was in command of the forward troops, continued the advance; on hearing of Sikandar's approach with his main army, he entrenched himself at Sirhind and asked Humayun for reinforcements. Humayun, still in Lahore and feeling ill, sent all the troops he had with the twelve-year-old Akbar to Bairam Khan's assistance and himself followed a few days later.

For nearly four weeks the armies remained in their camps, fighting daily skirmishes, until the Moguls managed to intercept a large train of supplies coming for the Afghans and to defeat the accompanying detachment. Now the Afghans attacked, but being unable to force Bairam's defences they were charged by the enemy in the flank and rear in an enveloping movement; they were reduced to confusion and finally fled, in spite of their vast numerical superiority, leaving behind the baggage and the artillery. It was a decisive victory as it opened the road to Delhi, and as soon as the hot winds and torrential rains abated, Humayun proceeded to the capital, where after fifteen years the Khutba was again read in his name, and he himself entered the city on July 23, 1555.

Although he could claim to have reconquered his throne, not even the near-by provinces were safe in his hand. The fiefs which he apportioned to his men were still to be secured; the forts, in which the Afghan detachments were, had still to be taken, and the officers whom he sent out were more concerned with acquiring booty and maintaining themselves in princely splendour than with establishing any kind of government. And so it is said that Humayun, with some advisers, was busily occupied in Delhi with working out a plan for establishing a governmental system.

It was Sher Shah who had created a state out of a congery of lands in permanent army occupation, as it had been under Babur and Humayun. He had introduced a system which safeguarded the collection of revenue without excessively oppressing the cultivator. He had organized a provincial administration by which he could supervise the viceroys and fiefholders and prevent them from acquiring too much independence and power. His son, on the whole maintaining his father's administrative organization, had by his oppression aroused hatred against the central government, and in the chaos ensuing after his death the different rivals and their chieftains robbed and plundered the peasants. The cultivation of land nearly ceased and a terrible famine broke out, accompanied by pestilence. A new administrative system had to be introduced, and it is said that Humayun, on the whole maintaining Sher Shah's village and district administration, planned to divide the domain into provinces, each with its own capital. Each province should have a military governor with just sufficient forces to keep order in his region, and a kind of administrative board which would check any arbitrary actions on his part and report to the central government. Humayun himself, with a standing army of about 12,000 men under his immediate command, would visit the provinces in turn and inspect and supervise activities there. As usual with him, he started with devising embroidered gold and silver emblems and chains denoting the rank of these men of distinction.

However, long before Humayun could start to realize this scheme in practice an accident occurred. He had been sitting on the terrace roof of his library, giving audience to some officers, and just as he started to walk down the steps, he heard the call to evening prayers. He stopped to kneel down, but his staff slipped, his foot was caught in the skirt of his robe and he fell down the sharp and slippery stairs, receiving a violent contusion on the right temple. When he was picked up and carried into the palace, he was unconscious and blood oozed out of his ear. He seemed to recover, could speak, but later relapsed into a coma, and after four days, on January 26, 1556, he died in his forty-eighth year, after twenty-five years of kingship, more than half of which had been spent either in distress or in desperate fight for some shadow of sovereignty.

Official presentations written by the courtiers of the Mogul dynasty ascribe all his sufferings to the wickedness of his brothers and his own eagerness not to betray the dying Babur's bequest. Less inhibited historians give him a sterner appraisal. One of them sums up thus: 'He stumbled out of life as he had stumbled through it'. An Indian historian, while most affectionately considering his foibles and the vicissitudes of his career, characterises him as 'the most quixotic figure that has ever occupied the Mogul throne in Hindustan'.

By all standards he was of a complicated nature, affectionate and ostentatious, forebearing and cruel, and there are dozens of stories showing the conflicting traits in his character. He maintained the established custom of visiting the royal ladies with aunts and sisters for a kind of family entertainment, where naturally a strict rank order prevailed—in the timing of the visit, in the seating and so on. When one of the ladies complained that she and some others had lately been neglected, he informed them that he was an opium-eater and that there was therefore often a delay in his comings and goings, and they must put it to him in writing that, whether he came or not, they would be content and thankful to him. Another story goes that when he entered Kabul for the first time after Kamran's flight, he asked one of the royal aunts for something to eat, and when all she could offer was a beef curry, he wept and was disgusted with Kamran that he had omitted to send a goat for her kitchen. On the other hand, when in the revelries after the fall of Champanir in Gujarat, a drunken band of secretaries, librarians, clerks and so on in Humayun's army suddenly mounted their horses and set out for the conquest of the Deccan in Southern India, they were pursued, brought back, and Humayun sentenced them—for something which was only a drunken frolic—to be mutilated, have their hands, noses or ears cut off, or even had them beheaded. And when the Imam at a religious service in the mosque read a chapter of the Koran in which Humayun saw an allusion to these sentences, he ordered the Imam to be trodden to death by an elephant.

After his return to Hindustan and the re-occupation of Delhi he put one of his favourites in command of the Punjab, who began to squander the treasure and the revenue, offending and dismissing the governors and officers whom Humayun himself had appointed. To replace him, Humayun, shortly before his accident, sent his son Akbar to the Punjab with Bairam Khan as his mentor and a strong force to take over the government there, and also to keep Sikandar Shah in check, who after his defeat had fled into the hills, collected his adherents and was now raiding the low country. Immediately after Humayun's fall a firman was sent to Akbar informing him of the accident, adding that his father was recovering; then a second messenger followed with information of the relapse, and a third brought the news of the Emperor's death.

Humayun's death was kept secret until all preparations for the suppression of any possible local disturbances were completed, then the Khutba was read in Akbar's name, and on February 14, 1556, the thirteen-year-old Akbar was crowned in the small provincial town of Kalanaur, where he was encamped.

PART THREE

AKBAR

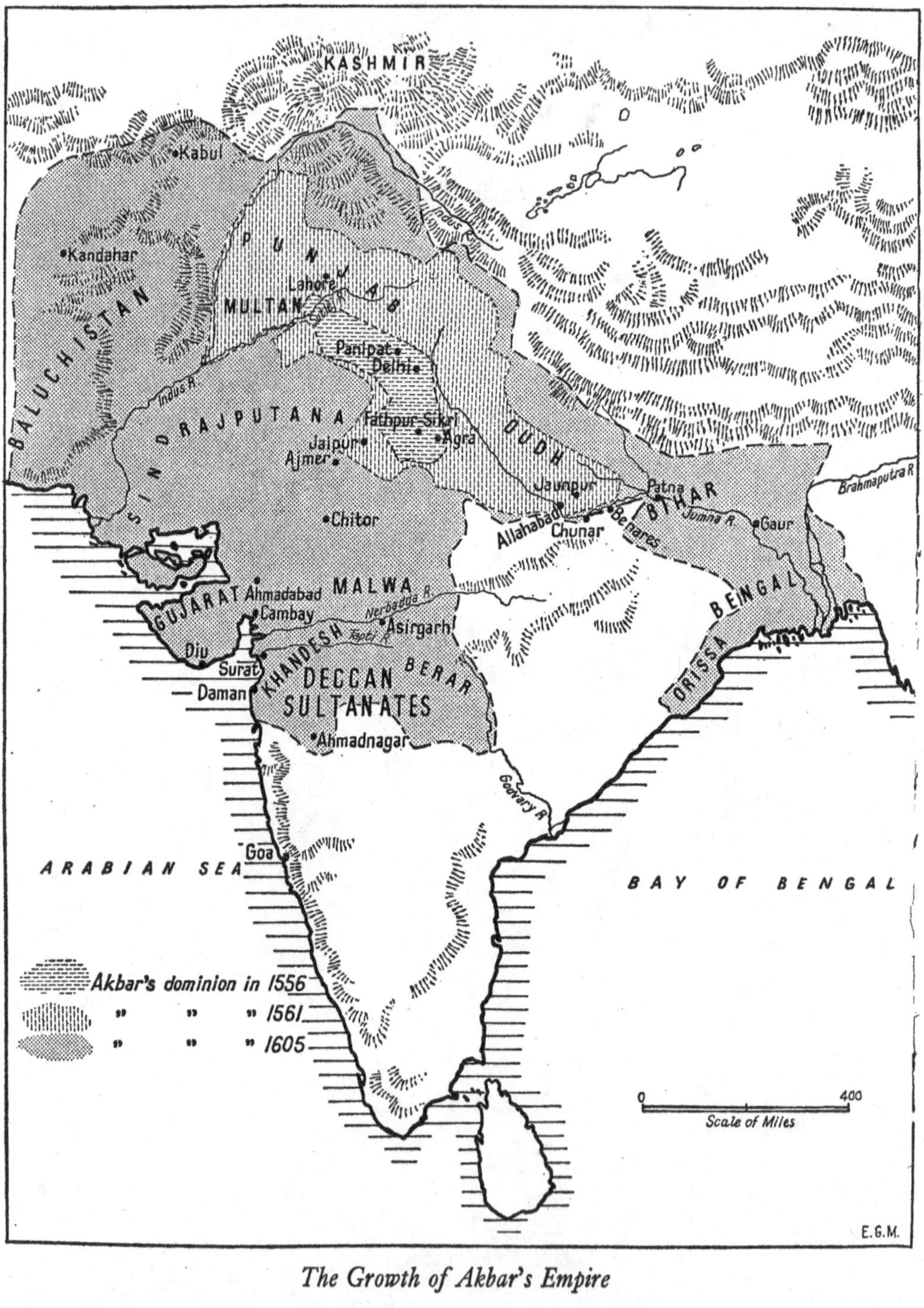

The Growth of Akbar's Empire

1
UNDER TUTELAGE

WHEN the thirteen-year-old Akbar was enthroned on a makeshift throne, a brick structure three feet high built on a platform in the garden of Kalanaur, his Empire was even less real than his throne. What he actually possessed were the few districts of the Punjab which were held by Bairam Khan's army. In the mountains of the East Punjab he was still being challenged by Sikandar Shah and his Afghans. In the south he depended on the goodwill of the chieftains who wielded power there. Tardi Beg, the governor of Delhi, had had the Khutba read in Akbar's name and sent the royal insignia to him, together with Akbar's cousin, who as Kamran's son might have been a rival claimant to the throne. That was sufficient proof that he intended to remain loyal and defend this southern part of the domain, devastated as it was by famine and the wars of the Afghan rivals. The chiefs from the various districts between Delhi and the Punjab also came to wait upon the boy king and were duly confirmed in their ranks and possessions, and that was all. Even Kabul was being administered, as arranged by Humayun, in the name of Akbar's younger brother, Mohammed Hakim, under the tutelage of a governor.

However, at the time of his enthronement Akbar was not yet very interested in state affairs. He occupied his time with all kinds of sport and was very fond of animals. As a child he had been taught the art of pigeon-flying by one of his teachers and he enjoyed it; in India he had learned to hunt with cheetahs—hunting leopards. These were his pleasures. All the efforts of his tutors to teach him reading and writing had been in vain, nor had the admonitions of his father Humayun had any effect. But he liked having books read to him; he learned by heart the verses of poets which he heard recited, and he revealed an outstanding memory, keeping complicated facts and details in his mind without the aid of the written word. Thus the affairs of government and army, for the time being, were in the care of Bairam Khan, who became Khan-Khanan, the chief minister, and all orders were issued by him in the name of Akbar.

The immediately most dangerous enemy seemed to be Sikandar Shah, who was making inroads into the lowlands of the Punjab; Bairam Khan was preparing a campaign against him when the news arrived that the chief commander of the other Afghan rival, Adil Shah, a Hindu named Hemu, had occupied Agra and, after beating the Mogul forces there, had taken possession of Delhi too. A war council was held and most of the officers recommended a total retreat to Kabul, there to await a new opportunity for the invasion of Hindustan; but Bairam Khan opposed any retreat and Akbar naturally agreed with him. Thus the whole army advanced in the direction of Delhi, meeting on the way the forces retreating from the city, who also advised returning to Kabul. Their main spokesman was Tardi Beg, a brave and experienced commander, who did not see any possibility of resisting Hemu's five-times superior forces with their artillery and five hundred war elephants.

Tardi Beg was Bairam Khan's rival in every respect. Already during Humayun's invasion of Hindustan they clashed in every war council. Now, as the commander of the defeated troops after the loss of Delhi, of which he had been governor, he was at the mercy of Bairam Khan; Bairam Khan, invited him into his tent and had him murdered while Akbar happened to be out on a hawking party. When Akbar returned, Bairam Khan informed him that he had had to punish Tardi Beg because of his flight, and could not delay the act as that would have infected the morale of the army.

Bairam Khan was now the undisputed commander-in-chief, and he ordered the army to continue the march towards Delhi. He sent out a strong advance troop and at the field of Panipat this group met the enemy's artillery, which Hemu had sent in advance, under light cover. Bairam's riders attacked immediately and seized the guns. In spite of this loss, when the two main armies met at Panipat, Hemu still possessed an immense superiority; attacking the Moguls he threw both their flanks into confusion and then pushed against the centre with his war elephants. But at this moment an arrow struck him in the eye and penetrated his brain. He slumped unconscious on his elephant. At the loss of the commander his soldiers scattered, and when Hemu with his elephant was brought before Akbar, Bairam Khan asked the boy to slay him and, as the slayer of the infidel, become a Ghazi. Some reports say that Akbar severed the head with a sabre stroke; others maintain that he refused to strike a helpless and unconscious prisoner and that Bairam Khan himself killed Hemu. In any case, this second battle of Panipat, fought on November 5, 1556, gave Akbar Delhi, as the first had done for Babur.

The fleeing enemy was relentlessly pursued, the entry of the new Emperor into Delhi was made in state, and a tower was erected of the heads of the slaughtered enemies. After a month in Delhi, Akbar and Bairam Khan went back to the Punjab, riding now against Sikandar Shah, who had defeated the small force they had left there; but as at the news of their approach Sikandar Shah quickly withdrew into a prepared fortress in the hills, this march proceeded in a leisurely fashion, with hunting expeditions and with much feasting and pleasure. While the siege of Sikandar's fortress began, the royal ladies from Kabul arrived with their escort. That was a great event and an occasion for more festivities. Then the news came that the Afghan rivals, who had not ceased fighting one another, had met in a battle and that Adil Shah had been killed by the Shah of Bengal. Thereupon Sikandar Shah surrendered on condition that he would be pardoned, and he received a fief in Bihar, where he died two years later.

Now the domain of the sixteen-year-old Akbar extended from the province of Agra to the province of Lahore and he went with Bairam Khan to Lahore to receive the allegiance of various chiefs. On the way he married his cousin, a daughter of Hindal, and at about the same time Bairam Khan celebrated his marriage with Salima Begam, a daughter of Humayun's sister, and also a cousin of Akbar. Thus the all-powerful Khan-Khanan became a relative of the Emperor. Nevertheless, since the arrival of the court in the Punjab, Bairam Khan's position was not quite as unchallenged as before. Tension had been building up between him and what was called the Harem party, based partly on a natural antipathy, because Bairam Khan, who came from Persia, was a Shiite and seemed to give preference to his co-religionists, while the whole of the Harem party were Sunnites. Moreover, the court was full of men who aspired to the highest posts in the government and in the army, and the driving force behind them was their wives or mothers, who had been wet-nurses of Akbar.

The relation between a child and the woman who had suckled him was regarded as so close that she was honoured with the title 'Anaga', foster-mother, and this relationship extended to her family. Her husband was 'Atga' (foster-father) and her sons 'Kuka' (foster-brothers). And this foster-father-cohort ('Atga Khail') saw no chances of advancement so long as a man of such intolerant and domineering character as Bairam Khan was at the top. He appointed and dismissed commanders, governors and officials with complete indifference to the fact that he created adversaries for himself who rallied round the Harem party.

At first they proceeded carefully, just representing any changes made by Bairam Khan as arbitrary; then they started to accuse him of assuming rights which were Akbar's. Akbar himself did not seem to care too much. He found a new amusement in riding elephants and in arranging elephant-fights. After six months in Lahore, the court went to Delhi, and after another six months in Delhi they made a river-trip to Agra, occupying themselves with fishing and water-fowling. And during the whole time more forts, towns and districts were taken by the troops sent out by Bairam Khan, and Akbar had to distribute dresses of honour, new titles, new fiefs. However, Bairam Khan, feeling himself the founder of this new Empire, became heedless and forgot that it was only natural for Akbar, as he was growing up, to get annoyed with too strict a tutelage, all the more so as Bairam Khan held a tight purse and Akbar's household complained that they were paid worse than the servants of the Khan-Khanan.

In the spring of 1560, when Akbar was in his eighteenth year, the Harem party decided to go into action. The occasion was a hunting trip on which Akbar went while Bairam remained in Agra. So they were separated, and under the pretext that his mother was ill and wanted to see him, Akbar was induced to go to Delhi. There, after receiving him with all royal honours, the Harem party prevailed upon him to send to Bairam a message saying that he, Akbar, was now determined to take the government into his own hands; at the same time the message promised Bairam a suitable fief and recommended him to make a pilgrimage to Mecca, as he had intended to do for a long time.

Bairam Khan submitted, against the wishes of his partisans, who advised him to seize Akbar by force. He returned the insignia of his office and went to collect his private hoards. It was only then, when troops were sent after him, under a man whom he himself had raised to the post of commander, with the order to get him out of the country, that he rebelled. A battle was fought, he was defeated and ultimately captured and brought before Akbar, who as usual was on a hunting expedition. Akbar received the penitent dignitary with all signs of favour and provided him with a magnificent equipage, so that he should make the pilgrimage in a state suited to his rank. However, on the way, while still in Hindustan, he was murdered by an Afghan, his camp was plundered, and it was only with difficulty that his retainers managed to save his family. When Akbar heard of the disaster he had Bairam's four year-old son Abdurrahim brought to court, while he himself married Bairam's young widow, Salima Begam, who soon ranked as one of the most important ladies of the harem.

Bairam Khan's dismissal made little difference to Akbar's activities. He occupied himself as before with hunting, field sports and other dissipations. The business of government passed into the hands of the Harem party, which was headed by Maham Anaga, the head-nurse, a scheming and ambitious woman who actually wielded power and put her friends into all important positions. Her main care was the advancement of her son, Adham Khan, and an army under his command was sent for the re-conquest of the kingdom of Malwa, still ruled by an Afghan chief. When the chief was defeated such cruelties were committed under Adham Khan's command that they appalled even the Moguls. The captives were slaughtered troop after troop, and even sayyids and sheikhs, who came out of the conquered fortress with Korans in their hands, were killed. Moreover, this foster-brother of Akbar sent only a few elephants to the court, keeping the rich spoils and the women of the Afghan ruler's harem, famous for their dancing and singing, for himself.

That was an imposition and insolence, and the eighteen-year-old Akbar showed for the first time that he was not to be trifled with. He set out post-haste, with a small escort, and although delayed on the way by accepting the submission of some strongholds, he surprised Adham Khan in his camp by his completely unexpected arrival. The foster-brother assumed an attitude of humble servitude, but his fawnings did not reconcile Akbar. Next day, Maham Anaga herself arrived in all haste, arranged a great entertainment; all the treasures and all the women were presented to the Emperor, so that he might choose whom and what he wanted, and he was appeased.

However, Adham Khan had still not learned the lesson. As the royal cortege was leaving, he stole two special beauties from the Afghan's harem. When they were later reported missing, Akbar stopped the march. The girls were found, but on Maham's order they were put to death before they could disclose the truth to Akbar; also by having them killed she could maintain that they had eloped of their own accord and had been punished. Akbar said nothing, but from this moment on his belief in her devotion and truthfulness vanished.

On the way back he amused himself as usual with hunting, showing exceptional courage and strength. He encountered a tigress with her cubs and immediately, on foot, attacked and killed her with one stroke of his sword. In Agra he mounted a particularly savage elephant and made it fight another one just as vicious. Akbar's elephant proved stronger, put the other to flight, pursued it and, to the dismay of the courtiers, the two maddened beasts raced down the steep bank of the Jumna and over the swaying pontoon bridge across the river, with the Emperor still sitting on his elephant. On the other side of the river Akbar, unperturbed, quietened and stopped his beast.

He also showed particular interest and skill in all mechanical crafts. Within the palace enclosure, and even in camps, workshops were maintained and often visited by him. It was said that 'there is nothing that he does not know how to do', and that he 'takes particular pleasure in making guns and in founding and modelling cannon'. He always used his inventive spirit: a keen polo player, he was annoyed that the game had to stop as soon as it became dark. Then he heard of a wood that would not burn but only smoulder when ignited, and ordered polo balls to be made of it so that play could continue after dark with a luminous ball, adding a new thrill to the sport.

But now, while pursuing his pleasures and sports, Akbar began to take a personal share in state affairs. And here he proved himself just as dashing and surprising as in his sports. In the middle of summer and in terrific heat he rushed with an army to the east and brought two rebellious governors to obedience. A few months later, just as he became nineteen, he discovered that the Harem party was not as united as it seemed, but was riddled with jealousies and rivalries; and to the dismay of Maham Anaga and her clique, he suddenly appointed his foster-father Shams-ud Din to the post of Khan-Khanan. Shams-ud Din was the husband of Ji-Ji Anaga, his principal wet-nurse, who was disliked by Maham, and Shams-ud Din promptly took the governorship of Malwa away from Adham Khan and recalled him to court—under the pretext that his loving mother should have him near her.

Shortly afterwards Akbar, having heard Indian minstrels sing the praises of a saint buried in Ajmer, made a pilgrimage to his shrine, and on his way he received the Raja of Jaipur, Bihar Mal, and married his daughter, a Hindu Princess, without making her accept the Moslem faith. He went even further and took her brother, Bhagwan Das, and her nephew, Man Singh, into his service and appointed them to high office.

That was an extraordinary act at that time. Akbar and the motley crew who had come with Humayun from Kabul were foreign intruders who, by force of arms, had taken the possessions of the earlier intruders, the Afghans. While the Afghans still maintained a closely knit unity within each of their clans, Akbar's troops were composed of Jagatais, Uzbegs, tribes from Persia and from the Afghan hills. Each group had come to make its own fortune at the cost of the infidels who inhabited the vast country, and now the man in whose name they had fought and conquered and from whom they expected their tenures and possessions had by marriage related himself to an infidel local prince, placing the infidel relatives among the high dignitaries at court.

This was the result of the teachings of the man whom Bairam Khan had chosen as tutor to Akbar, naturally a refugee from Persia, who had there been accused of being a Sunnite and was here believed to be a Shiite and who taught Akbar the principle of 'sulh-i-kull'—peace for all, the principle of universal toleration. And as if Akbar wanted to stress this point of toleration still further, he issued a decree forbidding the enslavement of the women, children and relatives of a beaten enemy. They should not be taken prisoner, but should be allowed to return freely to their homes and relations. As Akbar's chronicler, Abul Fazl, later wrote, he argued: 'If the husbands have taken the path of insolence, why shall it be the fault of the wives; and if the fathers have chosen the road of opposition, what fault have the children committed? Moreover, the wives and innocent children of such factions are not munitions of war!'

Of course, such a decree could not stop the customary practices of war, but the chronicler was able to write: 'The blissful result ensued that the wild and rebellious inhabitants of portions of Hindustan placed the ring of devotion in the ear of obedience'. For the first time the new sovereign showed that he did not want to be regarded as the lord of the savage invaders alone but as the ruler of all peoples. The Hindus were not to be treated as infidels against whom every crime was meritorious.

This attitude was in no way attributable to the new Khan-Khanan's doings, but neither had he used his influence to restrain the Emperor; besides, he stood in the way of certain ambitions of the Maham clique, and at this point the dissensions within the Harem party came to explosion point. Adham Khan, with a number of his adherents, rushed into the palace hall, where Shams-ud Din was sitting in conference with other high officials, and attacked him. When Shams-ud Din ran out into the courtyard, he was killed there; then Adham Khan tried to rush into the harem rooms on the upper floor where Akbar was asleep, but the eunuch guarding the entrance bolted the door. Nevertheless, none of the officials and servants present took any action against Adham Khan, who impudently demanded that the door should be opened. Meanwhile Akbar, awakened by the uproar and hearing what had happened, came out through another door and, meeting Adham, called out: 'You son of a fool, why have you killed our Atga?' Seizing Akbar's hands, which held a scimitar, Adham demanded an inquiry; when Akbar withdrew his hands, Adham grasped his own sword. With a blow of his fist, Akbar knocked Adham unconscious and then ordered him to be thrown headlong from the terrace. When the servants did this in such a way that Adham was still alive after the fall, they had to fetch him up and throw him down again, so that his skull was shattered.

Then Akbar went to Maham Anaga, who lay ill, and told her that her son had killed the Atga and that retaliation had been effected. Maham, who did not quite understand that her son had been killed, replied: 'You did well'. When she realized the truth, she died broken-hearted. But by his quick retaliation Akbar prevented tribal warfare from breaking out; the relatives of Shams-ud Din were gathering to take vengeance on the relatives of Maham Anaga, and were only quietened when they were shown the body of Adham Khan and saw the quick execution of the Emperor's justice. Nevertheless, Akbar thought it safer to use them for an expedition to the Puñjab, where the fiefs of the clan were situated. The bodies of Maham Anaga and her son he ordered to be buried with honours in a tomb which he commanded to be built; similar mourning and similar honours were also accorded to the body of Shams-ud Din. With the death of the culprit the affair was finished, so far as Akbar was concerned, and he allowed the courtiers who were implicated in inciting Adham Khan and who had fled in fear of retribution to come back. He reinstated them in their positions.

2

CONQUERING AND ORGANISING

EMERGING from the tutelage of the Harem party with the intention of deciding for himself how his country was to be governed, Akbar, at the age of twenty, already showed some of the characteristics which were typical of him throughout his life and may have contributed to his success. One of them was that he did not disdain to discuss any problem that occupied him with everyone in his entourage and he never tired of listening to the opinions of others. If he received advice which seemed to him reasonable, the position of the man who gave it was of no consequence, he was afforded the opportunity to prove himself. When he had found the treasury empty and no revenues coming in, because under the regency of Maham Anaga everything was embezzled, it was a eunuch among his servants, who had once been in the employ of Islam Shah, the son of Sher Shah, who now told him of the measures by which Sher Shah had checked embezzlement and regulated financial affairs. Akbar honoured the eunuch with the title of Khan and put him in charge of crown lands. The rules and regulations of Sher Shah were re-introduced, the officials put under strict control, their behaviour investigated, and after a thorough weeding out, the revenue improved to such an extent that next year Akbar could again show the Hindus that he was not unmindful of their feelings.

He heard that the Hindus who wanted to make pilgrimages to their holy places had to pay a special due, and he abolished this due although the amount was estimated at millions of rupees, because, as he said, it was contrary to the will of God to tax people who went to worship the Creator, even if their mode of worship was mistaken. A year later he issued a decree abolishing the poll-tax on non-Moslems, thus raising them to equal status with the Moslems. This measure seems to have met with strong resistance and could not be put through in practice. Therefore he waited; but later, when his power became absolute, he re-issued the order.

We have the testimony of foreign observers, such as the Jesuit Fathers, that also in his later years Akbar was always willing to consult others about his affairs and often took advice in private from persons near to him, but the decision invariably remained with him alone. They say that he 'never gave anybody the chance to understand his sentiments . . . and was in all his business—a man apparently free from mystery and guile, as honest and candid as could be imagined—but in reality so close and self-contained, with twists of words and deeds so divergent one from the other, and most times so contradictory that even by much seeking one could not find the clue to his thoughts . . . Even an attentive observer, after long and familiar intercourse with him, knew no more of him on the last day than he had known on the first.' His panegyrist and chronicler, Abul Fazl, while ascribing to him superhuman visionary abilities, continuously repeats that for the most part he kept his nature 'behind the veil'. But in reality, as a man who had never learned to read or to write, he had to use every opportunity to inform himself on all problems in order to get acquainted with the solutions which had been used by other sovereigns in the past or in other lands, and he had to keep his thoughts secret until he had decided how to act. Even when he acted, he often could not dare to disclose the reasons for his actions without grave danger.

When he first married an Indian princess and began to draw her relatives into his service, it was not only to show the Indian princes that it was to their advantage to join him but, perhaps more important still, to free himself from the complete dependence upon the turbulent and selfish chieftains. The historians note with astonishment the great numbers of Hindu names in the lists of his chief officers who accompanied him in his campaigns, and he relied on many of them as observers and organizers, because it was in their interest to work for him, while the men from the north, to whatever position he might appoint them, thought mainly of extending their own power and gaining advantages for a clan. When he abolished the poll-tax on the Hindus, it was not only to awaken in the native population the feeling that it was of great importance for them not to have his sovereignty replaced by that of another Moslem ruler, but also to take from the fiefholders a

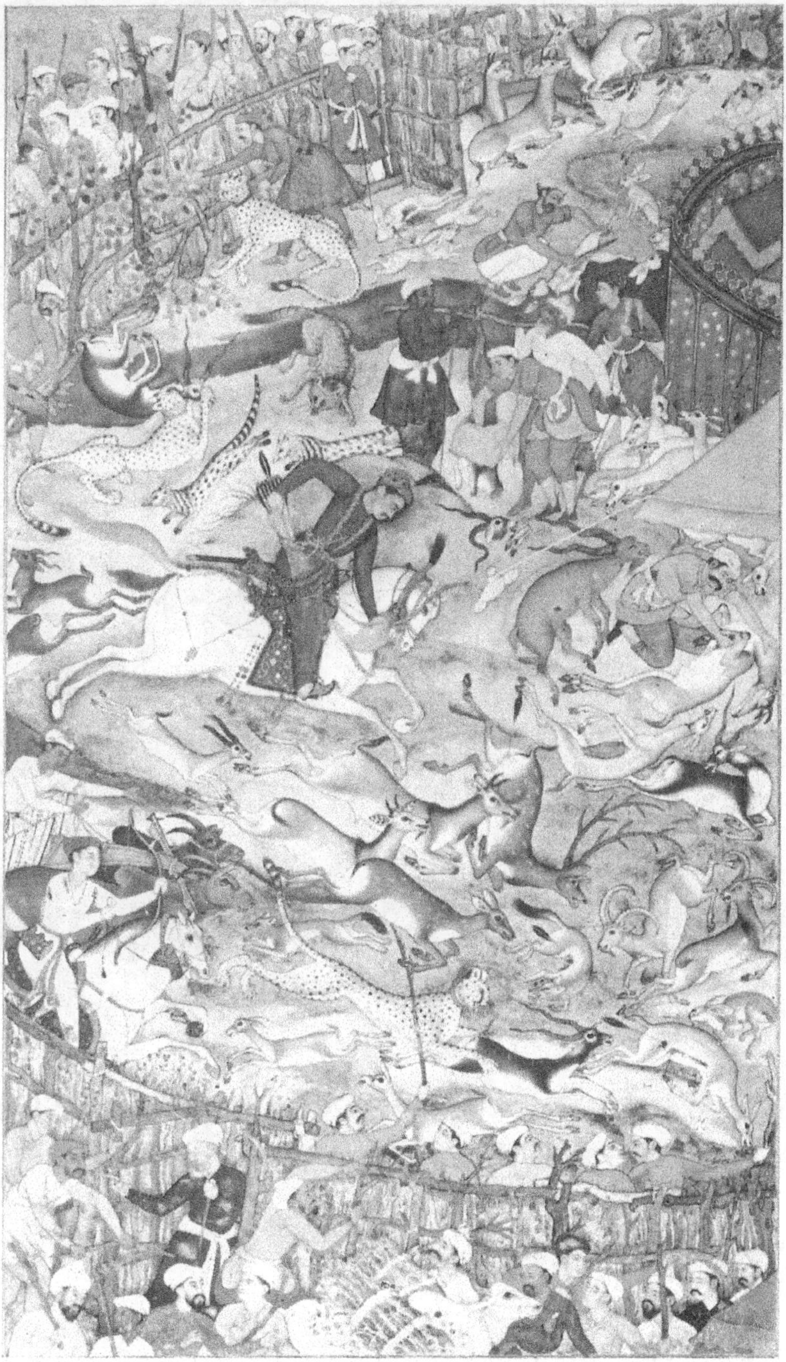

9. Akbar hunting after the Mongolian fashion, but with cheetahs.

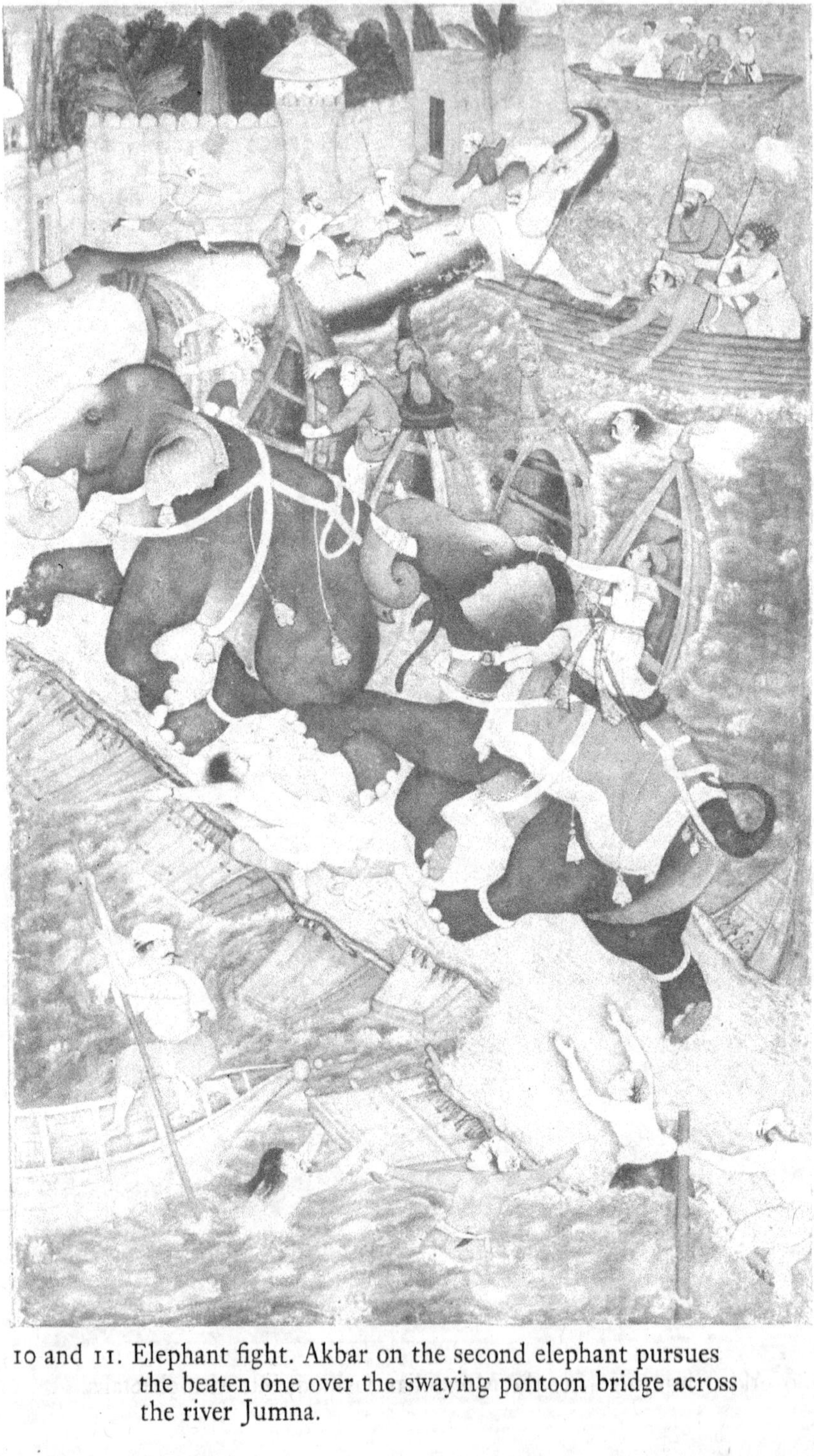

10 and 11. Elephant fight. Akbar on the second elephant pursues the beaten one over the swaying pontoon bridge across the river Jumna.

The courtiers look on in dismay at Akbar's adventure.

12. Akbar orders his foster-brother Adham to be thrown from the terrace to his death.

means of extortion and enrichment which increased their self-importance and gave them the feeling of being actual rulers.

It was his intention that whomsoever he chose for any position he was not to rule on his own, but only had to execute orders. In later years he confessed his feelings to Abul Fazl: 'It was by the grace of God that I found no capable minister, otherwise the people would have considered that my measures had been devised by him'. It was his pride that all decisions were his. His rule had to be absolute—that was the only way in which he could hold together the diverse tribes which constituted his army. When he appointed Jagatai commanders, the Uzbegs became jealous; when he appointed Persians they both felt hurt, because most of the Persians were Shiites; and the appointment of a Hindu commander often led to a distinct weakening of the army's efficiency, so that, at least in the earlier stages of his long reign, he had to appoint beside the Hindu a generally acknowledged Moslem governor. Again, almost every khan or beg whom he sent out to conquer some district thought of retaining the booty for himself or, if appointed governor, tried to assume a role of semi-independence.

Thus, the years showed Akbar himself continually on the move westwards or eastwards into far-off provinces to fight rebellious chiefs and to beat down mutinous governors. Even though he was always victorious, he knew that he was not able to enforce continuous obedience, and therefore showed himself, after each victory, satisfied with a professed submission. The only precaution he took was to see that there was no near relative of his whom the dissatisfied commanders or governors could declare Emperor in his place. This policy cost the life of Kamran's son, whom Humayun, after blinding the father, had taken into his court.

On the other hand, in order to occupy the chieftains and their troops not immediately needed for a great war, Akbar sent them out to conquer more and more of the small Rajput principalities which had not submitted to his overlordship. There was no question that any of these could constitute a danger to him, but they possessed riches accumulated in generations; there was booty to be taken, and there were lands which could be given as fiefs to his ever-greedy followers. Moreover, Akbar's saying was always: 'A sovereign should be ever intent on conquests, otherwise his neighbours will rise in arms against him. The army should be exercised in warfare, lest for want of training they become self-indulgent.' Thus the Rajas, who had the misfortune that their principalities adjoined his frontiers, fought heroic battles against overwhelming forces, sacrificing their lives and burning their women and children when their strongholds fell. In one case it was a Rani, a woman, who led her troops into the battle on an elephant and, twice wounded by arrows, stabbed herself to death when defeated. In another case, at the conquest of Chitor after long and desperate resistance, three-quarters of the population of 40,000 were slaughtered.

Such deeds remained in the memory of the people. The name of Rani Durgavati was long revered, the 'sin of the slaughter of Chitor', which for a long time remained a desolate ruin, became proverbial, and in later years Akbar himself honoured the two main defenders of the fortress by erecting their statues, mounted on stone elephants, at the entrance to the fortress-palace of Delhi.

Yet whatever campaign Akbar undertook, in whatever part of his dominions he was, he always found an occasion for one more extraordinary personal feat. If it was not an elephant hunt in the forest, it was a hunt of wild asses in the desert; if he did not kill tigers, he ordered a hunt in the old Mongolian fashion in which for weeks tens of thousands of beaters drove all game into a circle of a few miles, where he then hunted for days with sword, lance, musket, arrows or even lasso. If he did not cross the Ganges in full flood on an elephant, he performed a long distance march of about thirty-six miles on foot in one day, an undertaking in which, of the multitude who had been with him at the start, only three of his companions were able to finish. He rode distances in a single day which others took two or three days to cover. He seemed to be impervious to heat, rain or storm, beginning his campaigns regardless of the weather at any time of the year.

Yet one thing troubled the young athletic sovereign: he had no children. When he had gone on his pilgrimage to the shrine of the saint in Ajmer, he had ordered Maham Anaga to bring the whole harem there. It was while on the return journey to Agra that he had married the first Indian princess, but although neither she nor the other wives immediately produced children, Akbar repeated his pilgrimage to Ajmer every year. Nearly two years later he saw in Delhi an extremely beautiful woman who was the wife of a sheikh. He sent a messenger to the sheikh, reminding him of an order of Jenghiz Khan, that if the sovereign desired a wife of one of his subjects, the husband had to divorce her and surrender her to his lord. The sheikh obeyed and retired to the Deccan, in the still independent part of India. Shortly afterwards, some of Akbar's servants advised him that among the leading families in Delhi there were more such beautiful ladies, and eunuchs were secretly inspecting the harems of leading men in search of them. It was on his return to Delhi from the shrine of another saint that, from the platform of Maham Anaga's mausoleum, a man shot an arrow at Akbar which pierced his shoulder. The assailant was a slave, but when the retinue wanted to take him for questioning about the instigators, Akbar ordered him to be killed on the spot. The wound itself was not dangerous, and ten days later Akbar was able to travel to Agra in a litter. Nevertheless, the search for other people's beautiful wives was stopped. At the end of the year one of his wives gave birth to twin sons, but within one month both of them died.

Four years later Akbar visited a holy sheikh, Salim, who lived near Sikri, where Babur had fought his battle against Rana Sanga and his Rajputs. The sheikh predicted that Akbar would have three sons, and shortly afterwards the first Indian princess whom he had married became pregnant. To ward off evil spirits she and most of the harem were sent to the monastery built by Sheikh Salim, and there on August 30, 1569 a son was born whom Akbar, in recognition of the prayers of the holy man, called Salim. Three months later a daughter was born, also in Sikri. The next year, in June, another of Akbar's wives gave birth to a second son, Murad. As all the children lived and grew, 'free from the evil spirits of Agra', Akbar began to build on the spot a city of gardens and palaces, naming it Fathpur-Sikri—the victory city of Sikri—and made it the residence of the court. Two years later a third son, Daniel, was born to him by a concubine in Ajmer, in the house of the saint called Daniel, and shortly afterwards he had two further daughters.

By this time the thirty-year-old Akbar could regard his dominion as established and start to think of conquests. He had succeeded in crushing at last the insurrections which had flared up again and again, caused either by some Mirzas, descendants of Sultan Husain Baikara of Khorasan, or by his Uzbeg chieftains. To rid himself of the scattered Uzbeg remnants he paid a gold-piece to 'whoever brought a Mogul rebel's head'. He had prevented internal strife, breaking up the 'foster-father clan' in the Punjab by assigning to each of the chieftains some governorship far removed from the others. By marrying more Rajput princesses and placing their relatives in high positions he had gained recognition as overlord of more and more Rajput principalities, and had subdued others which tried to resist him. And so he now set out for the conquest of Gujarat, which his father Humayun had taken from Bahadur Shah and lost again.

This time Gujarat had no sovereign of Bahadur's calibre. The country was prey to various chieftains who were fighting one another, while its richest part, the south, was in possession of the rebellious Mirzas who after their defeat had fled from Akbar's domain to Gujarat. The campaign was an easy one. The puppet king, who had been driven out from his own capital, was found hiding in a cornfield, made his submission and received a small allowance. The chieftain holding Ahmadabad surrendered the capital and was given the governorship of the still unconquered province where the Mirzas had established themselves. Then Akbar went to Cambay to see the sea and is reported to have made a short sailing trip. He also used the occasion to give audience to Portuguese, Turkish and Persian merchants, and did not fail to make ample enquiries from them. Afterwards he marched against the Mirzas, beat them on the battlefield and laid siege to their main stronghold, the port of Surat, the usual point of departure for Mecca pilgrims. The defenders asked for help from the Portuguese; a Portuguese warship arrived from Goa, but seeing the difference in the strength of the two parties, the Portuguese preferred to visit Akbar as friendly envoys and to offer presents. Akbar, in accordance with his habits, had a long conversation with them, 'enquiring about the wonders of Portugal and the manners and customs of Europe', and finished by sending an envoy to the viceroy of Goa. He was interested in establishing friendly relations with the Portuguese, who dominated the sea, in order to secure a safe-conduct for the pilgrims to Mecca.

After seven weeks of siege Surat capitulated and Akbar became lord of Gujarat. The Mirzas managed to flee, two to the Deccan, and two others to the Punjab, but two of them were caught. One was beheaded, the other was brought before Akbar with his eyes sewn up. Akbar ordered the stitches to be cut before imprisoning him. The commandant of Surat, who had previously been in Humayun's service, was granted his life, but as 'he had used his tongue indiscreetly', it was cut out.

Crimes did not need to be serious to merit such punishments. Mutilation and death were stakes in the large hazard of the play of life; one had to show that one deserved to take part in the gamble. At one of the drinking parties in Akbar's camp the bravery and contempt of life shown by the Rajputs were praised and stories told that when two rivals claimed to surpass the other's courage, they made a third one hold a double-headed spear and then ran from opposite sides against the points, piercing themselves on the spear until its ends came out at their backs. Akbar remarked that these Rajputs were rivals and at feud with each other; he had no rival and was at feud with no one, but he would match their bravery. He proceeded to fasten the hilt of his sword against a pillar and was about to fling himself against the point of the sword. At the last moment, when he was really rushing against the sword, Man Singh, the Rajput chief in his service, struck the sword down and it fell, cutting Akbar's hand between the thumb and the forefinger. Flying into a rage, Akbar threw himself on his saviour and would have strangled him, had not others of his companions wrenched the Emperor from his victim, though they succeeded only by twisting his wounded thumb.

When he had cooled off, he in no way showed displeasure with the man who had prevented him from demonstrating his bravery or with the others who had wrenched his wounded finger. Such outbreaks of temper were very rare with Akbar. He usually kept himself well under control, and his natural vehemence mostly came to the fore only in the performance of his often extraordinary feats; sometimes he exacted similar exploits also from the others with him.

A short time after his return to the capital he received the report that the Mirza who had fled to the Deccan had reappeared with an army in Gujarat and, together with some rebellious local chieftains, had started a rising. It was the hottest time of the year, the second half of August, and Akbar's khans and begs having gone to their fiefs, he had no army with him except for a few hundred men of his special guard. With these he set off, and changing from horses to camels and from camels to horses, he rode over 450 miles in eleven days, on the way collecting troops which he had called from neighbouring fiefs, so that he arrived before the Mirza's camp some four miles from Ahmadabad, with 3,000 riders. When the Imperial kettle drums were beaten, the Mirza did not believe his ears. He had the reports of his spies that two weeks earlier Akbar had been in Fathpur-Sikri, and the attackers had neither artillery nor royal elephants. Nevertheless Akbar was there, led the charge against the superior forces of the Mirza, and in hard hand-to-hand fighting won the battle. The Mirza was wounded, and when his horse fell as he tried to flee he was captured.

An hour later a fresh troop was seen to advance; Akbar's men believed that these were the men of the governor of Ahmadabad arriving too late, but the new force of 5,000 horses was that of the Mirza's ally, who had been besieging Ahmadabad and was now coming either to help or to revenge the Mirza. A second battle started and again ended with Akbar's victory. Both the rebels were beheaded, and a pyramid was erected of the heads of slain enemies, the reports mentioning 1,000 to 1,200. Now Akbar allowed himself and his men ten days rest in Ahmadabad before starting the return journey. This journey he completed more comfortably, in three weeks, and in forty-three days altogether, after riding out from Fathpur-Sikri, he re-entered his capital in triumph.

As Akbar's dominions had now reached the western sea he decided to extend them in the same way to the eastern coast. The ruler of Bengal, an Afghan who, after the death of Sher Shah's relatives, had ascended the throne and placated Akbar by nominal recognition of his sovereignty, occasionally sending some presents as tribute, had died. After his death in 1572 and the usual unrest, his young son, Daud, who had been raised to the throne by Afghan nobles, ordered the Khutba to be read in his own name and even occupied a frontier stronghold belonging to Akbar's domains. Akbar ordered his governor in the east to punish the presumptious youth. After some fighting an agreement was reached, then broken; the king was besieged in Patna, but in the end the governor had to implore Akbar to come himself.

The reports from the east had been unsatisfactory for a long time and Akbar had enough time to make thorough preparations. This campaign did not need to be a bolt out of the blue, and he ordered a whole fleet of river ships to be built, 'so wonderfully fashioned as to be beyond the powers of description. There were delightful quarters on the decks, and there were gardens on the boats such as clever craftsmen could not make on land. The bows of every one of these waterhouses were wrought in the shape of animals, so as to astonish spectators. Large boats were arranged for every office which is required for administrative purposes, and all courtiers had boats suitable to their status'. As usual, Akbar did not take any account of the weather and the magnificent procession of boats, starting in June at the height of the rainy season, 'amidst the roar of thunder and the flashing of lightning', soon ran into difficulties. Already on the Jumna 'many of the river-houses were sunk by the waves'. When the Ganges was reached, 'there blew a hurricane, and eleven boats sank. The orchestra boat was damaged, but the musicians were saved by Divine help'. As the boats were approaching Chunar, 'the naval authorities became alarmed. A large number of persons left the boats and came on dry land.' But Akbar continued his river journey undismayed, landing every day for a hunt with cheetahs and otherwise letting himself be entertained by songs of minstrels or by having books read to him. From Benares the ladies and the children, whom he had taken on the journey, were sent on to Jaunpur, while the Emperor proceeded down the river and at last, after hazardous travel of seven weeks duration, landed near Patna.

The besieging army was in a poor state, the camp was flooded, the animals exhausted. But the reinforcements brought by Akbar changed the situation. At first he proposed to the ruler of Bengal that the war should be decided by single combat between the two kings, and when this proposal was declined, he ordered his troops to storm Hajipur on the opposite bank of the Ganges, from where the garrison of Patna received their supplies. It was a difficult undertaking as the flooded river was miles wide, but in three days the fort was captured, and a boat loaded with the heads of dead Afghan warriors was sent by Akbar to Shah Daud. Two days later Daud fled by night in a swift boat, making for Bengal. The garrison, who attempted to follow him by ship or land, suffered severe losses, and it is said that for a long time people would pick up purses filled with gold and articles of armour which they kept finding in the river and on the banks. Akbar tried to pursue the enemy, but failed to overtake them. Then he detached an army of 20,000 men for the conquest of Bengal and went to Jaunpur. There he remained for a month, appointing officers for the administration of territories which he declared crown-lands and receiving reports of successes from his Bengal army, and then returned to Fathpur-Sikri after a campaign which had lasted altogether seven months.

Now, as his domain was about to reach from the western to the eastern seaboard over the whole width of India, he decided to give it a unified and regular administration, and the organization with which he had already started after the conquest of Gujarat became the structure that held the Empire of the Great Moguls together for many generations.

The chronicler, Abul Fazl, characterized its main features as 'the branding regulation, the conversion of the imperial territories into crown-lands, and the fixing of the grades of the officers of state'. Up to that time the districts and provinces were granted to the chieftains as 'jagirs' (fiefs), and according to the revenue that the 'jagir' was expected to produce, the holder ('jagirdar') had to keep a certain number of cavalry and defray all expenses, maintaining the roads, forts and so on. It was not the land that belonged to him, but only the taxes which were exacted from the people. The 'jagirs' were not hereditary, and often enough the 'jagirdar' was transferred from one 'jagir' to another, deliberately in some completely different part of the empire in order to prevent the formation of a coalition, a practice which led to much abuse. The 'jagirdars' lent each other riders to make up their quota, or mounted some idle vagrants on the first baggage horse to hand, to present them as soldiers when a review of their troops was due. Already, Sher Shah, to prevent this fraud, had issued an order that the military horses must be branded so that the same horse could not be presented a second time by somebody else, and now Akbar again introduced the branding regulation.

Moreover, the 'jagir' system contributed to the development of two contradictory tendencies among the nobles. As the 'jagir' was only a temporary grant, the 'jagirdar' had little interest in it and was always on the look-out for a larger one. Larger 'jagirs' could only be expected when more provinces and districts were to be distributed, so he was eager for a strong government which could undertake new conquests. On the other hand the 'jagirdars', particularly in the outlying provinces, endeavoured

13. Akbar, mounted on an armoured elephant, receives a horse-tail-standard and kettledrums captured from Uzbegs.

14. Akbar with a hawk.

Raja Man Singh.

to cheat the government by retaining for themselves most of the war booty, until they had enough money to be able to hire more soldiers and perhaps become strong enough to make themselves factually independent, thus converting the always revocable grant into a hereditary possession. The desire of these nobles was for a weak government.

Akbar's idea to 'convert the territories into crown-lands' was a measure designed to counteract this constantly equivocal attitude to his central power and make the chieftains completely dependent. The crown-lands were to be ruled and the revenues collected by government officials, and the chieftains were to be paid in cash for the maintenance of their troops. That in turn demanded the third reform, 'the fixing of the grades of the officers of state', so that everybody was paid according to his rank.

As the whole organization of the Empire was of a military nature, all officials were graded from the commander of ten to the commander of ten thousand, and the rank of commander of over five thousand was reserved for members of the royal family. These grades did not mean real command but were only titles signifying the position of the official in the hierarchy and the salary he was to receive. So, for example, the chief of the kitchen department ranked as a commander of six hundred. On the other hand everyone was expected to be able to provide military service according to his official rank. Abul Fazl, Akbar's personal friend and chronicler, who occupied the position of secretary of state and rose to the rank of commander of four thousand, in his later years also distinguished himself in war. The historian Nizam-ud Din was recalled from a campaign because he caused too much devastation in the province he was conquering. The court-jester Raja Birbal led a detachment against hill tribes and was killed in a battle.

This military organization of the state, which was borrowed mainly from the Persians, demanded an elaborate administrative system. A large record office was organized. In each district the cultivated land was to be measured and the land tax determined according to the kind of crop, with the corresponding records being kept. A large Ministry of Finance was needed to formulate all the rules and regulations and to scrutinize the transactions and payments. The payment of tax was permitted either in money or in kind at market prices.

Naturally such reforms were extremely unpopular among the holders of power who, before these new regulations, had ruled as kings in their provinces, and the new ordinances were sabotaged as far as possible. The 'jagirdars' were helped by corrupt officials appointed to the districts 'to encourage cultivation and to increase the revenue'. As one of the chroniclers says: 'They did not carry out the regulations as they ought to have done. A great portion of the country was laid waste through their rapacity; the wives and children of the peasants were sold as slaves and scattered abroad, and everything was thrown into confusion.' In Gujarat, where this administration was introduced first, a terrible famine broke out. But Akbar persisted. Many of the corrupt officials were exposed and punished, and died 'from severe beatings administered and from tortures of the rack and pincers'.

Slowly and piecemeal the system was extended, except in the far-off regions like Bihar and Bengal, and even in Gujarat it had to be abolished because of disturbances, but where it was carried through, it enhanced the autocracy and the wealth of the central government to whom all the higher officials were directly responsible. In later times Akbar devised a system of giving the great 'jagirdars' high appointments at the court, thus forcing them to live in the capital and having their 'jagirs' administered by some employees. In order to go to their 'jagirs' they had to obtain special leave, which was granted only for a short time.

It was a carefully considered policy, intended to make the court the real centre of the widespread Empire where the Emperor had his chief nobles at hand and could immediately assign them to any task required, and it was only the will of the Emperor which determined what function the individual noble had to perform.

Akbar himself took his duties as sovereign very seriously. Abul Fazl gives a picture of his daily routine when he was in the capital. At sunrise he showed himself to the people assembled in the outer court of the palace, listened to their complaints and held an open court lasting for over four hours, where people could state their cases, which were decided on the spot. In the afternoon another assembly was held to which only persons of distinction were admitted and where state business was transacted, appointments, promotions and grants made. In the evening, and often during the night, he received his ministers and advisers for the discussion of confidential matters. Always scribes stood by, to take accurate notes of every word of his. In each case he announced his decision and the reason for it; if anyone had any doubts he was allowed to express them, and Akbar listened to the objections before he gave the definite order of what had to be done. Altogether he is said to have devoted about sixteen hours a day to state business.

3

THE REFORMER

On his return from his lightning campaign to Gujarat, Akbar was greeted by Sheikh Mubarak, one of his most trusted spiritual advisers, with a speech proposing that the Emperor might now soon become the spiritual as well as the temporal head of his people. This suggestion was probably the outcome of long private talks and reflected Akbar's intention to bring about a change in the relations between the political and the religious authorities; for, in spite of his position as an absolute monarch, his powers were severely curtailed by the rules and pronouncements of the Ulema, the Moslem divines, whose regulations controlled the whole way of life of the people and obstructed many of the reforms which he thought necessary.

The head of all the ecclesiastical offices was the Chief Sadr, who not only distributed grants for ecclesiastical and benevolent purposes, which he did completely arbitrarily without any reference to the treasury, but also combined the power of Chief Inquisitor with that of the highest judicial authority. He used this power, with the assistance of the Sheikh-ul-Islam, for the persecution of every deviating group, and Sheikh Mubarak himself, before he became Akbar's friend, had had to flee for his life because he was associated with a sect holding unorthodox views. The third duty of the Chief Sadr was to act as the religious adviser to the Emperor and to watch that all government actions were strictly in accordance with the Islamic law, of course as he interpreted it.

However, it was just the question of interpretation which gave Akbar the opportunity to act against this restraining control without immediately running dangerous risks. The law of the Koran had as many interpretations as there were Moslem sects. Each one maintained that it represented the only true following of the Prophet, and so there could be no objection if the Emperor asked the highest representatives of all sects to come together to discuss their interpretations. The wrong and heretical ones would be exposed while the true faith would triumph.

Thus, immediately after his return from the eastern campaign, Akbar ordered the building of a Hall of Worship in which the discussions on theological and philosophical problems of a religious nature were to take place, in all freedom and under his own presidency.

The men who were to take part in these debates or listen to them were Sheikhs—holy men in possession of special spiritual gifts, Sayyids—reputed descendants of the Prophet, Ulama—the jurists and doctors learned in the sacred law, while the nobles of the court interested in theological questions were also invited to attend. Each class of guests was assigned a separate space, and only Akbar himself moved freely from one to the other in order to be able to chat with anybody he selected. The debates started on Thursday after sunset—when the Mohammedan Friday began—and continued sometimes until noon on Friday. Akbar said that this kind of discourse had such charm for him that it distracted him from everything else; up to now he had restrained himself from listening too much to such debates, as he would otherwise have neglected necessary duties, but now he had time.

Sheikh Mubarak, who was probably the instigator of this experiment, very soon had the pleasure of seeing his expectations realized. He was a learned theologian who had often changed from one sect to another and finally come to share the views of a group which believed that the 'just order' on earth could not be expected from the teachings of some divine but could only be introduced by a godly sovereign who would come to the throne, and quite understandably this view pleased and intrigued Akbar. He was prepared to act as this godly sovereign as soon as the truth was established what this godly order should be.

However, the truth did not reveal itself. The controversy raged not only between the various sects and schools but even the orthodox Moslems proved to be divided among themselves. The one group was headed by the Sadr, the other by the Sheikh-ul-Islam. Instead of leading to mutual understanding the discussions sharpened the existing disagreements. Everyone was accusing everyone else of heresy, the debates degenerated into quarrels, abuse, threats, and Akbar sometimes had to intervene to prevent brawls and fist fights.

He was still a pious Moslem; he visited all the holy places he could, he allowed the royal ladies who had the desire to go to Mecca to make the pilgrimage under a safe escort, sending with them enormous gifts. As he himself could not go on the pilgrimage, he accompanied them a short distance in pilgrim's garb. He had talks with saintly hermits in their sanctuaries, and he may have hoped sincerely that the free discussions would clarify the points of discord and provide a basis for a generally accepted theological view which could provide a unifying religious force for his empire.

Moreover, besides the religious question there were purely practical ones to be solved of a highly political character. By marrying Hindu princesses and drawing their relatives to his court he had obtained important service, but the position of his wives needed clarification. The Sunnites did not recognize the legality of these marriages, maintaining that only four wives could be legally married. The Shiites recognized them as legal 'Mut'a' (temporary) marriages. The acceptance of the orthodox Sunni view would relegate these princesses to the position of concubines and this disgrace would be a deadly insult to all his Rajput commanders; it might raise the whole of Rajputana against him. On the other hand, the declaration on his part that he was following the Shiite law might lead to a rebellion of most of his army chieftains. The appointment of a Shiah commander to Bengal had already caused great difficulties. A proposal that the Chief Kazi—judge of Koran law—should decide on the question led to the dismissal of the Kazi who did not dare to offend the Sadr and the Ulama, whereupon a newly appointed Kazi promptly acknowledged the legality of these marriages. Even so, Akbar could not leave such and similar matters to be decided by the pronouncement of some zealot. He needed well-defined rules which would somehow reconcile the views of the heterogeneous elements in his empire. Somewhere it should be possible to find just and clearly stated solutions which would satisfy human reasoning, and privately, outside the scope of this assembly, he began to consult adherents of other religions: Hindus, Jains, Parsees.

At this time he himself had a strange spiritual experience which convinced him that a mysterious direct communion with God must exist. It was in the Punjab, when returning from the visit to one of the pilgrimage shrines that he had ordered preparations for a Mongolian type of hunt in which the game from a circumference of about forty miles were driven together into a small enclosure. While the arrangements were nearing completion, Akbar seems to have been seized by a visionary extasy. It was probably a particularly severe epileptic fit, as his chroniclers give examples of similar fits, although not of such intensity or enchantment. Abul Fazl describes it in these words: 'A sublime joy took possession of his bodily frame. The radiance of the cognition of God cast its ray.' Another chronicler says: 'Suddenly a strange state and a strong frenzy came upon the Emperor, and an extraordinary change was manifested in his manner, to such an extent as cannot be accounted for. And everyone attributed it to some cause or other.'

In the end, 'when he had for a long time received the Divine rays, and the stewards of the hidden chamber of the Divine decrees, brought down him who had obtained his desire in the spiritual kingdom for the sake of the government of the world', he countermanded the hunt, and the animals were left to disperse. Under the tree under which he had had his seizure he distributed much gold to fakirs and the poor and ordered that a 'lofty building and an extensive garden' should be made on the site. A peculiar sequel was that he had his hair, 'which was long and beautiful, in sympathy with the natives of India', cut short, and Abul Fazl comments; 'Would it be surprising if through the miracle of the Divine power he should change his mind and bring some inhabitants of this country to follow our custom?' But Akbar's feelings seem to have been deeper, as 'he was near abandoning this state of struggle and entirely gathering up the skirt of his genius from earthly pomp' —that meant retire to the contemplative life, which does not sound improbable, since Akbar is quoted as having said that already, as a youth of twenty, he 'experienced internal bitterness, and from the lack of spiritual provision for my last journey my soul was seized with exceeding sorrow'.

The news of the event must have been reported to the court at once, as his mother journeyed to the camp with all speed. But her fear proved groundless. Akbar stayed on for some time 'in the pleasant abode where the magical musicians came forth with their melodies, and his august heart was engaged by this', and then he started again to attend to the matters of government. He only gave an order that in the courtyard of the palace of Fathpur-Sikri a tank of twenty by twenty yards and twice a man's height deep should be filled to the brim with coins, and for three years afterwards the contents of the tank were distributed among the needy.

On his return to Fathpur-Sikri, the debates in the Hall of Worship were resumed. As Akbar's yearnings had become widely known, religious and wise men from Persia, Khorasan and Arabia, certain of a magnificent reception and bountiful presents, flocked to his capital to take part in them. The result was that the discussions became still more heated and controversial. 'The bigoted Ulama and the routine-lawyers, who reckoned themselves among the chief philosophers and the leaders of enlightenment, found their position difficult. The veil was removed from the face of many of them'. Angered by the arrogance of the mullahs, Akbar countered their arguments with the allusion that Mohammed's illiteracy served as proof of his divine mission, saying that 'the prophets were all illiterate and the true believers should therefore retain one of their sons in that condition'.

Then came a surprise. Probably under the impression of direct contact with the supernatural in his fit and, on hearing that 'legitimate Caliphs did not leave worship to others, but took this weighty matter upon their own shoulders', Akbar himself mounted the pulpit of the chief mosque of Fathpur-Sikri and recited the 'Khutba' put for him into verse and ending, as usual: 'Exalted be His Majesty, Allah Akbar!'. 'Allah Akbar' means: God is great, but it could also mean: Akbar is God. Did he claim divinity? 'On every side there arose the dust of commotion and the black smoke of darkness. The wicked crowded together'.

Akbar kept aloof, but a short time afterwards there came the answer. Sheikh Mubarak found that at last the time was ripe for his masterstroke. He submitted to the assembly a document stating that, as Akbar was a 'most just, most wise, and most God-fearing king', whenever religious questions should come up on which the opinions of the interpreters were at variance, his ruling on the case should be binding on them and on all people 'for the benefit of the nation and as a political expedient'.

In accordance with the commandment of the Koran: 'Obey God, and obey the Prophet, and those who have authority among you', all Ulama and Sheikhs were forced to sign this declaration acknowledging that the Emperor stood higher in the eyes of God than an interpreter of the Moslem law. Thus, about fifty years after Henry

VIII in England, Akbar in Hindustan became not only the Head of the State but also the Head of the Church, with the same restraining provision: in Henry's case 'as far as the law of Christ will allow', in Akbar's case 'provided that the order is in accordance with some verse of the Koran'.

Still, Akbar took care not to hurt the feelings of the orthodox unnecessarily; he made his usual annual pilgrimage to Ajmer, and on the way back he ordered a special tent to be set up as a mosque and made a point of praying in it five times a day as a most pious Moslem. And a little later, when a pilgrim to Mecca brought back a stone which was supposed to bear the imprint of the Prophet's foot, he ordered that the relic should be received and conveyed with due ceremony and went himself to meet it. But at the same time he dismissed the zealous Sadr and the Sheikh-ul-Islam by sending them to Mecca with the order not to return. Appropriating to himself religious authority over his Moslem subjects, Akbar was preparing to pursue, without obstruction from anyone, the line of policy which he considered necessary for the unification of his Empire. When later on, the Sadr and the Sheikh-ul-Islam came back from Mecca, in spite of the order to stay away, care was taken that they did not survive for long.

Akbar could not suffer any further interference on their part, since during the whole time that he was grappling with the administrative and religious problems, military operations proceeded unabated. The campaign in Bengal had been at first successful. After a pitched battle in which the army of King Daud of Bengal was defeated, he submitted and was allowed to retain Orissa, the land south-west of Bengal. The imperial army established itself in Bengal, but its climate proved deadly to the warriors from the north. An epidemic of malaria broke out and 'things came to such a pass that the living were unable to bury the dead' and threw them into the river. When the commander died too, the officers had only one thought: to get out of the country with all the booty they had taken. Encouraged by the prevailing confusion, Daud reoccupied Bengal. Akbar appointed the governor of the Punjab as the new commander, but he was a Shiite and most of the officers who were Sunnites resented his authority. When he at last succeeded in bringing them back to their duty, he engaged Daud in a fierce battle, took him prisoner and executed him as a rebel. His head was sent to Akbar, who was already preparing to take the field himself. That was the end of the kingdom of Bengal; it became a province of the Mogul Empire, called by the Moguls, because of its climate, 'a hell full of good things'.

While this war continued, another army under Raja Man Singh was sent against the Rana of Mewar. Mewar, once the leading principality of Rajputana, had after the loss of its capital Chitor and other important towns become poor and small, but the Rana still upheld the traditional pride of the Rajputs. When Man Singh sought a discussion with him in the hope of persuading him to acknowledge Akbar's suzerainty, the Rana refused to receive him, because Man Singh had accepted service with a Moslem and agreed to his aunt marrying one, even if it was the Emperor Akbar. The result of the encounter was a foregone conclusion, as the Rana had only three thousand horsemen to occupy the pass leading into the hills where he had collected all his adherents. Nevertheless, it was a desperate battle, a furious hand-to-hand combat, until the Rana, severely wounded, fled into his inaccessible mountain refuges. As Rajputs were fighting on both sides, the men of the northern tribes in Akbar's army were not sure how they could distinguish between enemies and allies, and their officers gave them the advice that they could not be wrong in shooting, because 'on whichever side the infidels were killed, it would be a gain to Islam'. Man Singh seems not to have pressed the pursuit of the Rana eagerly enough and to have failed to devastate the Rana's land. For a time he was in disgrace, but then Akbar must have recognized that it had been his own fault and that it had been asking too much from Man Singh to fight against a Rajput prince who still upheld the Rajput tradition and to devastate Rajput land. Therefore he restored Man Singh to favour. The Rana still maintained his undaunted resistance in his mountain fastness for nearly twenty years, until his death, and his heroic deeds became legendary.

In these circumstances it seemed to be an almost superhuman task to create among the discordant elements of Akbar's Empire, who had nothing in common except hatred for the rest, a feeling of unity and common interest. However, prompted by Sheikh Mubarak and his son Abul Fazl, the chronicler, he continued to speak of universal toleration, declaring that by taking from every religion that which appeals to reason, he might 'in this way open the lock, the key of which has been lost'. As Abul Fazl writes:

'The Shahinshah's court became the home of the enquirers of the 'seven climes', and the assemblage of the wise of every religion and sect'.

He now had around him representatives of all the different religions in his Empire, and in listening to them he found in every religion some features that attracted him. He liked the teaching of the Parsees of India that one can approach God through any religion and that the prophets had been so numerous in order to show that there were different ways to God; and he delighted the Parsees by paying reverence to the Sun and by ordering that a sacred fire should be lit and kept burning in the charge of Abul Fazl. In their turn, the Jain divines impressed him by their learning and their ascetic life. Their belief that the transmigration of the soul, once it is completed, ends in a state of bliss appealed to him, and he satisfied them by ordering the release of caged birds and by prohibiting the slaughter of animals on certain days. He even declared that he would abstain from eating flesh on Fridays. He let the Hindu scholars explain to him the mysteries of their religion: the doctrine of Karma, that one's deeds determine one's lot in the next reincarnation, caught his imagination and he adopted various features of Hindu practices and began to celebrate some of their festivals.

His acceptance of certain rites from each religion awakened in their adherents the belief that he was on the point of conversion, but he continued with his enquiries and even despatched an envoy to the Portuguese authorities at Goa, requesting them to send Christian missionaries to him, 'who should bring the books of the law, and above all the Gospels, because I truly and earnestly desire to understand their perfection'.

His first information about Christianity was very favourable; he had heard that two missionary priests who had arrived in Bengal had refused to absolve their converts because they had committed fraud by withholding shipping dues and harvest taxes. Thereupon he let the Portuguese vicar-general of Bengal come to his court, then had consultations with a Portuguese envoy sent from Goa to negotiate about some trouble involving the pilgrim ships. But these men were, of course, unable to satisfy his curiosity, and his request to the Goa authorities raised great hopes of the conversion of the king and of the whole kingdom. Two Jesuit fathers, Rodolfe Aquaviva and Antonio Monserrate, set out for

Fathpur-Sikri, accompanied by a third one, a converted Moslem, who was to act as interpreter.

When the Jesuit Fathers arrived they were immediately received in private audience. The Emperor placed the Bible which they had brought on his head, after removing his turban, and then kissed it. He ordered court painters to copy their pictures of Christ and the Virgin, and allowed them to set up a chapel and to preach and make conversions. He was impressed when they refused a large sum of money which he offered them and would not accept anything beyond bare sustenance; and he enjoyed his discussions with them so much that he made Father Monserrate, the historian of the mission, tutor to his ten-year-old second son Murad, to instruct him in the Portuguese language and in Christian morals.

This favouring of the infidels naturally inflamed the Moslems at court. A letter which Father Aquaviva wrote to Goa, complaining that 'our ears hear nothing but that hideous and heinous name of Mahomed' shows to what extent feelings were roused against the Emperor, for the Father confessed: 'If we go too far, we endanger the life of the king'. As at the same time the administrative reforms curtailing the independence and incomes of the chieftains were being introduced further and further afield, unrest grew and finally a revolt broke out in Bihar and Bengal, the most distant and therefore most independent of the territories.

A mullah in Jaunpur, in his capacity as Kazi—law officer—issued a ruling that rebellion against a sovereign who has abandoned the true path of a faithful Moslem was lawful. The rebels were successful. They captured and killed the hated local governor and plundered the treasury. Moreover, they made contact with Akbar's brother, Mirza Hakim, the ruler of Kabul, and invited him to Hindustan in order to raise him to the throne. That was much more dangerous, and in addition Akbar discovered a conspiracy even among his courtiers. Now he could not risk leaving the capital and travelling to Bengal himself; so he placated the insurgents, softening his administrative measures, replacing the most unpopular officials and even giving new appointments to some of the ringleaders. Having won over some of them, he sent troops against the others. A boat which carried the Kazi of Jaunpur with other similarly minded mullahs conveniently foundered on the river; a few courtiers of doubtful loyalty were executed, and in the meantime Akbar was collecting one of the largest armies he had ever led. Hakim had invaded the Punjab, crossed the Indus and encamped before Lahore, expecting that the city would open its gates to him. Akbar decided to march against him.

At the first news of Akbar's move Hakim fled in haste over the Indus. Akbar followed him, deciding that the Kabul question must be settled once and for all. When he invaded Hindustan Humayun had left the land of Kabul in the possession of his youngest wife and her infant son Hakim. After his death she had dismissed three regents, one after the other, in quick succession, and then had the next three killed. Afterwards she married her daughter to one of Humayun's favourites and after a short time was herself murdered by him. Having Hakim in his power, this man began to rule in the prince's name. Hakim managed to ask Suleiman Mirza of Budakhshan for help; Suleiman defeated the impostor and sent him as prisoner to Hakim, who had him strangled. Then Suleiman gave Hakim one of his daughters in marriage, but afterwards tried several times, although unsuccessfully, to get the upper hand in Kabul. As both Kabul and Badakhshan figured as imperial domains, it sometimes needed Akbar's authority and the threat of his army to maintain a relative peace there. But now Akbar saw that in the case of difficulties within Hindustan, a menace could come from the north. This menace had to be ended.

As there was no need for a lightning stroke the campaign was to be comfortable one, and Akbar took part of the harem with him as well as the two elder princes Salim and Murad. Father Monserrate also had to accompany him, and we have from him and others a vivid description of the campaign and of the court on the move.

The royal ladies were carried in decorated covered litters on the backs of elephants, followed by their female servants riding under white umbrellas on camels. The treasure was also carried on elephants and camels, ordnance stores, furniture and other belongings in carts or on mules. The procession was protected by a guard of five hundred chosen riders under the command of senior officers. On the place selected for the encampment the imperial seraglio, the audience hall and a musicians' gallery were pitched on a space of about 1,500 yards in length. At about a hundred yards to the right, to the left, and behind, the tents of the royal ladies and of the princes were erected, and then a free space of about two hundred yards was left which no one except the guards was allowed to enter. Behind it the offices and workshops were placed, and at the four corners of the camp bazaars were put up. On all sides around this space the nobles were encamped, also according to their rank. Monserrate expresses his astonishment that, in spite of the multitude, the movement of the camp was executed with admirable precision, all provisions were plentiful and cheap, and he remarks that the dealers supplying the army were relieved from the payment of all dues and customs.

The rivers were crossed on pontoon-bridges, and where boats were scarce on ferries, in which case the crossing occupied several days. At the Indus, which was in flood, most of the officers recommended abandoning the campaign, but Akbar sent a strong advance troop of several thousand men with the eleven-year-old prince Murad across the river while waiting himself with the main army for the building of a pontoon-bridge. At the same time, envoys were dispatched to Hakim demanding that he should come and make his submission, and promising full pardon. The Mirza responded by sending other envoys with regrets over his past errors and promising loyal service in future, but he did not appear himself. The reasons on both sides were clear. Akbar was apprehensive that his brother might go to seek help from Persia or from the Uzbegs, while Hakim did not trust the promises of safety, and that not without reason, because Akbar's officers openly advocated a plan to waylay and kill him.

Thus the campaign went on. Having at last crossed the Indus, Akbar ordered the main army to proceed slowly, stage by stage, and himself rushed with a small select force into Afghanistan. On the way he received the report that Hakim had attacked the advance force accompanying Murad, but had been beaten off thanks to the gun-carrying elephants. Murad entered Kabul a few days before his father reached the capital. Here Akbar heard that Mirza Hakim had fled into the hills and was preparing to seek refuge with the Uzbegs if he were pursued. Akbar foresaw the complications which would arise if his brother became a refugee at the court of the Uzbeg Khan and stopped the campaign. He entrusted the government of Kabul to Hakim's sister, his own half-sister, who had come to visit him; he declared that he was pardoning Hakim, but warned him that if he misbehaved again he could expect no more clemency. Otherwise Akbar did not mind whether his brother resided in Kabul or elsewhere. After Akbar's departure he returned to Kabul and was allowed by his sister to resume the government until his death three years later, although all orders were issued in her name.

4

THE DIVINE FAITH

After his return from Kabul, the forty-year-old Akbar felt that he no longer needed to placate the feelings of his unruly vassals. The importance of the Kabul campaign was that it had cut all possibility of contact between the rebels in the south-east with the lands in the north and had removed the danger of being faced with war on two sides. Moreover, the revolt in Bengal and Bihar was as good as quelled, and he had trustworthy men there with enough troops to deal with any possible resurgence. And so he could now proceed with any administrative measures, however much they might be disliked.

He ordered a census to be taken of all people, their occupation and their income, in every city and town, and also village by village. The control of crops was to be strengthened and measures taken to increase the area of cultivated land. To avoid trading abuses, supervisors for each branch should control the selling and buying and receive one-half per cent of each deal from the purchaser and one per cent from the seller, half of which the controller had to pay into the treasury which set up separate departments for horses, for elephants, for camels, for sheep and goats, for armour, for gold and silver, for dyes, for intoxicants, for drugs, for leather goods and so on. He had divided his territories into twelve provinces, each with a complete regional government for finance, police, justice, transport, and in each there sat a viceroy as the commander-in-chief. Now he also abolished the office of Sadr, substituting for it six provincial ecclesiastical officers with much curtailed powers, and appointed a chief Kazi for each of the larger cities. All the grants given for learned and pious purposes had to be re-examined.

Naturally his quest for religious truth continued unabated. Badaoni, a zealous Moslem condemning all these speculations and dissensions, wrote in a diary which he secretly kept: 'Day and night people did nothing but enquire into and investigate the profound secrets of science, the subtleties of revelation, the curiosities of

15. Audience at Akbar's Court with Jesuit Fathers in the foreground.

16. Akbar receiving books from court poets.

history, and the wonders of nature . . .' Nevertheless he gives a true picture of Akbar's efforts and state of mind by writing: 'His Majesty collected the opinions of every one, especially of such as were not Mohammedans, retaining whatever he approved of, and rejecting everything which was against his disposition and ran counter to his wishes. From his earliest childhood to his manhood, and from his manhood to old age, His Majesty has passed through the most varied phases and through all sorts of religious practices and sectarian beliefs, and has collected everything which people can find in books, with a talent for selection peculiar to him, and in a spirit of enquiry opposed to every Islamic principle. Thus a faith based on some elementary principles has traced itself on the mirror of his heart, and as the result of all the influences brought to bear on His Majesty, there grew, gradually as the outline on a stone, the conviction in his heart that there were sensible men in all religions, and abstemious thinkers, and men endowed with miraculous powers among all nations. If some true knowledge was thus to be found everywhere, why should truth be confined to one religion, or to a creed like Islam which was comparatively new, and scarcely a thousand years old?'

Akbar was also disappointed with the performance of the Jesuit Fathers, who in their religious zeal attacked Islam and the Prophet at the assembly in the Hall of Worship in such language and in such a way that he had to give them a protective guard. In their behaviour he saw the same intolerance and the same presumption that they alone possessed the true faith as in the Moslem scholars, but he liked to have these men from such a different world around him at his court and to hold discussions with them. He treated them as personal friends, but that did not deter him from sometimes confusing them with, in their view, irrelevant answers. So one day he told them: 'Since you reckon the reverencing of women as a part of your religion and do not allow more than one wife to a man, would it then not be a wonderful thing if such fidelity and lifelong sacrifice were also to be found among your women? The extraordinary thing is that it occurs among the women of the Hindu religion. Here there are numerous concubines, and many of them are neglected and unappreciated and spend their days unfructuously in the private chamber of chastity, yet in spite of such embitterment of their lives they die as flaming torches of love and fellowship.'

It was not that he approved of the Indian ritual of 'suttee'; he even forbade the burning of widows if they did not demand it themselves. When he heard that the widow of a Raja was to be forced to 'suttee' by the family, against her will, he himself rushed to the place in one of his lightning rides and saved her. But he had to set the proud self-sacrificial spirit of Hindu women against their privileged European counterparts.

There are different versions, too, of a story that a trial by fire was proposed between the Jesuits and the Mullahs. The one says that Father Aquaviva suggested to a Mullah that they both, he with the Bible and the Mullah with the Koran in the hand, should go through fire to prove which book contained God's truth; the other version is that the proposal came from the Mullah and that Aquaviva declined it, although Akbar assured him that he would arrange the test in such a way that he would remain unhurt while the Mullah, whom Akbar disliked, should be burnt.

From the Emperor's whole attitude, however, it became clear that the hopes of converting him to Christianity were in vain and Father Monserrate expressed his disappointment when he reported to Goa that Akbar had been moved to summon the missionaries 'not by divine inspiration but by a certain curiosity and an excessive eagerness to hear of new things, or by a design to devise something novel', as he naturally concluded, 'for the destruction of souls'. In addition, the relationship became somewhat strained because Akbar did not let his liking for the missionaries deter him from trying to dislodge the Portuguese on his territory, and he sent an army against the ports of Diu and Daman which they held. However, he was sincerely sorry when the missionaries were recalled after two years, although at this time he was already busy with drawing practical conclusions from his long effort to choose the best from all religions: he decided to proclaim a new kind of faith.

He had recognized that his attempt to achieve an understanding between the followers of different doctrines through discussion had failed. Instead of trying to understand and appreciate other people's points of view, the debates only increased their mutual hatred and led to even greater intolerance. In despair he discontinued the assemblies and closed his Hall of Worship. But, privately continuing the discussions with selected men from each creed, he found certain common essentials and principles in all beliefs and thought that taking reason and religious toleration as a basis he would be able to lay down a unifying code of spiritual conduct which the more enlightened leaders among his heterogeneous peoples would adopt.

He summoned a General Council, which included the learned men of the court and the military commanders, and addressed them to the effect that for an empire ruled by one head it was bad to have the people divided among themselves by many kinds of religious laws hostile to each other, and creating as many factions as there were religions. 'We ought, therefore, to bring them all into one religion in such a fashion that they should be both 'one' and 'all', with the great advantage of not losing what is good in any one religion, while gaining whatever is better in another. In that way, honour would be rendered to God, peace would be given to the peoples, and security to the empire'. No objection was raised, only Raja Bhagwan Das, a brother of Akbar's first Hindu wife, expressed some concern, saying: 'I would willingly believe that Hindus and Moslems each have a bad religion, but tell us what the new sect is, and what opinion they hold, so that I may believe'. All were in agreement that Akbar as the spiritual as well as the temporal head should now prescribe 'the ceremonies, sacrifices, mysteries, rules, solemnities, and whatever else was required to constitute one perfect and universal religion', and it seems that he sent out Sheikh Mubarak 'to proclaim in all quarters that in a short time the new religious law to be professed would be sent out from the court', and everyone would have to accept it with reverence.

However, the orders and rules which started to appear in the name of 'Din Ilahi'—the new 'Divine Faith'—and with some interruptions continued to come out for over a decade did not amount to much, except that they reveal Akbar's view of kingship as a gift of God, with the consequence that 'the divine will manifests itself in the intuition of kings'. His daily performance of showing himself to the people was maintained because 'the very sight of the kings has been held to be a part of divine worship. They have been conventionally styled as the shadow of God, and to behold them is a means of calling to mind the Creator'. Accordingly, the adherent to the Divine Faith must accept four grades of devotion to the Emperor, declaring his readiness to sacrifice to him Property, Life, Honour and Religion—the four goods of the world's market.

Usually this acceptance resulted in favours and promotion, and Badaoni wrote in his secret diary that if the Emperor had been prepared to spend a little more money 'he would easily have got most of his courtiers, and many more of the vulgar people, into his devilish nets', but in fact Akbar chose very carefully whom he admitted as disciple to his Divine Faith. The adherence to the Divine Faith seems to have been regarded more as an initiation into a religious brotherhood than a new belief, and the introductory ceremony was performed by Akbar himself. The novice, with his turban in his hands, put his head on the feet of the Emperor, who raised him and replaced the turban on his head and gave him a medal which bore the 'Great Name'—probably some epithet of the name of God—and the engraving 'Allahu Akbar'. By this he became a disciple and was expected to follow every ordinance.

The ordinances themselves, 'the devilish nets' of Badaoni, had quite simple features: The members should greet each other by saying 'Allahu Akbar' and answer 'Jalla Jalaluhu'—meaning 'God is Great' and 'Glorious in His Glory', but forming a paraphrase, too, of the Emperor's name Jallal-ud Din Akbar. Instead of giving a dinner in remembrance of a man after his death, each believer should arrange a feast on the anniversary of his birthday and bestow alms, thus gathering good deeds for the last journey. They should, at least during the month of their birth, abstain from eating flesh; later on, this abstinence from meat was extended to a hundred days a year, and the slaughter of cows was made a capital offence. They should not cohabit with pregnant, old or barren women, nor with girls under the age of puberty. People should be buried with their heads towards the east and their feet towards the west—contrary to the Moslem custom. He himself even began to sleep in this direction, probably in reverence to the rising sun. The prostration which was considered lawful only in divine worship was declared to be due also to the Emperor; and gold and silk dresses which were forbidden by Moslem law were declared obligatory at public prayers. Beards were to be shaved.

It is possible that the institution of the Divine Faith was influenced by the approach of the millenium of the Hejira era, with the attendant expectation of changes at the end of the millenium and the appearance of a Mahdi—Saviour—who would supersede the ancient prophets. At least, Akbar also ordered the writing of a history of the thousand years and the preparation of millenial coins.

But in spite of the fact that this new belief was in the sharpest contradiction to Islam and incorporated many of the Hindu rites, there was only one Hindu among the prominent 'disciples', a wit who acted as a kind of court jester. When Akbar tried to win over Raja Man Singh, he received the answer: 'If discipleship means willingness to sacrifice one's life, I have already carried my life in my hand: what need is there of further proof? If, however, the term has another meaning and refers to faith, I am a Hindu. If you order me to do so, I will become a Moslem, but I do not know of the existence of any other religion than these two.' And it is interesting that this refusal in no way impaired Man Singh's position or Akbar's friendship for him. On the other hand Akbar's milk-brother, who in order not to be forced to become a disciple made a pilgrimage to Mecca, which had now been prohibited by the Divine Faith, was fleeced there in such a way that he returned disgusted and enrolled as a disciple in the new order.

To draw the conclusion, however, that Akbar ceased to be a Moslem and became an enemy of Islam, as some historians do, would probably be wrong. His remarks in this respect presumably only mean that he gave up the intolerant practices which orthodox Islam demanded and was prepared to pay reverence to everything in other creeds that appealed to his 'reason', which he considered to be the true criterion of belief. As conqueror and autocrat he felt himself rather like God's viceregent on earth, in a special and nearer relationship to God than other beings. He explained that, when in his youth he undertook hair-raising adventures, he had done so in order that God might end his life, if he had taken any step displeasing Him. He believed that 'between the Creator and the creature there existed a bond which is not expressible in language'. To visualize God is only 'apprehensible by force of imagination', and when 'each person gives a name to the Supreme Being it is according to his own condition; but in reality to name the Unknowable is vain'.

And just as he allowed the Jesuits to build a church, he issued an order that 'if any of the infidels chose to build a synagogue, or an idol temple, or a Parsee tower of silence, no one was to hinder him'. If a Hindu, as a child or otherwise, had been made a Moslem against his will, he was to be allowed, if he pleased, to go back to the religion of his fathers, and anyone was to be allowed to go over to any religion he wanted. When it is reported that he used Mosques as storage places, or even destroyed some, this may have been because Islam, as the ruling religion, demanded absolute authority, and the mullahs did not cease to fight any move on his part which was directed against their predominance. It may even be that the proclamation of the new religion was made by the forty-year-old Akbar in the spirit of hair-raising adventure in order to try the will of God; for Father Monserrate wrote in the same year, 1582, at the beginning of the reform, that it was surprising that Akbar had not been killed by the Moslems. Akbar himself expressed his views in the following terms: 'Although I am the master of so vast a kingdom and all the instruments of government are in my hand, yet since true greatness consists in doing the will of God, my mind is not at ease in this diversity of sects and creeds; and apart from this outward pomp of circumstances, with what satisfaction, in my despondency, can I undertake the sway of empire? I await the coming of some unknown man of principle who will resolve the difficulties of my conscience.'

Thus, the introduction of his new religion in no way satisfied Akbar's desire for more information and knowledge in spiritual and philosophical problems, and he used every occasion to get it. When a Greek priest was passing through his lands, he immediately placed a few young men under his instruction and tried to employ him in the translation of Greek books; and when the Padre wanted to go to Goa, he employed him as ambassador, sending with him rich gifts for distribution among the poor at Goa while asking for a second mission of 'the most learned and the most virtuous of the Fathers, that they may help me to a true knowledge of the Christian law, and of the royal highways by which they travel to the presence of God'. Typical in his letter are the words: 'I have knowledge of all the faiths of the world', and he wants them to come 'so that they may dispute with my doctors, and that I, by comparing the learning and other qualities displayed on either side, may be able to see the superiority of the Fathers over my learned men, who by these means may be taught to know the truth.'

This mission arrived at Akbar's court shortly before the millenial year of the Hejira era was to begin—October 9, 1591, to September 27, 1592; and whether the expectation of the Mahdi had made the nobles more intolerant, or whether the missionaries were not selected with enough care, they were recalled to Goa before the millenium year was over, in spite of Akbar's protest and in spite of the fact that he had given them domicile in the palace itself and made them start a school for the teaching of Portuguese and the Christian religion.

Akbar's promulgation of Din Ilahi should not be therefore taken as the half-insane act of a vain-glorious autocrat, imagining himself to be God's representative on earth, but as an effort to introduce some framework of law and custom which would justify his rule and make him the righteous sovereign of a foreign country in which he was making his empire. Because at this time all laws were based on religion, this framework had to be a religious one, a divine pronunciation of truth, but just because it had to be religious it was bound to fail. It is reported of Abul Fazl, who with his father was one of the chief architects of Din Ilahi, that while propagating it he at the same time employed a dozen scribes to copy the Koran for him.

5

IN THE NORTH

As the rebellions in Bihar and Bengal were now crushed, Akbar could think of extending his rule over the adjoining countries and his attention was directed to the north. His brother Hakim had just died in Kabul, leaving only small children; the situation there called for no more than the sending of some troops to maintain order and to bring the children to court to forestall any ambitious nobles who might attempt to rule in their name. But to the north-east of the Punjab there lay Kashmir, which Haidar Mirza, a relative of Humayun, had conquered after the expulsion of the Moguls from India by Sher Shah. He had been a vassal of the Emperor, but the present ruler had avoided going to court and doing homage; therefore his country was to be subdued. To the south-west of the Punjab there was Sind, where Humayun had undergone such difficulties and hardships, and the definite inclusion of the whole Indus valley in Akbar's Empire would round off his domain in the north and extend it to the frontiers of Persia. With these two quests in mind Akbar transferred his whole court from Fathpur-Sikri to the Punjab to be near the areas of action.

The conquest of Kashmir proved more difficult than was expected. Rain and snow cut off the supplies of the invading army. However, the Sultan, feeling that in spite of the mountain barriers he would not be able to withstand the onslaught for long, started peace negotiations and was granted easy terms: the Khutba was to be read and the coins were to be minted in Akbar's name. The cultivation of saffron and the manufacture of shawls, famous Kashmir products even at that time, should come under the control of Akbar's administration, while the Sultan was to come to Akbar's camp and pay homage. The commander of the army, Raja Bhagwan Das, guaranteed him his life and freedom, but Akbar was dissatisfied with this peace agreement and, although confirming it, imprisoned the Sultan when he came, and ordered a second invasion. The Raja, whose sister was married to Akbar, felt his honour besmirched by this violation of his promise of safe-conduct; he stabbed himself with a dagger; the wound, however, was not fatal and under the care of the court physicians he soon recovered. The Sultan was sent to Bihar, where he was freed after a short while and given a 'jagir'. Kashmir was annexed and attached to the province of Kabul.

Less successful were the expeditions undertaken at the same time against Afghan hill tribes. The imperial troops suffered various defeats, and some of the tribes even combined and for over a year cut the connection with Kabul through the Khaibar pass.

Thus more than three years passed since his departure from Fathpur-Sikri before Akbar could visit Kashmir, and he was so delighted with the country and with its natural beauties that he called it his paradisial garden. This did not deter him from demanding such a high revenue that his own fief-holders in Kashmir rose in arms, because if they had to deliver the amount of the assessment they would not have been left with enough money for themselves and their troops. But Akbar could no longer be forced to yield: the rebellion was crushed and the whole of Kashmir declared crown land.

In the meantime the annexation of Sind was achieved. After two engagements on the Indus, in which gun-carrying river-ships were used, the ruler of Sind submitted, accepted the obligation of war service and even enlisted as an adherent of the Divine Faith. In compensation he was granted a high rank and the rule of his country as a fief.

The conquest of Sind was followed by a war against the Baluchi tribes in the mountains to the north-west of the Indus valley, who were forced to hand over their strongholds on the approaches to the passes leading to the province of Kandahar. This province had been taken by the Persians immediately after Humayun's death, as belonging to them according to the treaty between Humayun and Shah Tahmasp. Akbar, on the other hand, regarded it as a part of Babur's kingdom of Kabul and was preparing to fight for it when it suddenly came peacefully into his possession.

The Persian prince who ruled the province, nominally as a fief from the Shah, saw himself menaced by the lately growing Uzbeg power. The Uzbeg ruler, Abdullah Khan, had not only invaded Khorasan and taken Herat but also had annexed Badakhshan, which was one of Akbar's vassal states. Badakhshan was too far away to risk a war there against the Uzbegs, and Akbar only gave refuge to its ruler and made him an army commander. But in the last instance it was the fear that the Uzbegs would irrupt into Kabul which kept him for a tenth year in the north, where he had made Lahore his capital. Now the prince in Kandahar, faced with the Uzbegs in Khorasan and with Akbar's troops in the Baluchi mountains, offered Kandahar to Akbar and came himself with two thousand riders to receive a fief in Hindustan.

This decade in the north brought not only expansion through conquest but also the internal consolidation of Akbar's Empire. The rebellious spirits were cowed, at least in the more centrally situated provinces, and if some foolhardy chieftains in the outlying domains still dared to attempt risings, there were governors and troops stationed near-by to deal with such disturbances. They no longer called for the Emperor's personal intervention.

While pursuing his conquests in the north, Akbar did not forget the south. There his dominions now bordered on the small sultanates of the Deccan plateau, the rulers of which, some of them Shiite Moslems, were always in conflict with each other. True to his saying that 'a sovereign should be ever intent on conquest', Akbar decided that they should be incorporated into his empire, and sent missions to the sultans inviting them to accept his suzerainty. The missions were honourably received, presents were sent, but they were too poor to be regarded as tribute. This meant that the sultans did not want to surrender their independance, so Akbar decided on conquest.

During this decade he had lost some of his best advisers and commanders, but a new generation had grown up and filled high posts. His own sons were now young men with several wives and children, and Akbar showed more affection for his grandchildren than for his sons, with whom he had enough reason to be dissatisfied.

His eldest son, Salim, was so violent and irritable that Akbar felt he could not entrust him with an independent governorship or command but preferred to keep him near by, and often enough the prince was excluded from the audience hall for misbehaviour. When in his fiftieth year Akbar fell ill with stomach trouble and colics, he even had the suspicion that Salim had poisoned him. Under these circumstances the second son, Murad, cherished hopes for the throne and was kept under observation by Salim's spies. But when he received Malwa as a fief and was then appointed governor of Gujarat, all the good advice and the instructions given to him by Akbar proved to have been wasted. By his overweening manners Murad offended the nobles and quarrelled with the commanders. Then Akbar appointed his third son, Daniel, to command an army against the Deccan, whereupon Murad wrote to his father an impetuous letter that the command against the Deccan principalities was due to him. However, when the letter arrived in Lahore Akbar had already recalled Daniel, because the prince, instead of proceeding south and collecting the army, had dallied on the way holding drinking parties. And when Murad was really appointed in his place and invaded the Deccan, the discord between him and the commander of the second army rendered the military operations unsuccessful. Akbar foresaw that in the end he himself would have to go to the south to lead the campaign, but he did not feel safe enough to leave the north yet, with Kashmir still discontented, the hill tribes semi-pacified and the Uzbeg menace looming in the background. And so he decided first to go to Kashmir to see how the settlement there was working.

At this time a terrible famine had broken out in the Punjab because of the lack of rain. This was followed by a plague which 'depopulated houses and cities, to say nothing of hamlets and villages. In consequence of the dearth of grain and the necessities of ravenous hunger, men ate their own kind. The streets and roads were covered with dead bodies, and no assistance could be rendered for their removal'. The departure of the extremely populous court, with all the adherents and followers, to the less afflicted country of Kashmir was therefore very opportune.

The visit to Kashmir lasted about six months. It brought a lighter assessment of revenues, public works were introduced, some relief measures to alleviate distress were taken and a number of customs duties abolished. Then, shortly after the return to Lahore, the news arrived that the Uzbeg ruler, Abdullah Khan, had died in Samarkand. Immediately, Babur's old dream of the reconquest of Transoxiana was revived in Akbar. He himself could not leave the empire for this far-off land, but might not one of his sons want to avail himself of the opportunity? Salim, when approached, did not want to hear of Transoxiana; he saw the whole idea as a conspiracy to remove him from his position as heir to a remote, unknown land, there to fight a mortal struggle against an unknown enemy, while his ageing father was surrounded by servile sons and grandsons striving to win the throne. When an envoy was sent to Prince Murad, he at once eagerly resumed the Deccan campaign; and Prince Daniel hastened away from Allahabad on the Ganges on a joyful tour of his fiefs. The great-grandsons of Babur no longer had the hardy adventurous spirit of the Timurids; the wonders of Samarkand did not awaken in them any longing: to them that was a foreign, cold, Central-Asiatic land; India's riches and pleasures were their domicile. Akbar had to abandon his dreams of the conquest of the land whence his ancestors came. His future conquests had to be in India.

It was thirteen years after his departure from Fathpur-Sikri that Akbar returned to the south, but he did not go back to the town of splendid palaces which he had built at the abode of the saint who had predicted the birth of his three sons and where his two elder sons and a daughter had been born. Agra again became the capital. Father Jerome Xavier, the leader of the third Jesuit mission to Akbar, had the occasion to see Fathpur-Sikri a few years later and he wrote: 'We might say "Here stood Troy", for it is totally demolished; only a few edifices made by the Emperor still stand firm'.

With the same rapidity with which the buildings had been erected at the Emperor's command—about which Abul Fazl wrote: 'The Emperor plans splendid edifices and clothes the work of his mind in the garment of stone and clay'—they also decayed as soon as he lost interest in a particular place; no care was taken to preserve them, for new edifices of equal splendour and magnificence were rising elsewhere. The requirements of the imperial court, wherever it was, provided the architects with ever new and challenging tasks in the construction of palaces and public buildings, and just as he drew philosophers and 'wise men' of every religion and creed to his court, Akbar also patronized artists and poets of all schools. The buildings erected during his reign were beginning to combine the Persian-Moslemic with the Indian style, and the art of painting was changing in the same way. Humayun had brought two famous Persian painters with him to Kabul and then to India, and under their guidance an Indo-Persian art school developed, with high achievements particularly in miniature painting and in frescos. Akbar himself regularly examined the works they produced and distributed rewards to the artists. When the third Jesuit mission brought with them a copy of a picture of the Madonna, probably from Santa Maria del Popolo in Rome, and exhibited it on the altar of the church, people thronged to see it. Three times they had to bring the painting to Akbar so that he could show it to his wives, then to his mother, and finally have it copied by his painters.

The Jesuits naturally attributed this enthusiasm to the miraculous power with which the original picture was supposed to be endowed, and described how 'a great captain, who came accompanied by more than sixty men at horse and many others at foot, stood as one in a trance as soon as he saw the picture, so overcome was he with admiration'. In fact, not only this but other Renaissance paintings, too, were eagerly copied and also engravings collected by the high nobles, who competed with each other to attract painters, poets and musicians to their residences. Abul Fazl writes: 'Most excellent painters are now to be found, and masterpieces may be placed beside the wonderful works of European painters who have attained world-wide fame', and he adds that the Emperor and all the Grandees of the court sat for their likenesses, and these portraits were preserved in an immense album.

Persian being the language of the court, calligraphy was also highly prized as a branch of art, and a multitude of calligraphers used their artistry to produce countless books, illustrated by the best painters, particularly for Akbar's enormous library. He ordered the most famous Sanskrit, Greek, Arabic and other works to be translated into Persian and had them read to him, and they were preserved in magnificently adorned volumes. The inventory of his library at his death showed 24,000 such manuscripts.

Music and song were equally cultivated, and among the famous musicians there were 'Hindus, Iranis, Turanis and Kashmiris, both men and women', and again the Hindu and the Moslem music mingled and became fused.

A new kind of culture was developing. The nobles who ruled the country, of whatever race or clan, no longer felt themselves strangers. Many were intermarried and related with Hindus, and even if they were not, the Indian surroundings had left their mark upon them; new generations had grown up who had been born in India, and their whole mode of life had become in many ways akin to that of the native nobility. Some of them spoke Persian, Arabic, Turki, Sanskrit and Hindi, others patronized learning and literature and founded schools of music. While the nobles continued to live and hold their feasts in tents, these were now luxury tents, kept sweet with pleasant perfumes, decorated with velvet and brocades, their floors covered with rich carpets.

This life of luxury among the courtiers and high dignitaries naturally contrasted with the poverty of the population, albeit the chroniclers state that a great increase in cultivated land took place under Akbar and the cheapness of the food may have provided somewhat better nourishment for the labourer and peasant; but they still depended entirely on the state of the harvest, and when the rains failed terrible famines were usual.

The oriental historians scarcely mention them, even such a disaster as the famine and the plague of 1595 to 1598, partly because it was regarded as the will of God, against which nothing could be done, and partly because such a calamity might throw an unnecessarily dark shadow on the glory of the ruler. The misery and the suffering of the masses were not the concern of the sovereign; his repute depended on the just distribution of rich rewards to his loyal servants, and it was quite an unusual act that Akbar appointed a great noble to undertake relief measures. Even the Jesuit Fathers of the third mission describe the calamity mainly in order to relate how mothers brought their dying children to them for baptism, thus ensuring that the souls of the infants would go straight to heaven.

This third Jesuit mission was, like its predecessors, sent at Akbar's request, about two years after the second mission had returned to Goa. In the meantime the millenial year of the Hejira era had passed without the appearance of the expected Mahdi; in the following year Sheikh Mubarak, who was the spiritual originator of the Divine Faith, had died, and although a flood of new ordinances concerning the Divine Faith continued to appear, Akbar missed the stimulating talks which he had had with these foreign ecclesiastics from a completely different world and again wanted them at court. Though the authorities in Goa must by now have realized that the pious hope of converting the Emperor of Hindustan to Christianity would never be fulfilled, the maintenance of a mission in a privileged position at his court was highly desirable, if only as a means of obtaining precise information regarding happenings and movements there, and they willingly complied with the Emperor's wish and were this time very careful in selecting the missionaries.

The head of the mission was Father Jerome Xavier, who had already done evangelistic work in India for many years and for whom Akbar soon developed a particular liking, keeping him always near wherever he went. The second missionary was Emmanuel Pinheiro, who was less in personal touch with the Emperor, devoting himself mainly to the creation of a considerable congregation of converts in Lahore, but who later displayed much zeal in countering the influence of the English merchants who arrived at the court. The third missionary, Benedict à Goes, who was helping Pinheiro in Lahore, was afterwards sent to Tibet and played no part in activities at the Mogul court.

In general, the relations between Akbar and the Portuguese had become very peculiar. Until his death he cherished the hope of capturing the Portuguese settlements and driving out the foreigners. Nevertheless, as long as he lived he continued to accord the missionaries an exceptionally favourable treatment, provided in Lahore, and later in Agra, a suitable site and funds for church and school, and allowed them to make converts. On the whole, in spite of some incidents of fanaticism, when zealous mullahs incited the populace to the slaughter of the infidels, the religious tolerance in Akbar's empire had become remarkable. When the church in Lahore was consecrated, the Mohammedan viceroy honoured the ceremony by his presence, and when a beautiful display of the Nativity scene was arranged at Christmas, great crowds of Hindus thronged the chapel.

In Kashmir, of which Father Xavier gives a glowing description, he fell severely ill, and Akbar 'showed him much kindness, giving orders for the liberal supply of all his wants, and sending his own physician to attend him; he even went in person to see him, which was a very special favour, for it is his custom never to visit anyone'. Shortly afterwards Akbar himself became ill, and 'on several occasions during his illness, he sent for the Father, and had him brought to the chamber where he lay, which even the greatest lords of his court were seldom permitted to enter.'

In spite of this privileged treatment, discord sometimes developed. After his return to Agra, Akbar had started on his campaign in the Deccan and laid siege to a particularly strong fortress, the walls of which he could not breach. His previous attacks on the small Portuguese ports had failed because Portuguese artillery was much superior to his own, and so he asked Father Xavier to write to the Portuguese authorities that they should send him their more powerful guns and battering engines if they wished to gain his friendship. Father Xavier replied diplomatically that 'the Christian religion forbade him to seek such things or to arrange for their being sought by others'. Akbar flew into a rage and ordered him to leave the court with his companions and to return to Goa. One of the courtiers advised the Jesuit not to leave but only to keep out of sight for a while, and after a short time he was completely restored to favour. When the fortress finally surrendered, Akbar put the Portuguese artillery officers, who had become Mohammedans and served the Deccan king, into the care of Father Xavier instead of executing them; they very quickly became Christians again and ultimately were allowed to return to Goa.

Nevertheless, the Portuguese authorities were perfectly aware of Akbar's design to get hold of their possessions. When he sent an embassy to Goa with some choice gifts and the request that his envoy should be assisted to buy precious stones, fabrics and other goods and hire skilled craftsmen, the embassy was received with imposing honours, but had to return without the 'skilled craftsmen', who would have been employed to improve his implements of war. And in honour of the embassy 'a terrific salute of artillery was fired and continued throughout the day, both from the guns in the city and from those in other parts of the island, and the ambassador fully appreciated the significance of this music.'

It was in 1603, less than two years after this mission, that Akbar received a letter from Lahore, from an Englishman named John Mildenhall, who introduced himself as a merchant and claimed to carry a letter from Queen Elizabeth of England. Akbar summoned him to Agra and granted him an audience. Mildenhall produced a recommendation by Queen Elizabeth, similar to the one which eighteen years earlier had been presented by another English traveller, John Newberry. It was the kind of letter commonly issued by the Queen to the merchant-adventurers for delivery to some legendary or actual potentate if occasion arose. Newbery's letter had been addressed to 'The most invincible and most mighty Prince, Lord Zelabdin Echebar, King of Cambaia; Invincible Emperor . . .' And it ran: 'The great eagerness which our Subjects have to visit the most distant places of the world (not without good will and intention to introduce trade of merchandise of all nations whatsoever they can; by which means the mutual and friendly traffic of merchandise on both sides may come) is the cause that the bearer of this letter, John Newbery, jointly with those that be in his company, with a courteous and honest boldness do repair to the borders and countries of your Empire.' Then followed the request that the bearers, in view 'of the hard journey they have undertaken to places so far distant may be honestly entreated and received and such privileges granted as to you shall seem good'.

Newbery had arrived at a time when Akbar was preparing to leave Fathpur-Sikri for the north, and besides, the English traveller was just passing through his country to further lands. But he had in his company a clever jeweller, whom Akbar kept in his service, giving him 'a house, and five slaves, a horse, and every day six shillings in money', as the other companion of Newbery, Ralph Fitch, reported. Otherwise this first English visit had a sequel only in England when Fitch returned home and conveyed the knowledge of India's riches to other merchants. The Levant Company was granted a charter, and later on the merchants succeeded in getting leave from the Queen to form a company for trading with India direct by sea. This first charter to the East India Company was granted on December 31, 1600.

Now, eighteen years after Newbery, Mildenhall was coming to Akbar with much greater pretensions. He presented twenty-nine good horses, Persian ones because of the long distance from his country to Hindustan, received valuable presents in return and was allowed to state his case in the council. He expounded that the Queen wished to maintain friendship with the Emperor and was asking permission for her merchants to trade with his Empire on equal terms with the Portuguese. Moreover, he expressed the hopes that the Emperor would not take offence if the English captured Portuguese ships in his waters or their ports on his coasts.

That was an extremely interesting statement. Akbar had seen the superiority of the Portuguese artillery, and all his efforts to get their guns had failed. The envoy whom he had sent to Goa told tales of the power of their fleet and the efficiency of their war instruments, and now these merchants of the Queen of England, who were eager to trade with him, felt strong enough to capture Portuguese ships and even to take Portuguese strongholds which he himself was unable to conquer. It was certainly worth having them here.

But how far could one believe these 'Feringhis'—unknown foreigners? Akbar tried to get some more information from the Jesuits, and, 'in an exceedingly great rage', they immediately denounced the English as thieves and spies, started to bribe the councillors and enticed Mildenhall's Armenian interpreter from his service. Actually Mildenhall was only pretending to ambassadorial dignity and was in certain ways a cheat. In reality he had been sent by the 'London Company of Merchants to the Levant' before they got the charter for the 'East India Company'; he had sailed to Syria, gone overland to Aleppo, where he stayed over a year, and then travelled with a large caravan through Persia to Kandahar. From there he came to Lahore, and skilfully used the Queen's letter to assume a higher status. Faced with the opposition of the Jesuits and being deprived of his Armenian interpreter, he stayed on six months to learn Persian and then asked for permission to state his grievances. The permission was granted, and now well acquainted with the customs and moods of the court, he expounded the advantages the Emperor would gain from trade and friendship with England. While the fifteen years' connection with the Jesuits had not brought a single embassy from Portugal, England would send embassies to honour the Emperor and also rich presents.

Jerome Xavier in his letters to Goa accused the 'English heretic' of devising a 'diabolical plot' and bribing the courtiers, but expressed the hope that he would not get the desired concessions. His pious hopes failed. Akbar ordered a 'firman' to be issued, granting Mildenhall's requests.

That was how European countries introduced themselves to Asiatic courts, vilifying each other, and, it is said, even using poison to do away with a competitor. Mildenhall himself continued to stay in Agra, then went to Persia and returned to Agra, where he is said to have died of poison, leaving his not inconsiderable possessions to a Frenchman whose daughter he intended to marry. Before his death he became a Roman Catholic and was buried in the Jesuit cemetery. But the information sent by him to London may have contributed to the efforts of the East India Company that culminated in the naval battle near Surat in 1612, in which they defeated the Portuguese rivals, and to the establishment of a factory in Surat. And his promise of an embassy was fulfilled by James I when he sent Sir Thomas Roe as accredited Ambassador to the Court of the Great Mogul, during the reign of Akbar's son and successor, the Emperor Jahangir.

6

THE END OF THE REIGN

THE thirteen years in the north brought Akbar's efforts to stabilize his Empire to fruition. These efforts were directed not only to conquests and the subjugation of the more or less independent principalities or clans but, more important still, to their adjustment to the forms of rule and administration which he had established in his domain. Everywhere there was an influx of officials. The cultivated land was measured, he introduced bamboo measuring sticks instead of the hemp rope previously in use, which contracted or extended according to heat and moisture; the land-tax was assessed according to an average crop over a ten year period. The statistical office, with all records, was in the charge of Abul Fazl. Whenever there was a failure of the harvest the tax in that area was repaid.

If Akbar was saying that 'the divine worship of monarchs consists in their justice and good administration', there were really only a few men who worked whole-heartedly with him. The majority of the higher functionaries hated the measures which made them nothing more than underlings who had to carry out precise orders, but Akbar was now an all-powerful despot and the fear of his wrath cowed them. His 'Din-Ilahi', having failed to become a generally accepted religion, developed into an exclusive order to which only few were admitted, and so Akbar ensured that the different races in his Empire could live in accordance with their different customs without being oppressed by the rest. Hindu judges decided the cases of Hindus, all religions were equally tolerated and allowed to be preached in public, and Akbar himself, while keeping the Jesuit missionaries at his court, received Jain divines with the same honours, and in accordance with their teachings not only gave up hunting but abstained almost wholly from eating meat, declaring: 'It is not right that man should make his stomach the grave of animals', and one of his 'Din Ilahi' orders was that the disciples must not 'use the same vessels as butchers, fishers and bird catchers'.

But whatever ideas or policies Akbar followed, practical considerations were always in his mind, and he never started anything before he was sure that he could achieve it. This unfailing success in all his enterprises was reflected in the saying which, as the Jesuits report, was in current use in the country: To be 'as fortunate as Akbar'.

Only in one respect did his luck seem to desert him, and that was in his sons. All three were incorrigible drunkards. Akbar himself, like all the Timurids, had freely indulged in drinking wine and using opium, although he became more abstemious in his later years, but with his sons drink had become a habitual vice. In addition, Salim, the eldest, had a vile temper and was so stubborn that Akbar always kept him near for better supervision; and the prince, now in full manhood, was chafing under this restraint and grew more and more impatient with his father's overlong reign. Murad, the second son, seems to have been more pliable when at court, but as soon as he was left on his own, he proved to be arrogant and intractable. And the third son, Daniel, was only out for dissipation and pleasure.

But Akbar did not give up hope. When he returned south from the Punjab, it was his intention to proceed immediately with the campaign against the Deccan kingdoms, but first he had ordered Prince Murad to report to him in the capital. However, when he reached Agra, Murad was not there. Akbar dispatched Abul Fazl to the Deccan to summon Murad to court, but Murad immediately marched further away to avoid meeting his father's envoy. Abul Fazl followed him and reached his camp, only to find Murad dying of delirium tremens. The prince's army was in a state of dissolution. Neither the officers nor the men had received any pay for months, no funds were available, nobody knew where they were bound for or the strength of the enemy.

Abul Fazl, with his contingent of three thousand riders, somewhat restored discipline. Akbar commanded the governor of Gujarat immediately to send all available treasure in the province to the Deccan army and added to this a large sum from Agra. Prince Daniel was appointed commander and ordered to march against Ahmadnagar, the capital of the kingdom of the same name, while Akbar himself was proceeding against the neighbouring kingdom of Khandesh. But behind the move of the fifty-eight-year-old Emperor there was no longer the drive of his previous campaigns. The army's march was a cumbersome proceeding, the Emperor had sometimes to be carried in a litter because of stomach pains, there were long halts at suitable spots, and it was only the size of the army, the number of his war elephants and guns and the immeasurable resources behind him, that in the end ensured his victory, in spite of the heroic efforts of the defenders.

While Prince Daniel laid siege to Ahmadnagar, Akbar found himself facing the much more difficult task of taking Asirgarh, the supreme fortress of the kingdom of Khandesh. The siege of Ahmadnagar lasted four months before some of the defence walls were destroyed by mines and the town could be stormed; but Asirgarh, built at the top of inaccessible cliffs, proved impregnable and it was here that Akbar had asked Father Xavier for Portuguese guns. This request having failed, he invited Bahadur Khan, the King of Khandesh, to come to his camp for peace negotiations, pledging his word that the visitor would be free to return. Bahadur Khan came, but was only prepared to submit on condition that he was to remain governor of his land and in possession of the fortress, whereupon Akbar broke his oath, took him prisoner and forced him to send a written order to the commandant to surrender the fortress. The order was not accepted; the commandant sent his own son to Akbar to remonstrate against his breach of faith and to tell him that, according to the country's tradition, seven princes of the royal family next in succession were staying in the fortress, so that one after the other could ascend the throne. According to some historians, Akbar had the young man killed; according to others he committed suicide, and while the siege went on Akbar started to bribe the defenders. Then a pestilence broke out in the fortress, causing paralysis from the waist downwards, and after ten months of siege Asirgarh surrendered. This time Akbar kept his word; all the garrison was spared, even the seven Portuguese artillery officers who had become Moslems and had conducted the defence. They were only entrusted to the care of Father Xavier and ultimately reached Goa as reconverted Christians. The king with his family and the other royal princes were distributed among different strongholds and received a small allowance. Khandesh, Ahmadnagar and a third sultanate of Birar were joined to Malwa and Gujarat as three new provinces, and Prince Daniel was appointed viceroy over the whole.

Akbar's great desire was to continue with the subjugation of the Deccan sultanates, as even of Ahmadnagar he possessed only the capital and a small part in the north while most of the land remained hostile under local chieftains; but his troops needed rest, his officers had to look after their fiefs, and most important of all, his own presence in Agra was suddenly most urgently required because of the conduct of his eldest son.

When Akbar had started the Deccan campaign he had made Prince Salim governor of Ajmer with the task of bringing to heel the Rana of Mewar, who was still holding out in his inaccessible hills, and from there continued to harass the country. Salim sent some troops against him and forced the Rana to withdraw into the hilly country, but he had no intention of pursuing him there. Instead he indulged in his drinking bouts in Ajmer. Akbar's remonstrances only infuriated him. He was already over thirty years old, and still nothing was his. His father would live for ever and keep him in subordinate jobs. He did not want to waste his time hunting down this little prince in his hills, grew obstinate and decided to go to the Punjab. He could make himself lord of the Punjab while his father was away in the south . . .

Akbar distrusted Salim and had never before given him an independent command. Even this time he had ordered Raja Man Singh to supervise him. As hereditary Raja of Jaipur, Man Singh had his residence near Ajmer, although he was the governor of the eastern provinces of Bengal and Bihar, which were supervised for him by relatives. Man Singh was also related to Salim, whose first wife was the Raja's adoptive sister. Just when Salim conceived the idea of going to the Punjab, Man Singh saw himself obliged to leave for Bengal, where some chieftains had rebelled. He managed to persuade his brother-in-law, instead of marching north, to go eastward too—either in the hope of continuing to influence him or because some of the land there was only nominally subdued and a large part still independent. If Salim wanted conquests of his own, there was still an opportunity for him there. Anyway, Salim left his post in Ajmer without Akbar's permission and journeyed eastwards. When he by-passed Agra, Akbar's mother, Hamida Begam, whose favourite grandson he had always been, hastened out of the town, in spite of the scorching summer heat, to meet him; but hearing of her approach, and afraid of long talks and of her pleadings, 'he left the hunting ground for his boat and went rapidly down the river'. But he travelled no further than Allahabad, where he seized the treasure containing the revenue from Bihar and began to redistribute the neighbouring fiefs and districts among his supporters. It was a clear case of rebellion, but in reply to Akbar's reproach Salim wrote a submissive letter with excuses, and Akbar preferred to leave things alone until his return from the Deccan.

Hearing that his father was leaving the Deccan, Salim raised additional troops, bestowed more titles on his adherents and then, pretending to be anxious to pay homage to his father, started to move with 30,000 troops in the direction of Agra. On the way he received a stern order that 'his peace and prosperity lay in returning to Allahabad. If a desire to serve had seized him he should come to court unattended'. He returned, and while he was still on the way back to Allahabad another letter from Akbar arrived, appointing him Viceroy of Bengal and Orissa, with the order to proceed there.

Salim took no notice of the new appointment, which would have banished him to the far-off provinces. Instead he assumed in Allahabad the style of an independent king and sent one of his adherents as envoy to negotiate with Akbar, excusing himself for his conduct, but demanding the right to visit his father at the head of 70,000 men, and the confirmation of all his grants to his officers.

Akbar still hesitated to use force against his rebellious son and summoned his friend and spiritual adviser, Abul Fazl, who had stayed behind in the Deccan, for consultation. It was known that Abul Fazl disliked Salim and had recommended strong action against him; and when Salim heard that he had been summoned and was about to proceed to Agra, he conceived the plan to have him murdered. He sent a message to a rebellious chief, promising him rewards and benefits if he would waylay and kill Abul Fazl, who would have to travel through his country. The chief intercepted Abul Fazl, scattered his small escort, killed him, and sent his head to Salim in Allahabad.

When Akbar heard of the murder of his friend, he was overwhelmed with grief and is said to have called out: 'If Salim wishes to be Emperor, he might have killed me and spared Abul Fazl', and for three days he abstained from appearing in public audience. An order went out to hunt down the actual murderer, but somehow the pursuit was always in vain; everyone accused someone else for the failure to catch him, and even the thorough investigation which Akbar ordered failed to detect whose fault it was that the murderer had been able to escape and hide. Later on, when Salim became Emperor, he promoted and raised the chief to a high rank because of this deed, as he himself admitted. About the murder itself he wrote:

'Although this event was a cause of anger in the mind of the late King, in the end it enabled me to proceed without disturbance of mind to kiss the threshold of my father's palace, and by degrees the resentment of the King was cleared away'.

In fact it was the royal harem that went into action to prevent open war between father and son. Salima Begam, Akbar's cousin, whom he had first married to Bairam Khan and, after Bairam's assassination, had married himself and who enjoyed a special position in the imperial household, declared that she would bring Salim to Agra repentant. She travelled to Allahabad and was able to persuade Salim to submit and come to Agra, guaranteeing his safety by placing him under the personal protection of Hamida Begam, Akbar's mother and the Prince's grandmother. When they approached Agra the old lady journeyed to meet them and took Salim to her own residence. It was here that Akbar saw the rebellious son who, as a sign of his submission, had brought an enormous amount of gold coins and, knowing his father's hobby, over 700 elephants as presents. A reconciliation of a kind took place, Salim was re-appointed to lead a campaign against the still unsubdued Rana of Mewar and departed to Fathpur-Sikri. But the idea of an unprofitable war in the Rajput hills, where little plunder but a lot of traps could be expected, did not appeal to him and he continuously demanded so many reinforcements and such supplies of funds that Akbar finally complied with his request to allow him to retire to Allahabad. In Allahabad, as a sign of his reconciliation with the Emperor, he started a series of brilliant festivities.

His rejoicings were suddenly interrupted by the suicide of his first wife, the adoptive sister of Raja Man Singh. About the cause of her suicide the chroniclers differ. Some say it was due to the behaviour of her son Khusru, who aspired to the throne in his father's place, and to some disloyal act on the part of her brother, which grieved her; others, more credibly, maintain that she felt disgraced by Salim's preference for another woman. The proud Rajput princess was not a person to be flouted by anyone, and she took a lethal dose of opium. Her death shook Salim so much that he noted: 'From the attachment I felt for her, I passed some days without any kind of pleasure in life or existence, and for four days I took nothing in the shape of food or drink'.

But soon he was again indulging in his old habits: 'He did not keep his lips from the wine-cup for a moment. When he got habituated to wine, he drank more, but the intoxication was less, and so he added to wine opium'. In this state of double-drunkenness he committed terrible cruelties, even flaying alive a man who had tried to flee from his service to Prince Daniel. The possibility that Prince Daniel might be proclaimed Emperor in his stead haunted him, and anyone desiring to serve his rival deserved the worst punishment.

At last Akbar decided to put an end to this behaviour. He assembled an army in a camp near the Jumna, and, officially stating that he was proceeding to Bengal, where Man Singh was still hunting down the Afghan rebels, embarked at Agra. It was August and the river was so dry that his boat got stuck in the sand. When it was refloated and he at last reached the camp, there came a sudden downpour which lasted three days and all the tents, pitched as they were on low-lying ground, except for the royal enclosure, were flooded. That caused another delay, and then the news arrived that the Emperor's mother, the seventy-seven-year-old Hamida Begam, was gravely ill. At first Akbar did not believe in her illness, because she had tried to prevent this punitive expedition against Salim with every means at her disposal; so he sent a trusted friend to see her, but on his report he hastened to the capital and found her dying.

Her death saved Salim. Akbar did not resume the campaign. Instead, an envoy was sent who persuaded Salim that now was his best chance for a reconciliation, and Salim set out for Agra to express his condolences to his father, taking with him precious presents but also his army. He was careful to leave his troops at a reasonable distance from the town and came only with his principal entourage to prostrate himself before the Emperor. It was an official, seemingly cordial reception, when Akbar, recognizing that his son's humility was once more only feigned, in order to deceive him, suddenly seized Salim, drew him into an inner apartment and there gave vent to his rage. It is said that he slapped his son's face, mocked him that in spite of his army of 70,000, he had to cast himself as a suppliant, and finally shut him in, in the charge of a physician and two servants, withholding wine and opium from him for some days. Then, probably on the intervention of the harem, he pardoned the Prince but kept him in Agra, assigning to him a separate residence, a suite and the revenue of Gujarat and Cambay, where Salim had no adherents.

That Akbar kept Salim in Agra and even allowed him to participate in the government to a certain extent may have been partly due to the conduct of Prince Daniel. For nearly a year Daniel had been ignoring Akbar's calls to come to him from the Deccan because, as all reports agreed, he was in a continuous state of drunkenness. All remonstrances and solemn pledges of abstinence on his part were of no avail. Even when Akbar sent the Khan-Khanan, who was Daniel's father-in-law, with the order to use any means to restrain him, and the Khan-Khanan put guards before Daniel's tent, the Prince bribed the guards to bring him liquor in small phials concealed in their turbans, or his servants put bags made of cow entrails but filled with wine under their clothes. Although he sent out a troop to prepare an advance camp for the journey to Agra, he himself did not follow it, and one of Akbar's agents reported that it was because 'the Prince had become suspicious and could not come to court so long as Prince Salim was there'. It seems that he was really afraid of his brother's ill-will, and so he stayed away and drank himself to death. Four months after Salim's arrival in Agra, Daniel died of delirium tremens.

Now Akbar had only one surviving son, Salim, and it could not be long before he would follow his aged father on the throne. Many of the courtiers, afraid for their safety and their lives, joined together to put Salim's eldest son Khusru on the throne. The rivalry between the two was well known, as also was Akbar's affection for his grandson. But it was clear that Khusru's accession could only be accomplished over the dead body of his father, because Salim would fight to the last.

About six months after Daniel's death, Akbar fell sick with dysentery. A strong astringent was administered and produced fever and strangury. All felt that the question of the succession should be settled, when Akbar suddenly ordered a fight to be arranged between the best elephants belonging to Khusru and Salim. A third elephant, from the Emperor's stable, was kept ready to protect the vanquished from too severe treatment. Salim and Khusru, mounted on horses, were in the arena, while Akbar with another grandson looked on from the window of his palace. Soon Salim's elephant had completely overwhelmed the other and began to illtreat it so that the umpires sent Akbar's elephant to intervene. But Salim's men resented the interference and bombarded the third elephant with stones, injuring both the animal and the driver. Akbar sent his grandson down to tell Salim that he must abide by the rules of the game, but the prince made the excuse that he had not given the order to throw the stones. In the meantime his elephant had completed its victory by driving both the others into the floods of the Jumna river. Was this the divine judgment that Akbar had longed for?

The next day, when Salim was expected to pay a visit to Akbar, the conspirators laid a trap to seize him as he arrived by boat, but at the last moment the Prince received a warning, did not leave the boat and escaped. A few days later, when there was no doubt that Akbar was dying, the question of the succession was raised in a meeting of the nobles. Some of the highest nobles proposed that Salim should be set aside and his son Khusru put on the throne. The proposal was immediately countered by powerful chieftains who held that it would be against all customs and laws of the Jagatai Mongols to let a son succeed to the throne while his father was alive, and they acted quickly. They put a strong guard around the treasury and another into Akbar's palace. They took care, however, to make Salim swear two solemn oaths: first that he would protect the Mohammedan religion, and secondly that he would refrain from any persecution of the nobles who had supported Khusru.

Having taken the oath, Salim ventured again to go to his father's palace. When he entered, Akbar was no longer able to speak, but after Salim had prostrated himself he made a sign that the Prince should put on the imperial turban and gird himself with Humayun's sword, which was hanging at the foot of the bed, thus designating him as his successor. Salim did as he was bidden and left the room as the acknowledged Emperor.

A few days later Akbar died, shortly after his sixty-third birthday, after a reign which had lasted nearly fifty years. The efforts of the men present at his bedside to move him to some kind of religious gesture had been in vain; he wanted no prayers to be said in the name of any religion or sect. The thirty-six year-old Salim ascended the throne, for which he had waited so long, as the Emperor Jahangir.

The Empire he inherited was no longer an unrelated patchwork of incidental conquests dominated by the arms of foreign invaders. In the fifty years of Akbar's reign it had grown into a coherent land mass stretching from the frontier of Persia to Assam and Burma, and from the Hindukush and the Himalayas to the Godavary river that flowed through the centre of the Indian peninsula. More than that, this land mass had been welded into a co-ordinated state, ruled through its length and breadth by one system of administration with the same methods, the same officials holding the same titles, the same revenue regulations, the same coinage. The diverse lands had become so many different provinces, held together by a highly organized bureaucracy in which Mohammedans and Hindus were equally eligible to the highest posts, carrying equal honours and privileges. No longer was an arbitrary rule of foreign chieftains imposed upon an alien population; the Hindus, once they had recognized that they were no longer regarded as infidels, and as such deprived of all rights, had begun to play a part in the building up of this empire and were proud of it. The Rajputs, who for over three centuries had desperately fought against the Turki or Afghan Sultans of Delhi, had in their majority become supporters of the Mogul throne and helped to spread the Mogul rule in the country. Not satisfied with political and economic unity, Akbar in unceasing efforts had also provided a unifying cultural basis. Having made Persian compulsory for all state officials, he brought it about that for the first time in medieval India Moslems and Hindus received their education in common schools and read the same books on all subjects from philosophy and history to mathematics and medicine, translated into Persian from all languages by a translation department.

On the basis of this new cultural knowledge a synthesis of the Hindu and the Moslem cultures was taking shape. Whatever the country or clan from which the families of the men in the imperial service came, or whether they were of the old Hindu nobility, everywhere there was the same demand for knowledge, for art, for poetry, for refinement in the way of life, and in all spheres a renaissance was manifesting itself.

It was an ostentatious life. The nobles and officers spent vast sums on costly dresses, precious jewelry and magnificent display, vying with each other in the multitude of their servants and retainers or in the decoration of their palaces and tents, and the trappings of their horses and elephants. This lavish spending brought expansion to the luxury trade. Silk clothes, velvet, brocades, perfumes, Chinese porcelain and Venetian glass were imported in great quantities. The inventory after Akbar's death estimated the value of his porcelain and glass alone at two and a half million rupees.

But the imports were covered by exports of cotton fabrics, pepper, indigo, opium and various drugs. Cotton cloth was dyed in beautiful and fast colours, of which the travellers reported that 'the flowers and figures could not be washed out'. Also important was the shawl and carpet-weaving industry. Akbar specially patronized the craft of silk-weaving. The internal demand of the firmly established upper classes made industry flourish. The towns were populous and prosperous, with large and beautiful gardens. In general, peace reigned and nowhere was there an enemy in sight who could threaten the might and the well-being of this great Mogul Empire, at the head of which stood the Emperor with complete autocratic power. Furthermore, he possessed immeasurable wealth. Akbar had accumulated in his hands not only the loot hoarded by generations of rulers in all the defeated kingdoms and principalities, but also the immense revenues that flowed into his treasury from all his lands. When he died, he was one of the richest monarchs ever known.

The future of the Empire now depended only on the ability of its sovereign to use his power wisely and judiciously. All that Akbar's successors had to do to achieve unprecedented splendour was to maintain the institutions and the administration which he had created in working order. And even when his descendants in later generations proved unsatisfactory and intolerant and broke all the rules and regulations laid down by their great ancestor, the Mogul Empire maintained its predominant position for a full century and enjoyed a cultural and artistic renaissance, the works of which we can only admire.

CHRONOLOGY

1483 February: Birth of Babur.
1488 War between Ahmed Mirza of Samarkand and Mahmud Khan of Tashkent. Mahmud gives the town of Turkestan to Sheibani.
1494 June: Omar Sheikh falls to his death, Babur succeeds to the throne. Ahmed Mirzà dies, Mahmud Mirza enthroned in Samarkand.
1495 Mahmud Mirza dies.
1497 Babur captures Samarkand.
1498 Jahangir enthroned in Ferghana.
1499 Babur regains Ferghana but is forced to agree to the division of the country.
1500 Babur takes Samarkand by surprise.
1501 Babur, beaten by Sheibani, flees from Samarkand.
1502 Ismail becomes Shah of Persia.
Babur and the Mongol Khans fight for Ferghana.
1503 Sheibani defeats the Mongol Khans.
1504 Babur takes Kabul.
1505 Babur's first invasion of India.
1506 Husain Baikara dies. Babur's expedition to Khorasan.
1507 Sheibani invades Khorasan and takes Herat.
1508 March: Birth of Humayun.
June: Revolt of the Mongols.
Babur assumes the title of Padishah.
1510 December: Sheibani's death.
Birth of Kamran.
1511 October: Babur's entry into Samarkand.
1512 May: Babur flees from Samarkand.
1514 Babur's return to Kabul.
Ibrahim Lodi becomes Sultan of Delhi.
1516 Birth of Askari.
1518 Babur invades the Punjab.
1519 Birth of Hindal.
March: Babur returns to Kabul.
1519–20 Invasion of the Punjab.
1520 Humayun sent to Badakhshan.
Siege of Kandahar.
1522 Babur takes Kandahar.
1524 Death of Shah Ismail.
Babur takes Lahore.
1525 Babur invades India.

CHRONOLOGY

1526 April: Battle of Panipat, Babur enters Delhi.
December: Babur poisoned by Ibrahim's mother.
1527 Babur's campaign against Rana Sanga.
March: Battle of Khanua.
April: Humayun's departure for Badakhshan.
1528 Babur captures Chanderi.
1529 January: Babur sets out for the eastern campaign. Maham leaves Kabul.
May: Battle of the Gogra. Peace with the Shah of Bengal.
June: Humayun and Kamran in Kabul. Maham arrives in Agra.
July: Humayun arrives in Agra.
October: Babur sends Suleiman Mirza to Badakhshan.
1530 February: Babur leaves Lahore.
April: Humayun's illness.
September: Babur's illness.
December: Death of Babur.
1531 Kamran marches into the Punjab. Bahadur Shah annexes Malwa.
1532 Humayun's campaign against the Afghans.
Siege of Chunar.
1535–36 Humayun's campaign against Bahadur Shah.
1537 February: Death of Bahadur Shah.
October: Humayun besieges Chunar.
1538 March: Surrender of Chunar.
April: Sher Khan takes Gaur.
October: Humayun enters Gaur.
1539 March: Humayun leaves Bengal.
June: Humayun defeated by Sher Khan at Chausa.
1539 July–1540 March: Humayun in Agra.
1540 June: Battle of Kanauj.
July–November: Humayun in Lahore.
1541 August: Humayun marries Hamida.
Hindal leaves for Kandahar.
1542 August: Humayun reaches Umarkot.
October: Birth of Akbar.
December: Hamida joins Humayun at Jun.
1543 April: Bairam joins Humayun.
July: Humayun leaves Sind.
December: Humayun crosses the frontier of Persia. Akbar brought to Kandahar.
1544 July: Humayun meets Shah Tahmasp.
1545 May: Death of Sher Shah.
September: Humayun conquers Kandahar.
November: Humayun takes Kabul.
1546 Kamran retakes Kabul.

1547 Humayun besieges Kabul.
1548 June: Humayun starts for Badakhshan.
August: Kamran submits to Humayun.
1549 Humayun's campaign against Balkh.
1550 Humayun re-occupies Kabul.
1551 Death of Hindal.
1553 October: Death of Islam Shah.
December: Kamran blinded.
1554 December: Humayun invades the Punjab.
1555 February: Humayun captures Lahore.
July: Humayun enters Delhi.
1556 January: Death of Humayun.
February: Proclamation of Akbar.
October: Hemu takes Delhi.
November: Battle of Panipat, Hemu defeated and killed.
December: Akbar and Bairam leave Delhi for the Punjab.
1557 May: Sikandar Shah surrenders.
October: Kamran dies in Mecca.
1558 Akbar moves to Agra.
1560 March: Dismissal of Bairam Khan.
1561 January: Assassination of Bairam Khan.
Invasion of Malwa.
April: Akbar's ride to Malwa.
July: Akbar's campaign against the rebels in the east.
November: Shams-ud Din appointed Prime Minister.
1562 January: First pilgrimage to Ajmer.
February: Akbar's first marriage to an Indian princess.
Prohibition of enslavement of captured women and children.
May: Murder of Shams-ud Din by Adham Khan.
1563 Remission of Pilgrim's Tax.
1564 January: Attempt on Akbar's life.
Decree abolishing the Poll Tax.
1564–67 Revolts of the Uzbegs and the Mirzas.
1567–68 Siege and slaughter of Chitor.
1568 Akbar visits Salim in Sikri.
1569 August: Birth of Prince Salim.
1570 June: Birth of Prince Murad.
Foundation of Fathpur-Sikri.
Revision of revenue assessment ordered.
1572 Invasion of Gujarat.
September: Birth of Prince Daniel.
1573 February: Capitulation of Surat.
Summer: Rebellion in Gujarat.
Introduction of cash salaries.

CHRONOLOGY

1574 Campaign to Patna. Akbar orders invasion of Bengal. Administrative reforms. Famine in Gujarat.
1575 Building of the Hall of Worship.
Pestilence in Bengal.
1576 Death of Daud. Bengal subdued.
1578 May: Visionary extasy.
1579 June: Akbar reads the Khutba.
September: Infallibility Decree.
1580 January: Beginning of the revolt in Bihar and Bengal.
February: Arrival of the first Jesuit Mission.
1581 Campaign against Hakim Mirza.
1582 Promulgation of 'Divine Faith'.
1584 Marriage of Salim.
1585 Newbery and Fitch in Agra.
Akbar departs to the north.
1586 Akbar arrives in Lahore. Campaigns against Kashmir and the hill tribes.
1587 May: Marriage of Murad.
August: Birth of Salims son Khusru.
1588–91 Conquest of Sind.
1589 May–November: Akbar in Kashmir and Kabul.
1590 Rebellion in Bengal and Bihar finally crushed.
1591 Rebellion in Kashmir quelled.
August: Arrival of the second Jesuit Mission.
1591 October–1592 September: The millenial year.
1592 Murad governor of Malwa and Gujarat.
1593 August: Death of Sheikh Mubarak.
Decision on war against the Deccan principalities.
1595 May: Surrender of Kandahar.
Arrival of the third Jesuit Mission.
1595–1598 Famine and pestilence in the Punjab.
1597 Akbar in Kashmir.
1598 Death of Abdullah Khan, the Uzbeg.
Akbar returns from the north.
1599 May: Death of Murad.
July: Akbar sets out for the Deccan.
1600 April: Siege of Ahmadnagar and Asirgarh begins.
July: Salim departs to Allahabad.
August: Fall of Ahmadnagar.
1601 January: Capitulation of Asirgarh.
April: Embassy to Goa.
May: Akbar's return to Agra.
1602 August: Abul Fazl waylaid and murdered.

CHRONOLOGY

1603 April: Salim brought to Agra by Salima Begam.
November: Salim returns to Allahabad.

1604 May: Suicide of Salim's wife.
August: Death of Hamida.
November: Reconciliation of Akbar and Salim.

1605 March: Death of Daniel.
September: Illness of Akbar.
October: Death of Akbar.

BIBLIOGRAPHY

Memoirs of Babur, trans. by A. S. Beveridge, 1921/22.

Erskine, William: *A History of India under the first sovereigns of the House of Taimur* 1854.

Edwardes, Stephen M.: *Babur, Diarist and Despot*, 1926.

Grenard, Fernand: *Baber, First of the Moguls*, trans. by H. W. White & R. Glaenzer, 1931.

Lane-Poole, Stanley: *Babar, The Founder of the Moghul Empire*, 1909.

Lamb, Harold: *Babur the Tiger*, 1962.

Rushbrook-Williams, L. F.: *An Empire Builder of the 16th Century*, 1918.

Mirza Haidar Dughlat: *Tarikh-i-Rashidi*—A History of the Moghuls of Central Asia. Trans. by Denison Ross & N. Elias, 1895.

Gul-Badan: Humayun-Nama—*The History of Humayun*. Trans. by A. S. Beveridge, 1902.

Ishwari Prasad: *The Life and Times of Humayun*, 1955.

Abbas Khan: *Tarikh-i Sher Shahi*, 1952.

Abul Fazl: *The Akbarnama*. Trans. by H. Beveridge, 1897–1939.

— *Ain-i-Akbari*. Trans. by H. Blochmann, 1873–1894.

Badaoni, Abdul-Qadir: *Muntakhab Al-Tawarikh*. Passages trans. by Edward Rohatsek, 1866.

Malleson, G. B.: *Akbar and the rise of the Mughal Empire*, 1915.

Smith, Vincent A.: *Akbar, The Great Mogul*, 1919.

du Jarric: *Akbar and the Jesuits*, an account of the Jesuit Missions to the court of Akbar. Trans. with intro. by C. H. Payne, 1926.

von Noer, Graf F. A.: *Kaiser Akbar*, 1880–85.

Antonova, K. A.: *Ocherki obschestvenykh otnoshenij i politicheskogo stroia mogolskoi indii vremen Akbara* (Sketches of social conditions and political establishments in Mogul India in Akbar's time), 1952.

Locke, J. Courtenay: *The First Englishman in India*, 1930.

Riley, J. H.: *Ralph Fitch, England's Pioneer to India*, 1899.

Moreland, W. Q.: *India at the Death of Akbar*, an economic study, 1920.

The Cambridge History of India, Vol. IV: *The Mughul Period*, 1937.

Srivastava, A. L.: *The Mughul Empire*, 1957.

Tripathi, R. P.: *Rise and Fall of the Mughal Empire*, 1956.

INDEX